The LAWRENCE DURRELL Travel Reader

The

LAWRENCE DURRELL

Travel Reader

EDITED BY
CLINT WILLIS

CARROLL & GRAF PUBLISHERS
NEW YORK

THE LAWRENCE DURRELL TRAVEL READER

Carroll & Graf Publishers
An Imprint of Avalon Publishing Group Inc.
245 West 17th Street
New York, NY 10011

Library of Congress Cataloging-in-Publication Data is available.

ISBN: 0-7867-1370-4

Printed in the United States of America
Interior design by Paul Paddock
Distributed by Publishers Group West

Contents

Editor's Note

Lawrence Durrell is best-remembered for his novels, including the four books that make up *The Alexandria Quartet*. He also wrote poems, stories, plays and books and essays on travel—or better, on place.

Durrell, was a compulsive traveler. Like many of that breed, he traveled in search of something elusive—perhaps some version of peace. He had a busy and fractious life: he served the British government in foreign postings that were usually stressful, often boring and occasionally dangerous; he married three times; he worried about money and had difficult relationships with his children; he drank too much. He detested dreariness, and left behind his youth in England in search of something opposed to it—something he had perhaps known during his early childhood in India.

Durrell found what he was looking for on certain islands and in certain provinces, where he encountered what he called "spirit of place". Such discoveries renewed him and his work; they made him happy.

The Lawrence Durrell Travel Reader reflects that spirit of place as well as Durrell's pleasure in engaging and appreciating it. His delight in certain places and his narrative skills together made him one of the most absorbing travel writers of the past century—an achievement overshadowed by his fame as a novelist. His best travel writing delivers to the reader Durrell's discoveries and the real though often fleeting happiness—the moments of peace—those discoveries brought him.

This collection is drawn largely from Durrell's four island books *(Prospero's Cell, Reflections on a Marine Venus, Bitter Lemons and Sicilian Carousel)*. Those books recall Durrell's extensive travels among the Mediterranean islands of Corfu, Rhodes, Sicily and Cyprus—islands which, beginning when he was very young, helped restore and sustain him as a man and an artist. This anthology also collects some of Durrell's short travel pieces— including several essays set in his beloved Provence, his home during the last three decades of an eventful, accomplished and well-traveled life.

SPIRIT OF PLACE

Lawrence Durrell found his spirit in the islands and countries of the Mediterranean: Corfu, Egypt, Rhodes, Cyprus, Sicily, Provence. What does that mean—to find your spirit in a place? Durrell explored that question in a 1960 essay, which ran in the *New York Times Magazine*.

LANDSCAPE AND CHARACTER
(1960)

'YOU WRITE', SAYS A FRIENDLY CRITIC in Ohio, 'as if the landscape were more important than the characters.' If not exactly true, this is near enough the mark, for I have evolved a private notion about the importance of landscape, and I willingly admit to seeing 'characters' almost as functions of a landscape. This has only come about in recent years after a good deal of travel—though here again I doubt if this is quite the word, for I am not really a 'travel-writer' so much as a 'residence-writer'. My books are always about living in places, not just rushing through them. But as you get to know Europe slowly, tasting the wines, cheeses and characters of the different countries you begin to realize that the important determinant of any culture is after all—the spirit of place. Just as one particular vineyard will always give you a special wine with discernible characteristics so a Spain, an Italy, a Greece will always give you the same type of culture—will express itself through the human being just as it does through its wild flowers. We tend to see 'culture' as a sort of historic pattern dictated by the human will, but for me this is no longer absolutely true. I don't believe the British character, for example, or the German has changed a jot since Tacitus first described it; and so long as people keep getting born Greek or French or Italian their culture-productions will bear the unmistakable signature of the place.

And this, of course, is the target of the travel-writer; his task is to isolate the germ in the people which is expressed by their landscape. Strangely enough one does not necessarily need special knowledge for the job, though of course a knowledge of language is a help. But how few they are those writers! How many can write a *Sea and Sardinia* or a *Twilight in Italy* to match these two gems of D. H. Lawrence? When he wrote them his Italian was rudimentary. The same applies to Norman Douglas' *Fountains in the Sand*—one of the best portraits of North Africa.

We travel really to try and get to grips with this mysterious quality of 'Greekness' or 'Spanishness'; and it is extraordinary how unvaryingly it remains true to the recorded picture of it in the native literature: true to the point of platitude. Greece, for example, cannot have a single real Greek left (in the racial sense) after so many hundreds of years of war and resettlement; the present racial stocks are the fruit of countless invasions. Yet if you want a bit of real live Aristophanes you only have to listen to the chaffering of the barrow-men and peddlers in the Athens Plaka. It takes less than two years for even a reserved British resident to begin using his fingers in conversation without being aware of the fact. But if there are no original Greeks left what is the curious constant factor that we discern behind the word 'Greekness'? It is surely the enduring faculty of self-expression inhering in landscape. At least I would think so as I recall two books by very different writers which provide an incomparable nature-study of the place. One is *Mani* by Patrick Leigh Fermor, and the other Miller's *Colossus of Maroussi*.

I believe you could exterminate the French at a blow and resettle the country with Tartars, and within two generations discover, to your astonishment, that the national characteristics were back at norm—the restless metaphysical curiosity, the tenderness for good living and the passionate individualism: even though their noses were now flat. This is the invisible constant in a place with which the ordinary tourist can get in touch just by sitting quite quietly over a glass of wine in a Paris *bistrot*. He may not be able to formulate it very clearly to himself in literary terms, but he will taste the unmistakable keen knife-edge of happiness in the air of Paris: the pristine brilliance of a national psyche which knows that art is as important as love or food. He will not be blind either to the hard metallic rational sense, the irritating *coeur raisonnable* of the men and women. When the French want to be *malins,* as they call it, they can be just as we can be when we stick our toes in over some national absurdity.

Yes, human beings are expressions of their landscape, but in order to touch the secret springs of a national essence you need a few moments of quiet with yourself. Truly the intimate knowledge of landscape, if developed scientifically, could give us a political science—for half the political decisions taken in the world are based on what we call national character. We unconsciously acknowledge this fact when we exclaim, 'How typically Irish' or 'It would take a Welshman to think up something like that'. And indeed we all of us jealously guard the sense of minority individuality in our own nations—the family differences. The great big nations like say the Chinese or the Americans present a superficially homogeneous appearance; but I've noticed that while we Europeans can hardly tell one American from another, my own American friends will tease each other to death at the lunch-table about the intolerable misfortune of being born in Ohio or Tennessee—a recognition of the validity of place which we ourselves accord to the Welshman, Irishman and Scotsman at home. It is a pity indeed to travel and not get this essential sense of landscape values. You do not need a sixth sense for it. It is there if you just close your eyes and breathe softly through your nose; you will hear the whispered message, for all landscapes ask the same question in the same whisper. 'I am watching you—are you watching yourself in me?' Most travellers hurry too much. But try just for a moment sitting on the great stone omphalos, the navel of the ancient Greek world, at Delphi. Don't ask mental questions, but just relax and empty your mind. It lies, this strange amphora-shaped object, in an overgrown field above the temple. Everything is blue and smells of sage. The marbles dazzle down below you. There are two eagles moving softly softly on the sky, like distant boats rowing across an immense violet lake.

Ten minutes of this sort of quiet inner identification will give you the notion of the Greek landscape which you could not get in twenty years of studying ancient Greek texts. But having got it, you will at once get all the rest; the key is there, so to speak, for you to turn. After that you will not be able to go on a shopping expedition in Athens without running into Agamemnon or Clytemnestra—and often under the same names. And if you happen to go to Eleusis in springtime you will come upon more than one blind Homer walking the dusty roads. The secret is identification. If you sit on the top of the Mena House pyramid at sunset and try the same thing (forgetting the noise of the donkey-boys, and all the filthy litter of other travellers—old cartons and Coca-Cola bottles): if you sit quite still in the landscape-diviner's pose—why, the whole rhythm of ancient Egypt rises up from the damp cold sand. You can hear its very pulse tick. Nothing is strange to you at such moments—the old temples with their death-cults, the hieroglyphs, the long slow whirl of the brown Nile among the palm-fringed islets, the crocodiles and snakes. It is palpably just as it was (its essence) when the High Priest of Ammon initiated Alexander into the Mysteries. Indeed the Mysteries themselves are still there for those who might seek initiation—the shreds and shards of the Trismegistic lore still being studied and handed on by small secret sects. Of course you cannot arrange to be initiated through a travel agency! You would

have to reside and work your way in through the ancient crust—
a tough one—of daily life. And how different is the rhythm of
Egypt to that of Greece! One isn't surprised by the story that the
High Priest at Thebes said contemptuously: 'You Greeks are mere
children.' He could not bear the tireless curiosity and sensuality of
the Greek character—the passionate desire to conceptualize
things metaphysically. They didn't seem to be able to relax, the
blasted Greeks! Incidentally it is a remark which the French often
repeat today about the Americans, and it is always uttered in the
same commiserating tone of voice as once the High Priest used.
Yet the culture of Greece (so different from that of Egypt) springs
directly from the Nile Valley—I could name a dozen top Greek
thinkers or philosophers who were trained by Egyptians, like
Plato, Pythagoras, Anaxagoras, Democritos. And the 'tiresome
children' certainly didn't waste their time, for when they got back
home to their own bare islands the pure flower of Greek culture
spread its magnificent wings in flights of pure magic to astonish
and impregnate the Mediterranean. But just to hand the eternal
compliment along they invented the word 'barbarians' for all
those unfortunate savages who lived outside the magic circle of
Greece, deprived of its culture. The barbarians of course were one
day to produce Dante, Goethe, Bach, Shakespeare.

As I say the clue, then, is identification; for underneath the
purely superficial aspects of apparent change the old tide-lines
remain. The dullest travel poster hints at it. The fascinating
thing is that Dickens characters still walk the London streets;
that any game of village cricket will provide us with clues to the
strange ritualistic mystery of the habits of the British. While if
you really want to intuit the inner mystery of the island try
watching the sun come up over Stonehenge. It may seem a dull
and 'touristic' thing to do, but if you do it in the right spirit you

find yourself walking those woollen secretive hills arm in arm with the Druids.

Taken in this way travel becomes a sort of science of intuitions which is of the greatest importance to everyone—but most of all to the artist who is always looking for nourishing soils in which to put down roots and create. Everyone finds his own 'correspondences' in this way—landscapes where you suddenly feel bounding with ideas, and others where half your soul falls asleep and the thought of pen and paper brings on nausea. It is here that the travel-writer stakes his claim, for writers each seem to have a personal landscape of the heart which beckons them. The whole Arabian world, for example, has never been better painted and framed than in the works of Freya Stark, whose delicate eye and insinuating slow-moving orchestrations of place and evocations of history have placed her in the front rank of travellers. Could one do better than *Valley of the Assassins*?

These ideas, which may seem a bit far-fetched to the modern reader, would not have troubled the men and women of the ancient world, for their notion of culture was one of psychic education, the education of the sensibility; ours is built upon a notion of mentation, the cramming of the skull with facts and pragmatic data which positively stifle the growth of the soul. Travel wouldn't have been necessary in the time (I am sure such a time really existed some time after the Stone Age) when there really was a world religion which made full allowance for the different dialects of the different races practising it: and which realized that the factor of variation is always inevitably the landscape and not the people. Nowadays such a psychic uniformity sounds like a dream; but already comparative anthropology and archaeology are establishing the truth of it. When we think about such formulations as 'World-Government' we always think of the matter politically, as groups of different people working upon an agreed agenda of sorts; a ten-point programme, or some such set of working propositions. The landscape always fools us, and I imagine always will. Simply because the same propositions don't mean the same in Greek, Chinese and French.

Another pointer worth thinking about is institutions; have you ever wondered why Catholicism, for example, can be such a different religion in different places? Ireland, Italy, Spain, Argentina—it is theologically the same, working on the same premises, but in each case it is subtly modified to suit the spirit of place. People have little to do with the matter except inasmuch as they themselves are reflections of their landscape. Of course there are places where you feel that the inhabitants are not really attending to and interpreting their landscape; whole peoples or nations sometimes get mixed up and start living at right angles to the land, so to speak, which gives the traveller a weird sense of alienation. I think some of the troubles which American artists talk about are not due to 'industrialization' or 'technocracy' but something rather simpler—people not attending to what the land is saying, not conforming to the hidden magnetic fields which the landscape is trying to communicate to the personality. It was not all nonsense what D. H. Lawrence had to say in his communion with the 'ghosts' in the New World. He was within an ace, I think, of making real contact with the old Indian cultures. Genius that he was, he carried too much intellectual baggage about him on his travels, too many preconceptions; and while the mirror he holds up to Mexico, Italy, England is a marvellous triumph of art, the image is often a bit out of focus. He couldn't hold or perhaps wouldn't hold the camera steady enough—he refused to use the tripod (first invented by the oracles in Greece!).

The traveller, too, has his own limitations, and it is doubtful if he is to be blamed. The flesh is frail. I have known sensitive and inquisitive men so disheartened by the sight of a Greek lavatory as to lose all sense of orientation and fly right back to High Street Clapham without waiting for the subtler intimations of the place to dawn on them. I have known people educated up to Ph.D. standard who were so completely unhinged by French plumbing that they could speak of nothing else. We are all of us unfair in this way. I know myself to be a rash, hasty and inconsiderate man, and while I am sitting here laying down the law about travel I feel I must confess that I also have some blind spots. I have never been fair to the Scots. In fact I have always been extremely unfair to them—and all because I arrived on my first visit to Scotland late on a Saturday evening. I do not know whether it is generally known that you can simply die of exposure and starvation in relatively civilized places like Inverness simply because the inhabitants are too religious to cut a sandwich or pour coffee? It sounds fantastic I know. Nevertheless it is true. The form of Sabbatarianism which the Scots have developed passes all understanding. Nay, it cries out for the strait-jacket. And sitting on a bench at Inverness Station in a borrowed deerstalker and plaid you rack your brains to remember the least pronouncement in the Old or New Testaments which might account for it. There is none—or else I have never spotted the reference. They appear to have made a sort of Moloch of Our Lord, and are too scared even to brush their teeth on the Sabbath. How can I be anything but unfair to them? And yet Scotland herself—the poetry, and the poverty and naked joyous insouciance of mountain life, you will find on every page of Burns's autobiographical papers. Clearly she is a queenly country and a wild mountainous mate for poets. Why have the Scots not caught on? What ails them in their craggy fastnesses?

(But I expect I shall receive a hundred indignant letters from Americans who have adopted Scotland, have pierced her hard heart and discovered the landscape-mystery of her true soul. Nevertheless, I stand by what I say; and one day when I am rich I shall have a memorial plaque placed over that bench on Inverness Station platform—a plaque reading 'Kilroy was here—but oh so briefly'!) But I must not fail to add that I have always admired the magnificent evocations of Scots landscape in the books of Stevenson; they are only adventure tales, but the landscape comes shining through.

So that I imagine the traveller in each of us has a few blind spots due to some traumatic experience with an empty tea-urn or the room-on-the-landing. This cannot be helped. The great thing is to try and travel with the eyes of the spirit wide open, and not too much factual information. To tune in, without reverence, idly— but with real inward attention. It is to be had for the feeling, that mysterious sense of *rapport,* of identity with the ground. You can extract the essence of a place once you know how. If you just get as still as a needle you'll be there.

I remember seeing a photo-reportage in *Life* magazine once which dealt with the extraordinary changes in physique which emigrants to the U.S.A. underwent over such relatively short periods as two or three generations. Some of the smaller races like Chinese and Filipinos appeared to have gained almost eight inches in height, over the statutory period investigated, while their physical weight had also increased in the most extraordinary way. The report was based on the idea that diet and environment were the real answers, and while obviously such factors are worth considering I found myself wondering if the reporters were right; surely the control experiment would fail if one fed a group of Chinese *in China* exclusively on an American diet? I don't see them growing a speck larger myself. They might get fat and rosy on the diet, but I believe the landscape, in pursuit of its own mysterious purposes, would simply cut them down to the required size suitable to homegrown Chinamen.

One last word about the sense of place; I think that not enough attention is paid to it as a purely literary criterion. What makes 'big' books is surely as much to do with their site as their characters and incidents. I don't mean the books which are devoted entirely to an elucidation of a given landscape like Thoreau's *Walden* is. I mean ordinary novels. When they are well and truly anchored in nature they usually become classics. One can detect this quality of 'bigness' in most books which are so sited from *Huckleberry Finn* to *The Grapes of Wrath*. They are tuned in to the sense of place. You could not transplant them without totally damaging their ambience and mood; any more than you could transplant *Typee*. This has nothing I think to do with the manners and habits of the human beings who populate them; for they exist in nature, as a function of place.

CORFU

Lawrence Durrell arrived on the Greek island of Corfu in March, 1935. He was accompanied by his wife, Nancy, and his young sister Margo. Durrell's mother, and two brothers—Leslie and Gerald—arrived two weeks later. Lawrence Durrell was 23 years old. He had spent his first 11 years in India (which he loved) followed by school in England (which he loathed). Durrell experienced Corfu as a rebirth of the spirit, and his residence there began his lifelong love affair with the Mediterranean. He spent parts of four years on Corfu, writing his second and third novels as well as poetry and notes for his first island book, *Prospero's Cell*. He left the island for Athens in 1939 and departed Greece in 1941, just ahead of the Nazi army.

DIVISIONS UPON GREEK GROUND

(FROM PROSPERO'S CELL, 1945)

'No tongue: all eyes: be silent.'

—*THE TEMPEST*

SOMEWHERE BETWEEN CALABRIA AND CORFU the blue really begins. All the way across Italy you find yourself moving through a landscape severely domesticated—each valley laid out after the architect's pattern, brilliantly lighted, human. But once you strike out from the flat and desolate Calabrian mainland towards the sea, you are aware of a change in the heart of things: aware of the horizon beginning to stain at the rim of the world: aware of *islands* coming out of the darkness to meet you.

In the morning you wake to the taste of snow on the air, and climbing the companion-ladder, suddenly enter the penumbra of shadow cast by the Albanian mountains—each wearing its cracked crown of snow—desolate and repudiating stone.

A peninsula nipped off while red hot and allowed to cool into an antarctica of lava. You are aware not so much of a landscape coming to meet you invisibly over those blue miles of water as of a climate. You enter Greece as one might enter a dark crystal; the form of things becomes irregular, refracted. Mirages suddenly swallow islands, and wherever you look the trembling curtain of the atmosphere deceives.

Other countries may offer you discoveries in manners or lore or landscape; Greece offers you something harder—the discovery of yourself.

10.4.37

It is a sophism to imagine that there is any strict dividing line between the waking world and the world of dreams. N. and I, for example, are confused by the sense of several contemporaneous lives being lived inside us; the sensation of being mere points of reference for space and time. We have chosen Corcyra perhaps because it is an ante-room to Aegean Greece with its smoke-grey volcanic turtle-backs lying low against the ceiling of heaven. Corcyra is all Venetian blue and gold—and utterly spoilt by the sun. Its richness cloys and enervates. The southern valleys are painted out boldly in heavy brush-strokes of yellow and red while the Judas trees punctuate the roads with their dusty purple explosions. Everywhere you go you can lie down on grass; and even the bare northern reaches of the island are rich in olives and mineral springs.

25.4.37

The architecture of the town is Venetian; the houses above the old port are built up elegantly into slim tiers with narrow alleys and colonnades running between them; red, yellow, pink, umber—a jumble of pastel shades which the moonlight transforms into a dazzling white city built for a wedding cake. There are other curiosities; the remains of a Venetian aristocracy living in over-grown baronial mansions, buried deep in the country and surrounded by cypresses. A patron saint of great antiquity who lies, clad in beautifully embroidered slippers, in a great silver casket, apt for the performance of miracles.

29.4.37

It is April and we have taken an old fisherman's house in the extreme north of the island—Kalamai. Ten sea-miles from the town, and some thirty kilometres by road, it offers all the charms of seclusion. A white house set like a dice on a rock already venerable with the scars of wind and water. The hill runs clear up into the sky behind it, so that the cypresses and olives overhang this room in which I sit and write. We are upon a bare promontory with its beautiful clean surface of metamorphic stone covered in olive and ilex: in the shape of a *mons pubis*. This is become our unregretted home. A world. Corcyra.

5.5.37

The books have arrived by water. Confusion, adjectives, smoke, and the deafening pumping of the wheezy Diesel engine. Then the caique staggered off in the direction of St. Stephano and the Forty Saints, where the crew will gorge themselves on melons and fall asleep in their coarse woollen vests, one on top of the other, like a litter of cats, under the ikon of St. Spiridion of Holy Memory. We are depending upon this daily caique for our provisions.

6.5.37

Climb to Vigla in the time of cherries and look down. You will see that the island lies against the mainland roughly in the form of a sickle. On the landward side you have a great bay, noble and serene, and almost completely landlocked. Northward the tip of the sickle almost touches Albania and here the troubled blue of the Ionian is sucked harshly between ribs of limestone and spits of sand. Kalamai fronts the Albanian foothills, and into it the water races as into a swimming-pool: a milky ferocious green when the north wind curdles it.

7.5.37

The cape opposite is bald; a wilderness of rock-thistle and melancholy asphodel—the drear sea-squill. It was on a ringing spring day that we discovered the house. The sky lay in a heroic blue arc as we came down the stone ladder. I remember N. saying distinctly to Theodore: 'But the quietness alone makes it another country.' We looked through the hanging screen of olive-branches on to the white sea wall with fishing-tackle drying on it. A neglected balcony. The floors were cold. Fowls clucked softly in the gloom where the great olive-press lay, waiting its season. A cypress stood motionless—as if at the gates of the underworld. We shivered and sat on the white rock to eat, looking down at our own faces in the motionless sea. You will think it strange to have come all the way from England to this fine Grecian promontory where our only company can be rock, air, sky—and all the elementals. In letters home N. says we have been cultivating the tragic sense. There is no explanation. It is enough to record that everything is exactly as the fortune-teller said it would be. White house, white rock, friends, and a narrow style of loving: and perhaps a book which will grow out of these scraps, as from the rubbish of these old Venetian tombs the cypress cracks the slabs at last and rises up fresh and green.

9.5.37

We are lucky in our friends. Two of them seem of almost mythological quality—Ivan Zarian and the arcane professor of broken bones Theodore Stephanides. Zarian is grey, eminent and imposing with his mane of hair and his habit of conducting himself as he intones his latest love-song; he claims to be Armenia's greatest poet with a firmness and modesty that completely charm. He has spent nearly two years here intoning his work to anyone who would listen, and making an exhaustive study of the island wines. He has managed to convert the top floor of the St. George Hotel into a workroom— indeed a wilderness of manuscript and paintings. Here, looking out upon the blunt fortifications of the Eastern Fort, and pausing from time to time to relish a glass of wine, he compiles his literary column for some new world Armenian newspapers. On Friday, the 8th of March, he sent me a friendly message reading:

> Dear Durrell: we miss you but most your beautiful wife. Dear, boy, yes, certainly I have immortalized you this week. I have written this epoch of our lives. Great love from Zarian.

Zarian walks as if he wears a heavy cloak. A copious and extravagant figure it was he who instituted our literary meetings once a week at the 'Sign of the Partridge', off the main square of the town. Zarian possesses an extraordinary typewriter which enables him, by simply revolving the bed of type, to write in French and Italian as well as in Armenian and Russian. At these weekly meetings he rises to his feet and, in a beautifully controlled voice, recites the 'to be or not to be' speech from Hamlet, first in French, and then in Armenian, Russian, Italian, German and Spanish. He scorns to learn English properly.

From my notebook 12.5.37
For Theodore's portrait: fine head and golden beard: very Edwardian face—and perfect manners of Edwardian professor. Probably reincarnation of comic professor invented by Edward Lear during his stay in Corcyra. Tremendous shyness and diffidence. Incredibly erudite in everything concerning the island. Firm Venezelist, and possessor of the dryest and most fastidious style of exposition ever

seen. Thumbnail portrait of bearded man in boots and cape, with massive bug-hunting apparatus on his back stalking across country to a delectable pond where his microscopic world of algae and diatoms (the only real world for him) lies waiting to be explored. Theodore is always being arrested as a foreign agent because of the golden beard, strong English accent in Greek, and mysterious array of vessels and swabs and tubes dangling about his person. On his first visit to Kalamai house he had hardly shaken hands when sudden light came into his eye. Taking a conical box from his pocket he said 'excuse me' with considerable suppressed excitement and advanced to the drawing-room wall to capture a sand-fly exclaiming as he did so in a small triumphant voice 'Got it. Four hundred and second.'

17.5.37

Gulls turning down wind; to-day a breath of sirocco and the sea grinding and crushing up its colours under the house; the town gardens steaming in their rotten richness. The Duchess of B. abroad in a large hat, riding in a horse-carriage. Shuttered mansions with the umbrella pines rapping at the windows. On the great southern shelf you can see the road running white as a scar against the emerald lake; the olives are tacking madly from grey to silver, and behind the house the young cypresses are like drawn bows. Nicholas who was standing firm and square before us on the jetty a minute ago is now that speck of red sail against the mountains. Then at night it dies down suddenly and the colour washes back into the sky. At the 'Sign of the Partridge' Zarian gives a discourse on landscape as a form of metaphysics. 'The divine Plato said once that in Greece you see God with his compasses and dividers.' N. maintains Lawrence's grasp of place against an English boy who declares all the Lawrentian landscapes to be invented not described; while Theodore surprises by asking in a small voice for a glass of wine (he does not drink) and adding in an even smaller voice: 'What is causality?'

18.5.37

Causality is this dividing floor which falls away each morning when I am back on the warm rocks, lying with my face less than a foot above the dark Ionian. All morning we lie under the red brick shrine to Saint Arsenius, dropping cherries into the pool—clear down two fathoms to the sandy floor where they loom like drops of blood. N. has been going in for them like an otter and bringing them up in her lips. The Shrine is our private bathing-pool; four puffs of cypress, deep clean-cut diving ledges above two fathoms of blue water, and a floor of clean pebbles. Once after a storm an ikon of the good Saint Arsenius was found here by a fisherman called Manoli, and he built the shrine out of red plaster as a house for it. The little lamp is always full of sweet oil now, for St. Arsenius guards our bathing.

22.5.37

At evening the blue waters of the lagoon invent moonlight and play it back in fountains of crystal on the white rocks and the deep balcony; into the high-ceilinged room where N.'s lazy pleasant paintings stare down from the walls. And invisibly the air (cool as the breath from the heart of a melon) pours over the window-sills and mingles with the scent of the exhausted lamps. It is so still that the voice of a man up there in the dusk under the olives disturbs and quickens one like the voice of conscience itself. Under the glacid surface of the sea fishes are moving like the suggestion of fishes—influences of curiosity and terror. And now the stars are shining down frostblown and taut upon this pure

Euclidian surface. It is so still that we have dinner under the cypress tree to the light of a candle. And after it, while we are drinking coffee and eating grapes on the edge of the mirror a wind comes: and the whole of heaven stirs and trembles—a great branch of blossoms melting and swaying. Then as the candle draws breath and steadies everything hardens slowly back into the image of a world in water, so that Theodore can point into the water at our feet and show us the Pléiades burning.

28.5.37

At such moments we never speak; but I am aware of the brown arms and throat in the candlelight and the brown toes in the sandals. I am aware of a hundred images at once and a hundred ways of dealing with them. The bowl of wild roses. The English knives and forks. Greek cigarettes. The battered and sea-stained notebook in which I rough out my poems. The rope and oar lying under the tree. The spilth of the olive-press which will be gathered for fuel. The pile of rough stone for the building of a garden wall. A bucket and an axe. The peasant crossing the orchard in her white head-dress. The restless cough of the goat in the barn. All these take shape and substance round this little yellow cone of flame in which N. is cutting the cheese and washing the grapes. A single candle burning upon a table between our happy selves.

4.6.37

I have preserved the text of Theodore's first communication. It arrived on Sunday by the evening boat and was delivered at the door by Spiro the village idiot. Since it was superscribed URGENT I made the messenger the gift of a drachma.

   'I learn with considerable joy from our mutual friend Z that you are intending

a written history of the isle. It is a project which I myself have long contemplated but owing to the diffuseness of my interests and lack of literary talent I have always felt myself unequal to the task. I hasten however to place all my material at your service, and on Tuesday will send you (a) my synoptic history of the island, (b) my facts about St. Spiridion, (c) my fresh-water biology of Corcyra, (d) a short account of the geology of the island of Corcyra. This should interest you. It is only the beginning. Yours sincerely, Theodore Stephanides.'

It is on the strength of this that I have entered into a correspondence characterized on my part by flights of deliberately false scholarship, and on his by the unsmiling and fastidious rectitude of a research worker. Our letters are carried to and fro by the island boats. It is, as he says, only a beginning.

7.6.37
At night the piper sometimes plays, while his grazing sheep walk upon the opposite cape and browse among the arbutus and scrub. We lie in bed with our skins rough and satiny from the salt and listen. The industrious and rather boring nightingales are abashed by the soft liquid quarter-tones, the unearthly quibbles of the flute. There is form without melody, and the notes are emptied as if drop by drop on to the silence. It is the wheedling voice of the sirens that Ulysses heard.

9.6.37
We have been betraying our origins. N. has decided to build a garden on the rock outside the house. We will have to bring the soil down in sacks, and employ the Aegean technique of walled boxes and columns. The design is N.'s and its execution is in the hands of John and Nicholas, father and son, who are the best masons in the village. The father builds slightly lopsided because,

he says, he is blind in one eye; and his son comes silently behind him to rectify his errors and admire his facility in pruning the mountain stone into rough blocks. John is most comfortable squatting on his haunches in the shadow cast by his wide straw hat and talking scandal; he moves along the wall in a series of hops like a clipped magpie. His son is a fresh-faced dumb youth with a vivid smile and excellent manners. He dresses in the hideous cloth cap and torn breeches of the European workman, while his father still wears pointed slippers. It is worth perhaps recording the traditional island costume, now seldom seen except at festivals and dances.

> Blue embroidered bolero jacket with black and gold
>   braid and piping.
> A white soft shirt with puffed sleeves.
> Baggy blue breeches called Vrakes.
> White woollen gaiters.
> And pointed Turkish slippers with no pom-pom.
> Either a soft red fez with a blue tassel
> Or a white straw hat.

11.6.37

The straw from the packing-cases will go to cover the floor of the magazine where the goat is tethered. The rooms look lovely and gracious with their white-washed walls, and the few bright paintings and books. The windows give directly on to the sea, so that its perpetual sighing is the rhythm of our work and our sleeping. By day it runs golden on the ceilings, reflecting back the bright peasant rugs—a ship, a gorgon, a loom, a cypress-tree; reflecting back the warm crude pottery of our table; reflecting back N. now brown-skinned and blonde, reading in a chair with her legs tucked under her. Calm eyes, calm hair, and clear white teeth like those of a young carnivore. As Father Nicholas says: 'What more does a man want than an olive-tree, a native island, and woman from his own place?'

13.6.37

The man and his wife are fine creatures. He is called Anastasius and she Helen. It is obvious from their children that the marriage was a marriage of love rather than convenience. She is most delicately formed in a deep silken olive-colour; their hair has that deep black which shines out in sudden hints of blue—the simile of the Klepthic poems says 'hair like the wing of a raven'. Beautifully formed eyebrows above their dark eyes, clear and circumflex. Only their hands and feet—like those of all peasants—are blunt and hideous: mere spades grown upon the members through a long battle with soil, ropes, and wood. Their daughters are called Sky and Freedom.

17.6.37

'Formal geology', writes Theodore in his treatise, 'will still find features of interest in Corcyra; and if the form of the island in general is conditioned by its limestone features, there are many interesting configurations worth the mature attention of field- workers.'

Southward the land falls gently away to the white cape, luxuriant and steaming; every curve here is a caress, a nakedness to the delighted eyes, an endearment. Every prospect is contained in a frame of cypress and olives and brilliant roofs. Inlets, lakes, islands lead one slowly down to the deserted salt-pans beyond Lefkimi.

Two great ribs of mountain enclose this Eden. One runs from north to south along the western ranges; while from east to west the dead lands rise sheer to Pantocrator. It is in the shadow of this mountain that we live. Here little vegetation clings to the rock; water, harsh with the taste of iron and ice cold, runs from the ravines; the olive-trees are stunted and contorted in an effort to maintain a purchase on this crumbling gypsum territory. Their roots, like the muscles of wrestlers, hang from the culverts. Here the peasant girls lounge on the hillside—flash of colour like a bird—with a flower between their teeth, while their goats munch the tough thistle and ilex.

'All epochs from the Jurassic are represented here. In the north the configurations of certain caves suggest volcanic origins, but this has not yet been proved.' The grottoes at Paleocastrizza are ribbed with jewels which smoulder purple and yellow and nacre in the reflected light of the intruding sea. Grapes from this mountain region yield a wine that bubbles ever so slightly; an undertone of sulphur and rock. Ask for red wine at Lakones and they will bring you a glass of volcano's blood.

20.6.37

Zarian sends me a poem about the island in Armenian to which he adds an English translation. Writing of Corcyra he says: 'The gold and moving blue have stained our thoughts so that the darkness is opaque, and we see in our dreams the world as if in some great Aquarium. Exiles and sharers, we have found a new love. This is Corcyra, the chimney-corner of the world.'

Since I have nothing else I reciprocate with my poem on Manoli, the landscape painter of Greece: 'After a lifetime of writing acrostics he took up a brush and everything became twice as attentive. Trees had been simply trees before. Distinctions had been in ideas. Now the old man went mad, for everything undressed and ran laughing into his arms.'

Theodore promises 'Maps, Tables, and Statistics'. I am making no attempt to control all this material. If I wrote a book about Corcyra it would not be a history but a poem.

World of black cherries, sails, dust, arbutus, fishes and letters from home.

24.6.37

Fragment from a novel about Corcyra which I began and destroyed: 'She comes down through the cloud of almond-trees like a sentence of death, all dressed in white and leading her flock to the very gates of the underworld. Our hearts melt in us at the candour of her smile and the beauty of her walk. Soon she is to marry Niko, the fat moneylender, and become a stout shrew drudging out to olive-pickings on a lame donkey, smelling of garlic and animal droppings.'

25.6.37

N. has been away for three days in the town, trying to buy a few odds and ends of furnishings for the house. The silence here is like a discernible pulse—the heart-beat of time itself. I am all day alone on the great rock; the sea is cold—its chill hurts the back of the throat like an iced wine; but blue as the grave, while the sun is blazing. To-night a letter by boat from her. 'I have bought us a twenty-foot cutter, carvel built, and Bermuda rigged. I am terribly excited—the whole world seems to be open before us. But O how wine-darkly she rides. Bringing her out to-morrow with Petros. Wait for me at the point.'

26.6.37

The problem of water for the garden is serious. The only spring is on the highroad a quarter of a mile up the ravine. All our water is carried down on the backs of womenfolk in huge earthen jars. We had Nick the douser down with his hazel-twig, but after walking backwards and forwards grumbling under his breath for a quarter of an hour, he pronounced the water 'too deep'—over five metres. As the house stands at sea-level we could not afford to dig and have the well turn brackish on us. It must be a mountain spring or nothing. Meanwhile my two erudites send their suggestions by water—each a model of its kind. Zarian suggests a machine that a friend of his invented for turning salt water into fresh; he forgets how it works but he will write to America at once for particulars. It costs rather a lot but would save trouble; we would simply put one end of the pump in the sea and spray the garden with fresh water. Theodore, on the other hand, suggests something more practical. In the droughty summer the natives of Macedonia construct themselves ice-boxes by pulping quantities of prickly pear which they bury in a hole to the depth of about two metres. The hole is filled with fine pebbles or stones, and when the rains come the absorbing pulp of the prickly pear sups up the water and retains it in its pores. He suggests that we should adopt this scheme for our walled garden-boxes. 'Be careful', he adds, 'to pulp the tree well. Count V. tried this in his country house garden on my advice but omitted to pulp the prickly pear so that by some unfortunate chance he found it growing up through his flower-beds. This, as you can imagine, was a catastrophe and he has not spoken to me since.'

3.7.37

The conventions of our weekly meeting at 'The Partridge' are charming; we share our food, our criticism, and even our mail. When Zarian gets a letter from Unamuno or Celine it is read out and passed round the table; and when I get one of Henry Miller's rambling exuberant letters from Paris the company is delighted. This is the real island flavour; our existence here is in this delectable landscape, remote from the responsibilities of an active life in Europe, have given us this sense of detachment from the real world. Over the smoking copper pans the face of Paul, the Cretan manager of the tavern, looms strangely. He watches over the dishes, pausing to wipe the sweat out of his great brown moustaches; his manner is that of one who has dealt with epicures for a lifetime. Later Luke, the blind guitarist, arrives, led by his small son—a child of great beauty and pallor. Its face is the face of a Byzantine ikon. Stiffly the old red-faced man sits down on a chair, and strikes his instrument; the small expressionless face of the boy is cocked over his cheap violin as he tunes it. Then they strike up one of the familiar Greek jazz songs—inevitably a tango; yet the words haunt, and the refrain is taken up to the accompaniment of knife and fork by the roystering Zarian, Peltours the lean Russian painter, Veronica and John, Nimiec, Theodore. The narrow whitewashed room with its ugly tables and cheap advertisements rings.

'Loneliness, Loneliness,
You are bitter company to us.'

Afterwards we walk down in the warm night to the dark slipway, and, as the moon is rising, shake out the jib of the *Van Norden,* start her engine, and put our noses northward into the night. Lights move on the darkness hardly grazing the surface of the consciousness. From the receding shore, clear on the water, we can hear Zarian still contending some majestic literary theme. N. curls in a rug and dips her grapes over the side in the shining sea. And hollow over the harbour, speeding us with the promise of a safe arrival, St. Spiridion strikes the hour of midnight.

4.7.37

We breakfast at sunrise after a bathe. Grapes and Hymettos honey, black coffee, eggs, and the light clear-tasting Papastratos cigarette. Unconscious transition from the balcony to the rock outside. Lazily we unhook the rowboat and make for the point where the still blue sea is twisted in a single fold—like a curtain caught by a passing hand. A shale beach, eaten out of the cliff-point, falling to a row of sunken rocks. A huge squat fig-tree poised like a crocodile on the edge of the water. Five fathoms directly off the point so that sitting here on this spit we can see the dolphins and the steamers passing within hail almost. We bathe naked, and the sun and water make our skins feel old and rough, like precious lace. Yesterday we found the foetus of an octopus, colourless ball of gelatine, which throbbed invisibly in the palm of the hand; to-day the fisherboys have found our beach. They have written Angli ("Αγγλοι") in charcoal on one of the rocks, we have responded with 'Hellenes' which is fair enough. We have never seen them. N. draws a little head in a straw hat with a great nose and moustache.

5.7.37

Yesterday was a fisherman's holiday; first a great glistening turtle was washed up on the beach at the cliff edge. It was quite dead and its heavy yellow eyelids were drawn down over its eyes giving it a sinister and reptilian air of being half asleep. It must have weighed about as much as the dinghy. I expected the fishermen to make some use of the meat but nobody has touched it—except the village dogs which have been worrying its flippers.

More exciting was the killing of the eel. We were unhooking the boat when a small boy who was helping us cast off pointed to something in the water and exclaimed 'Zmyrna'. I was about to probe about with an oar—for I could see nothing in the shadow of the great rock—when Anastasius came running like a flash from the carpenter's shop. He held two heavy four-pronged tridents. For a moment or two he stared keenly down into the water; we could see nothing beyond the movements of marine life, the swaying of the seaweed fronds and the strange flickering passage of small fish. Then Anastasius lowered a piece of wood—simply the unshod shaft of a trident—into the darkest patch of the shadow. There was a small audible snap—as of a rat-trap closing—and his shoulders became rigid; maintaining his pressure on the wood he picked up a trident and lowering the point slowly into the water suddenly struck home at an angle. There was a sudden convulsion among the seaweed and the head of the eel emerged; it seemed to our terrified eyes about the size of a dog's head and infinitely more senseless and wicked. The trident had pierced the skull and while it was still dazed from the blow Anastasius strove to dislodge it from its perch. Help, too, was at hand. Old Father Nicholas came racing down with a couple of sharpened boat-hooks and these were driven into the meaty shoulders of the eel.

It took three of them to lug it on to the rock, and for a quarter of an hour on dry land it fought savagely, with two tridents piercing its brain and two more in its sides. I can hear the dry snapping of its jaws on the stick as I write. It had muscle on it like a wrestler, and its tail tapered into a great finned bolster of brown gristle—a turbine; altogether the whole fish looked more like an American invention than anything from the water-world; and it had the ferocity and determination of Satan. It was interesting to see how *afraid* its evil aspect made one; long after it was dead the peasants were driving their tridents into it with imprecations; and everyone gave it a wide berth until it stiffened with an unmistakable rigor.

Another reflection of this anxiety: Helen was given a terrific scolding because she was in the habit to poking about in the rocks at low tide barefooted. 'And if such an animal got you?' Anastasius kept repeating. 'And if such an animal got you?'

The children stood like carvings by the sea in their red flannel frocks, never taking their eyes off the dead eel. They all had their thumbs in their mouths. Then Sky removed her thumb with a little sigh and said: 'Let's go,' and they trotted off up among the olive-trees.

To-night we shall have eel-meat with red sauce for supper.

6.7.37

At night the fishing-boats put out; they carry great carbide-flares to attract the fish to the nets, and the dark bulk of the Albanian shadow opposite is studded with their jewelled fires. Dark red and smoky, occasional fires glow on the hills themselves; yellow and small along the sealine shine the lights of the solitaries who hunt alone in boats with tridents. I must record the method and the instruments employed in carbide fishing—but to-night my mind is full of a story which Nicholas has been telling me. It concerns two lovers in Corcyra during the occupation of the Turks. He was an Albanian Moslem and she a Greek. During a political crisis he was banished from the island and she was kept guarded in a country-house on the coast; before he left they agreed to signal to each other by lighting fires—he on the tip of Cape Stiletto and she at Govino on the second Sunday of every month. For three years these fire-messages passed telling each of them that the other was well. Then one night the girl died and her attendants forgot to light the accustomed fire. The fire on the Cape, however, burned at the accustomed time. But when her Albanian lover saw no response to his message he knew that something serious was afoot and crossed over to the island to try and visit her. He was caught and murdered. Yet ever since then on the second Sunday of every month there is a fire alight on the end of Cape Stiletto; it burns brackishly for a few hours and then goes out. Sometimes it shows a greenish flame. It is *not* a carbide-fisher as there is no shallow beach off the cape; it is *not* a scrub-fire because on this bare promontory there is nothing but rock. It is, says Nicholas, the Albanian sending his message—a message to which there is never any answer, for Govino headland lies dark and unresponsive to the west, under the hump of shadow from the mountains.

7.7.37

The boat rides beautifully. N. has christened her the *Van Norden*. Now in the still weather we keep her anchored close under the balcony; she is smart in her black paint with brass fittings and a white awning. Yesterday we took her out in a fresh north-easterly wind up as far as the Forty Saints. I wanted to conquer my timidity about a following wind. But she ran before it like a knife. The wood around the lead keel however is puffed and cankered; she must come out and be painted against worms. I notice that we speak about her in the compassionate and familiar way that people speak about their pets. The young schoolmaster Niko is full of envy, and in order to show off we invited him for a sail in the evening. He handles her much more sensitively than either of us; with roughness and determination, with an unerring sense of what to ask her. She turns upwind like a dancer and falters into the still water under the house like a vessel of silk.

IONIAN PROFILES

(FROM PROSPERO'S CELL, 1945)

25.7.37

The sea's curious workmanship: bottle-green glass sucked smooth and porous by the waves: vitreous shells: wood stripped and cleaned, and bark swollen with salt: a bead: sea-charcoal, brittle and sticky: fronds of bladderwart with their greasy marine skin and reptilian feel: rocks, gnawed and rubbed: sponges, heavy with tears: amber: bone: the sea.

Our life on this promontory has become like some flawless Euclidean statement. Night and sleep resolve and complete the day with their *quod erat demonstrandum*; and if, uneasily stirring before dawn, one stands for a moment to watch the morning star, which hangs like a drop of yellow dew in the east, it is not that sleep (which is like death in stories, beautiful) has been disrupted: it is the greater for this noiseless star, for the deep scented tree-line and the sea pensively washing and rewashing one dreams. So that, confused, you wonder at the overlapping of the edges of dream and reality, and turn to the breathing person in whose body, as in a sea-shell—echoes the systole and diastole of the waters.

Nights blue and geometric; endearing and seducing moon; the sky's curvature like an impress of an embrace while she rises—as if in one's own throat, so pure and glittering. When you have stared at her until she chills you, the human proportions of your world are reasserted suddenly. Suddenly the man crosses the orchard to the seawall. Helen walks with a lighted candle across the grass to tend the goat. Abstract from the balcony Bach begins to play—absorbed in his science of unknown relations, and only hurting us all because he implies experience he cannot state. And because paint and words are useless to fill the gap you lean forward and blow out the lamp, and sit listening, smelling the dense pure odour of the wick, and watching the silver rings play on the ceiling. And so to bed, two enviable subjects of the Wheel.

27.7.37

Yesterday we awoke to find an Aegean brigantine anchored in the bay. She wore the name of *Saint Barbara* and two lovely big Aegean eyes painted on her prow with the legend θεὸς ὁ Δκαιος ('God the Just'). The reflected eyes started up at her from the lucent waters of the lagoon. Her crew ate melons and spoke barbarically—sounding like Cretans. But the whole Aegean was written in her lines, the great rounded poop, and her stylish rigging. She had strayed out of the world of dazzling white windmills and grey, uncultured rock; out of the bareness and dazzle of the blinding Aegean into our seventeenth-century Venetian richness. She had strayed from the world of Platonic forms into the world of Decoration.

Even her crew had a baked, dazed, sardonic look, and sought no contact with my chattering, friendly islanders. The brig put out at midday and headed northward to the Forty Saints in a crumple of red canvas. Like a weary dancer to the Forty Saints and the Albanian peaks, to mirror herself in some deserted and glassy bay like a mad butterfly. We could not bear to see her go.

29.7.37

My material is rapidly getting out of control once more. Theodore has been to stay for a few days. Characteristic of his shy heart he sends us presents. For N. a box of Turkish delight with pistachio-nuts in it; for me a flute made of brass, with the word Μοναξιὰ

('Loneliness') engraved upon it. It is impossible to get a note out of it so I have asked the peasants to find me the shepherd boy to teach me.

Theodore has recorded the latest miracle of St. Spiridion with sardonic humour. An old man from a country village appeared at the X-ray laboratory with what was diagnosed as an incurable cancer of the stomach; medicine having washed its hands of him, the old man and his family made a mass-petition to the Saint. Within three weeks he reappeared before the doctors. The cancer had been reabsorbed. Theodore is professionally downcast, but secretly elated to find that the Saint has lost none of his art. It gives him the opportunity for a long disquisition upon natural resistance. It appears that the peasants can stand almost any physical injury which can be seen; but that a common cold may carry off a patient from sheer depression and terror. He gives an instance of a peasant who had a fight with his brother and whose head was literally cloven with an axe. Tying the two pieces of his skull together with a handkerchief the wounded man walked three miles into town to visit a doctor. He is still alive, though feebleminded.

Zarian has contributed a wonderful piece of natural observation for our notebooks. He observed last Tuesday that the four clock-faces of the Saint's church all registered different times of day. Intrigued, he asked permission to examine the phenomenon, scenting an ecclesiastical mystery. But it turns out that the clock-hands are made of the flimsiest material and that the pressure of the wind upon the clock. . . . Therefore when the north wind blows the northern clock-face is slowed up considerably, while when the south wind takes up its tale the southern clock-face shows a loss of time.

Not that time itself is anything more than a word here. Peasant measurement of time and distance is done by cigarettes. Ask a peasant how far a village is and he will reply, nine times out of ten, that it is a matter of so many cigarettes.

30.7.37

It is important, when writing about the peasants, not to falsify them with sentimental humour. It is very much the fashion to represent them as comic and quaint abstractions attached to picturesque names like Paul and Socrates and Aristotle. The fact that they dress oddly seems to drive city-bred writers into a frenzy of romantic admiration. But really the average Balkan peasant is quite commonplace, as venal, cunning, or admirable, as a provinical townsman. And the sentiment which attaches to the pastoral life of these picturesque communities (which treasure amulets against the devil and believe in a patron saint), has been very much overdone. Anthropologists are only just beginning to visit the suburbs of our greater cities with their apparatus. Their findings should establish a greater sense of connection between the peasant and the townsman.

3.8.37

Theodore has one particular friend who is a so-called lunatic. He sits with the others most of the time under the trees outside the whitewashed asylum building, looking at his own fingers; but at times an abrupt desire to talk seizes him, and when it does he unerringly selects for audience the so-called sane who pass along the dusty white road outside the railings. His name is Basil and he has yellow dilated eyes and a deep voice. Theodore often pauses on his way out of town to greet him, rattling his stick against the railings to draw his attention, and shifting the great green bag of tree-spore and seed which he carries about him on his walks. The lunatic sticks his head through the bars and smiles artfully. He says:

'They say I am mad.'

'Yes,' says Theodore gravely.

'And here I am.'

'Yes,' says Theodore.

'I am fed and clothed and do not have to work.'

'Yes.'

'Well—am I mad, or are the people outside mad?'

This is in the purest vein of Ionian logic and is to be commended to students of sociology. Basil's dossier lists him as a melancholic. A novice in a nearby monastery he early showed a gift for casuistry—that melancholy science. But he dips his fingers into Theodore's little paper bag of sweets with a transfiguring smile of happiness before he goes back to his place on the garden bench among the others.

6.8.37

'If you had an opportunity to put a question to Socrates what would it be?' writes Zarian. 'I would ask him if he was a happy man. I am sure that greater wisdom imposes a greater strain upon a man.' At the 'Partridge' this view is contested bitterly by Peltours and N. Wisdom, they say, teaches the ratiocinative faculty how to rest, to attain a deeper surrender of the whole self to the flux of time and space. Theodore recalls Socrates' epileptic fits while I find myself thinking of a line from Donne prefixed to 'Coryat's Crudities': 'When wilt thou be at full, Great Lunatique?'

7.8.37

Fishing demands the philosophic attitude. We have been waiting a week for propitious nights to use the carbide lamp and the tridents and at last the wish has been granted: deep still water and a waning moon which will not rise until late.

After dinner I hear the low whistle of the man by the sea and I go out on to the balcony. He is shipping his basket and tridents and screwing his carbide-lamp to the prow. To-night I am to try my hand at this peculiar mode of fishing. The tridents are four in number and varying in size; besides them we ship the octopus hook—attached to a staff about the size of a billiard cue—for octopus is not stabbed direct but coaxed: whereas squid and fish are victims of a direct attack.

Small adjustments are made. He removes his coat which smells of glue and wood shavings and bales some of the water out from under the floor-boards. Then we cast off and move slowly out into the darkness. The night is deep and clean-smelling and utterly silent. Far out under the Albanian hills glow the little flares of other carbide-fishers. Anastasius circles in the margin of rocks below the house and begins to talk quietly, explaining his practice. Midges begin to fly into our faces and we draw down our sleeves to cover our arms. He rows standing up and turning his oars without breaking the surface—since it is into this spotless mirror that we must gaze, and the least motion of wind smears all vision.

Presently the carbide lamp is lit and the whole miraculous underworld of the lagoon bursts into a hollow bloom—it is like the soft beautiful incandescence of a gas-mantle lighting. Transformed, like figures in a miracle, we gaze down upon a sea-floor drifting with its canyons and forests and families in the faint undertow of the sea—like a just-breathing heart.

Now hoarse in the darkness beyond the point the Brindisi packet-boat brays once; and nearer a grampus gives a Blimp-like snort. Then we are alone again.

Anastasius talks quietly. When I am tired I must not hesitate to tell him, he says. He himself is indefatigable and in good weather fishes half the night. But he is not really talking to me; he is talking himself into the receptive watchfulness of the hunter—the unreasoning abstraction which will allow him to anticipate the movement of fish; he is like a chess player combining possibilities in his own mind and testing them, so to speak, upon futurity.

We move in a concave ripple. Deep rock-surfaces, yellow and green and moving like a human scalp with marine fucus. Fishes, a school, the silver-white of σπάρος dawdle to the entrance of a cave and goggle at us. Each wears a black dapple on the back, and they look, in their surprise, like a row of semiquavers. Then, as if frightened by some purely marine event they disappear with the suddenness of a thrown switch. An eddy of wind purls the surface and Anastasius dips his twig of almond into the bottle of olive oil hanging at the prow. He scatters a few drops before us and the water clears again and steadies. I catch my breath, for there, crouching on a patch of reddish sand is the famous and eatable σκορπειὸς (I take him to be the sea-scorpion) with his bulldog head flattened upon a stone. Anastasius gets him squarely through the body at the first lunge and soon he is fluttering and ebbing in the darkness at my feet—a small dying pulse, uncomfortably tapping against the dry wood. Twice I put him in the basket and twice he leaps out and beats against the wood like the pulse of a dying bird.

We do not speak now, but proceed slowly along the edge of the lagoon in silence, surveying the haunted underworld which seems so like a panorama of the moon's surface. We stop where the fig-trees overhang and he tells me to look down. I can see nothing. Gingerly he lowers the trident and strikes; it is buried in a small white shape which begins to flutter madly. The small frightened eyes of the squid. As it breaks surface it spits a mouthful of ink over his face and arms and begins to wheeze like a sick kitten. Cursing softly and laughing he scrapes it off the trident against the gunwale and lets it drop into the basket where the contact of its fluttering hardly dead body suddenly rouses the stiffened body of the Scorpion to a small fluttering gasp of life. The air is cold tonight, and the sudden chill is fruitful, for within an hour we have several squid and two unnameable white fish besides the scorpion.

Anchored in a tiny bay we smoke a cigarette and Anastasius breaks off a piece of dry bread in his teeth. The air makes one hungry. The lamp is guttering and he charges it again with rock carbide. Once more the underworld flares into bloom. It is time, says Anastasius, for us to land an octopus, and to this end he ships the tridents and lets down his hooked staff, with its floating decoy of parsley training dispiritedly from it. He begins probing gently under rocks, turning this way and that. From the darkness of the cliff-edge above us a fir-cone falls with a little plop into the water. 'Look,' says Anastasius suddenly between his teeth, and I lean down. From under a rock, lazily moving, is something which looks like a snake. He is touching it very gently with the sprig of parsley, flirting with it. The tentacle plays softly with the leaves and is joined coyly by a second tentacle: then a third. They make playful passes at the sprig of green which conceals the waiting hook. Presently the ugly gas-mask head of the octopus comes into view, peering with moronic concentration at the decoy. And the moment has come. Anastasius slips the hook under the hood and tugs. There is a sudden strain and convulsion. The tentacles of the beast become rigid, but it is too late. Up it comes, writhing and grovelling, carrying two small boulders in its paws which it drops into the boat with a tremendous clatter, alarming us both. He now grips it firmly, and the hideous thing wraps itself round his arm, fighting back strongly. His object is to find the critical central bone, and he gives a sudden movement of the wrists, turning the hood inside out and plunging his teeth into a certain place in order to break it. A convulsion, and the whole mechanism seems to falter and fall to pieces. The tentacles still frantically suck and writhe, but they are now attached to a paralysed and shattered brain which gives them no directions for escape. Thrown dully to the bottom of the boat, they suck along the wood with the dull tearing noise that medical tape makes when it is being torn from human flesh.

Anastasius laughs softly and washes his hands in sea-water to dry them on the edge of his coat. A fish is a fish, but squid and octopus are a delicacy for him.

We take up the hunt in a desultory way and I manage, under his tuition, to spear yet another squid, and to miss a red mullet.

It is past midnight, and a small wind has sprung up, forcing us to use more and more olive oil to still the surface. We retrace our path slowly indulging in afterthoughts: looking under rocks which we have missed, and probing the larger caves in the hope of rousing an eel. Soon we are back at the davits, slinging the boat. Helen is there to meet us with bread and wine. I lend her my torch and she exclaims proudly over the catch in the happy vein of a person whose lunch and dinner for the morrow has been provided for.

By now a thin slice of moon is up, and early morning winds are beginning to curl up and lie on the surface of the water for a minute at a time before disappearing. The cypresses stretch for a moment from their romance stillness, like tired and cramped human models. I pause irresolute at the still edge of the bay, wondering whether the water is too cold for a bathe. The taste of the Greek cigarette is light and heady.

To-morrow I am to be instructed in the art of fishing with the shoulder net—called δείχτι. This has a span of about six feet, and is loaded at the edge with lead. It is carried folded in a certain way on the left shoulder and is used to trap fish in shallow water. The throwing of it demands a special skill.

And so, confused by these shallow veins of thought, to the balcony and the bedroom. The *Van Norden* lies at anchor twenty feet from the house, her tall spars rigid and consciously beautiful on the lacquer of the sea.

Sleep, in this cool, still room, is like entering a cave.

LANDSCAPE WITH OLIVE TREES

(FROM PROSPERO'S CELL, 1945)

10.1.38

Dominant in a landscape full of richer greens, the olive is for the peasant both a good servant and a hard master. In the good olive year whose harvest stretches across from January to May, the whole country population is busy attending to the tree which provides the island with its staple diet—olive oil.

Throughout the spring months, through the gales of March and the hard sunspots of April, the tireless women are out with their soft wicker hampers gathering the fruit as it falls. In the other islands the fruit is beaten from the tree and the tree itself pruned; but in Corcyra this has been, for hundreds of years, considered harmful. Prolix in its freedom therefore the olive takes strange shapes; sometimes it will swell and burst open, ramifying its shoots until a whole clump of trees seems to grow out of the breast of the parent; in some places (there is one particular grove between Kouloura and Kassopi) the trees grow tall and slender, with bodies not rough, but of a marvellous platinum-grey, and branches aerial and fine of attitude. In the northern crags again the olive crouches like a boxer; its roots undermine roads; its skin is rough and wormy; and its pitiful exhausted April flowering is like an appeal for mercy against the conspiracy of rock and heat.

There is no estate without its oil magazine—a low building with stamped earthen floor which houses the presses and all the machinery of the trade. It is here that the long lines of coloured women come, bearing their baskets full of the sloe-shaped fruit, now covered in bloom. And here they stand, gorgeous as birds, they shake the rain from their dresses and receive their dole of bread and piercing garlic.

Built up against the wall of the magazine lie the cold stone bunkers which slowly brim with the fruit; while monstrous in the shadows stands the massive and primitive mill. This has a stone bed with a gutter about three feet high. From its centre a beam supports a granite millstone. A smaller beam standing at right angles to this can be harnessed to the neck of a pony which supplies the millstone's power.

On wet days when a big wood fire is built at which the women can dry themselves as they come in from olive-gathering, the shadows leap and flap against the gloom of the archways, throwing into sudden relief the strings of onions and tobacco hanging from the roof, the unruffled chickens lying in the straw, the weaving-loom, and perhaps the sagacious evil face of the billy-goat munching in a corner.

The olive-gathering is an all-weather business; in the blinding February storms you hear the little hard berries dropping to the ground, and, if you happen to be standing on high ground looking southward you can see the visible track of the north wind as it strikes the valley, turning the olive trees inside out—so that they change from green to silver and back to green. Under the shelter of archway and wall the women stoop in circles steadily filling their hampers while the rain rattles like small-shot in the leaves about them and the first thirsty wild flowers stir in the cold ground under their feet.

But the olive-tree has hardly suited its internal economy to its position, for its attenuated white flowering commences in April, just when it is most occupied with the ripening of its fruit: so that if its previous year's blossom has been prolific, it has hardly the strength to blossom again. Its crop is irregular, and the lean years for the harvesters are very lean indeed. Bread and oil as a diet hardly leaves any margin for thrift.

After the first pressing in the mill-bed the men come with their wide-mouthed baskets and gather up the magma, piling its greyish mass into a wooden press; the pony, whose efforts at the millstone are now no longer necessary, is unharnessed and turned loose in the paddock. Taking up the long wooden lever, the men begin to screw at the pulp, helping the oil away if the weather is cold, by pouring boiling water upon it. As the pressure becomes stronger, they fasten a rope to a sort of primitive windlass, and give the creaking structure their whole weight. It is like the birth of something in the gloom of the great magazine; their groans echo through the cypress floors of the house. The windlass creaks. The fowls cluck nervously about the feet of the men. Appreciatively sitting in the great fireplace with the light playing upon his beard, the abbot of the local monastery lends moral support as he sips his glass of wine.

The oil itself spurts dirtily in the stone gutters and slips drop by drop into the underground stone tanks where it will be left to settle itself into purity; while the madder coloured acid refuse is run off into the gutters—where its pungent smell and the scorched herbage of its course are familiar characteristics of the landscape.

After many settlings in the various stone tanks the oil is considered pure enough to send to the town to the bulk dealers, poured into leather skins, which bobble and gulp, it is loaded into carts which rumble slowly off down the circuitous paths to Corfu. Bright and greasy in the sunlight the skins jog hideously together like so many truncated corpses.

The cakes of the refuse, now dried brown and stiff, and empty of juice, are stacked in the dry corners of the magazine, to be used later for fuel. Broken up they burn with a subdued smouldering warmth, and added to wood and coal, give our winter stove fuel enough to carry us through the three worst months.

Though the olive is an undependable friend its role never varies; dipped into it, the coarse peasant bread tastes dense and foul—yet the children of the fishermen have warm brown skins and dazzling white teeth. Everything is cooked in it. And it is only poetic justice to observe that every saint's shrine has lamps which are replenished by the offering of the poor, who have slaved nearly the whole year round in varying weather to gathering the yield of the tree.

The whole Mediterranean—the sculptures, the palms, the gold beads, the bearded heroes, the wine, the ideas, the ships, the moonlight, the winged gorgons, the bronze men, the philosophers—all of it seems to rise in the sour, pungent taste of these black olives between the teeth. A taste older than meat, older than wine. A taste as old as cold water.

The olive in Corcyra is the smallholder's pride, and in the wooded parts of the island land values are usually computed on the basis of the number of olive-trees. It is usual for the larger proprietors to let out the season's oil crop to the peasant living on the property, who works the crop and receives half the oil in return. But in the poorer villages holdings can amount to as little as two or three trees—and prospective property speculators take great care when buying a piece of land, to find out who owns the olive-trees, as their possession confers right of way.

14.1.38
Abstemious in the matter of drinks, the Greeks produce their own light wines and cognacs in abundance. Yet during our whole stay here we have seen a drunk person not more than once; and more

endearing still, we have discovered that these people have so delicate a palate as to be connoisseurs of cold water. The glass of water appears everywhere; it is an adjunct to every kind of sweetmeat, and even to alcohol. It has a kind of biblical significance. When a Greek drinks water he *tastes* it, and pressing it against the palate, savours it. The peasants will readily tell you which wells give the sweetest water, while even the townspeople retain a delicate taste in water, and are able to recognize the different sources from which the little white town handcarts (covered in green boughs) are replenished.

Two days before Christmas we climbed the dizzy barren razorback of Pantocratoras to the monastery from which the whole strait lay bare, lazy and dancing in the cold haze. Lines of dazzling water crept out from Butrinto, and southward, like a beetle on a plate, the Italian steamer jogged its six knots towards Ithaca. Clouds were massing over Albania, but the flat lands of Epirus were frosty bright. In the little cell of the warden monk, whose windows gave directly upon the distant sea, and the vague rulings of waves to the east, we sat at a deal table and accepted the most royal of hospitalities—fresh mountain walnuts and pure water from the highest spring; water that had been carried up on the backs of women in stone jars for several hundred feet.

15.1.38

During the last summer visit to the Count D. we attended a ceremony which furnished the seed for a whole train of arguments about pagan survivals, which have since been incorporated in one of Theodore's many unpublished monographs. The Count was half-way down the avenue of cypress trees when we came upon him, carrying in his hand a beautiful Venetian dish, full of something which only Theodore recognized as Colyva—the offering to the dead. 'You will perhaps walk with me,' said the Count, turning aside after his usual greetings, 'and assist me. I am making a small reverence to a cousin of mine who died two years ago to-day.' Noticing Zarian's hungry eye upon the dish (for our walk had been a long and dusty one) he smiled and said: 'It is a peasant custom still—and descended from who knows what pagan rite.' He removed the lid for us to look at the contents. 'Pomegranate seeds, wheat, pine-nuts, almonds and raisins, all soaked in honey. Here, it really tastes rather nice. Try some.' Together we walked with him through the wood, following the bridle-paths, until we came to the small chapel, surrounded by tall cypresses. The Count undid the heavy iron padlock which secured the door to what appeared to be the family vault. The gloom was intense, and the shadow thrown by the cypresses gave it a greenish radiance. We entered down three earthen steps leading to the concrete floor upon which the uncouth stone tombs stood, primitive in their lack of ornament. 'There is no need for the unearthly hush,' said the Count quietly. 'For us death is very much a part of every thing. I am going to put this down here on Alecco's tomb to sustain his soul. Afterwards I shall offer you some more of it at home, my dear Zarian, to sustain your body. Is that not very Greek? We never move far in our metaphysical distinctions from the body itself. There is no incongruity in the idea that what fortifies our physical bowels, will also comfort Alecco's ghostly ones. Or do you think we are guilty of faulty dissociation?' Zarian and Theodore, more at home in the gloom now, potter the length of the vault. While Theodore characteristically examines the moss upon the walls and attempts to recall its medical name, Zarian concentrates upon a tomb in the corner which appears to be empty; the cracked stone lid lies beside it, as if it had fallen off in the struggles of the body to re-enter life. 'Ugly things, these tombs,' says the Count. 'Like the bunkers of a merchant ship. Ah! you are looking at the empty one. It used to belong to my Uncle John, who caused us a lot of trouble. He became a vampire, and so we had him moved to the church behind the hill, where the ecclesiastical authorities could keep an eye on him. You did not know that the vampire exists?'

Walking back to the house across the green grass of the meadow, Theodore and the Count exchange reminiscences of vampiredom. The vampire is still believed in. It is known as a Vrikolax (βρυκολαξ) and is the reward for an exceptionally evil life. In some cases vampires have been reported to have terrorized villages to such an extent that the Church has had to be called in to use its powers of exorcism. 'Uncle John," says the Count, 'whom I remember as an old grey-whiskered ruffian in jack-boots, appears to have been an exceptionally wicked man. His reappearance was fully borne out by over two hundred witnesses, some of whose children had actually died. It was unpleasant, but they dug him up and put a stake into his heart in the traditional fashion. I felt that it was more politic to move him off the estate into the precincts of a church in order to avoid gossip.'

This theme, sufficiently exciting to wake Zarian from the abstraction into which his weekly Armenian article always throws him, also wakens Theodore in whom there lives a vague Edwardian desire to square applied science with comparative religion. The Count listens with exquisite politeness to a dissertation upon peasant lore. No one could guess that he has already heard it on several occasions. Throughout lunch, which we eat in the shade of the grape-arbour, Theodore unloads his evidence of pagan survivals in Greece—information which Zarian notes down excitedly on his cuff, on the tablecloth, in the battered notebook. Zarian's inveterate note-taking is a charming trait in his character—especially as he has never yet been known to succeed in reading his own notes afterwards, so cramped and illegible a hand has he. Theodore spends hours helping him to decode his own notes every Tuesday when the massive and erudite Armenian article must be begun.

During the afternoon, while the worthies of my Corcyrean pantheon are sleeping in shuttered rooms, I slip down to the house of the peasant family and borrow the Count's placid little mare, which will take me through the vineyards and woods to what is perhaps the loveliest beach in the world. Its name is Myrtiotissa. Lion-gold sand, of the consistency of tapioca, lies smoothly against the white limestone cliff, thrown up in roundels by the force of the sea, which breaks upon a narrow sand-bank some sixty yards clear of the shore. The rocks here are pitted and perforated into natural cisterns, sluggish with weed, and which the receding tide has left full of sea-water and winking fishes; water which the sun has heated to greater than the temperature of human blood. Lowering myself into these natural baths, holding softly to the ladder of many-coloured seaweed, I feel the play of the Ionian, rising and falling about an inch upon the back of my neck. It is like the heartbeat of the world itself. It is no longer a region or an ambience where the conscious or subconscious mind can play its incessant games with itself; but penetrating to a lower level still, the sun numbs the source of ideas itself, and expands slowly into the physical body, spreading along the nerves and bones a gathering darkness, a weight, a power. So that each individual finger-bone, each individual arm and leg, expand to the full measure of their own animal consciousness in this beneficent and dangerous sun-darkness. The scalp seems to put forth a drenched thatch of seaweed to mingle with the weeds rising and falling around one's body. One is entangled and suffocated by this sense of physical merging into the elements around one. Blinded by this black sunlight, nothing remains of the known world, save the small sharp toothless kisses of fish on the hanging body—now no longer owned; a providential link with feeling, like the love of women, or the demands of the stomach, which tie one to the world of simple operations. One could die like this and wonder if it was death. The density, the weight and richness of a body without a mind or ghost to trouble it.

Here sometimes I come across Matthew, the lame dynamiter of fish, whose illegal operations in these bays have already cost him the sight of an eye and two fingers of his left hand. I help him to dive for those of his fish which for some mysterious reason sink instead of staying on the surface. On a fire of twigs in the evening we have often watched him grilling his fish with the absorbed air of a specialist, while Zarian stood by with the salt, and the Count with his little bottle of lemon-juice. Matthew chooses the afternoon for his fishing, as the noise of the detonations cannot then dissipate the heavy sleep of the policeman in the little guard house up the hill. He is an admirable companion because he never speaks. Clad in patched clothes and the conventional woollen vest, he moves slowly along the rocky galleries above the sea, his prehensile black toes (now swollen and bloated with damp) gripping the rocky ledges. In his right hand he holds the home-made depth-charge, which is made from a cigarette tin and short length of fuse wire. I follow him at a safe range, to allow for any mechanical faults in this piece of machinery.

At about three o'clock he will invariably climb the cliff above the bay, to where the monastery stands in its dazzling white sunlight, and fall asleep in the shadow of the main gate with his silver catch lying in his old felt hat upon the grass.

Three hundred feet below, I cross the margin of scalding white sand, to the shadow of the great rock, and lie panting for a moment, too exhausted by running to move. Above me, leaking from the heart of the cliff, runs sweet water, down a shallow lip of maidenhair, into a sand-bowl; further to the left a mysterious spring rises in the very sand itself with little regular gushes, as if from some severed artery in the earth. At each soundless pulse a small cone of sand rises in the hollow and slowly spins back to the bottom. Clear and cold, the water plays with the regularity of a clock. It is the sweetest of the island waters, because it tastes of nothing but the warm afternoon, the breath of the cicadas, the idle winds crisping at little corners of the inert sea, which stretches away towards Africa, death-blue and timeless.

In this little bowl I wash the grapes I have brought with me. They are the little early grapes, delicately freckled green, and of a pouting teat-shape. The sun has penetrated their shallow skins and has confused the sweetness with its own warmth; it is like eating something alive.

Then after a rest another burst of running across the sand to where the cliff-path winds upwards, vertiginous and rocky, among the myrtle-groves. At the top of the cliffs, if you look back, you see the sea has become a deep throbbing emerald; the sand is freckled by long roaming silver lines across which an occasional lazy fish will move, indulgent of still water. In the shadows under the cliff a piercing nitric green. Far out across the water a brig moves southward into the sun; the noise of its engine is carried in the empty spaces of the air—a sound rubbed out as soon as regis-tered, though nothing has breathed or stirred around one. A white butterfly wavers in across the blue spaces.

The mare snorts in the shadow of the peasant's house, glad to return. Half an hour later I am under the terrace upon which Zarian and Theodore sit, drinking tea from heavy Venetian-looking crockery, while the Count, an unfamiliar pipe alight in his mouth, sits and methodically cleans the coat of his favourite gun dog. It is inevitable that the discussion of this morning should be continuing. 'But, my dear Doctor,' the Count is saying placidly, 'I do not know how you can reconcile current religious beliefs without dragging in the ancient Pantheon. Our saints are not canonized and forgotten. They walk. The hagiography of St. Spiridion is still being written in those little two drachma books you buy outside the church. And then, the confusions. You have made a study of the folk-songs; have you found a very clear distinction made between the just and the unjust, or the idea of reward and punishment? No. The dead simply drink the waters of Lethe (τῆς Λυσρουνίας τα νερα) and enter into a sort of mirage life, troubled by vague longings for fleshly joys—everything which we sum up in that most beautiful of Greek words Νοσταλγία. And then, of course, you have the Underworld, the Abode of the Dead. It is also known as Hades and as Tartarus, just to complete our confusion. And Charon, as you know, still exists, though he has altered his habits. Sometimes black snake, sometimes black swallow or eagle, he is also the Black Cavalier of our modern imaginations, dragging the souls of the dead behind him into the netherworld. And even he is credited in modern mythology with a wife. No. The only return for the dead seems to be for the unlucky or the evil; they become vampires and roam for a short while, until the Church catches up with them.'

Zarian is wearing his spectacles which means that he is paying extra close attention. Meanwhile Theodore nods his golden beard and, pouring out his tea into a saucer, blows upon it to cool it. The methodical fingers of the Count move through the shaggy coat of the animal, pulling off the fat white ticks, pursed with blood, one by one. 'And then the naiads', says the Count again, with his peculiar sweetness of voice, 'and the nereids that haunt our fountains and wells—what would we do without them? The shadow of the cypress which at noonday can drive a sleeper mad? The sea-maiden that winds her arms about those poor fishermen whom the full moon has overtaken on the strands?' Theodore is giving his famous grunt of disapproval which we have all learned to imitate. It is a kind of humming behind closed lips. 'You cannot, my dear Doctor,' continues the Count ruthlessly, 'make them compare with your scientific findings, yet we are glad to own them, even if they are lapses from the material attitude. They are part of the fantasy of this remarkable country and island, are they not?'

The dog whimpers softly as the strong antiseptic is applied to the little raw wounds left by the ticks; the Count's shapely hands cherish and soothe it. He looks up smiling, and watches Zarian disposing of a cake in short order. 'And think of the piercing lamentations of the professional mourners. I have made a collection of them—all spontaneous poetry, and some of the best known to the language. But there is no trace of the good-and-evil preoccupation. No, we Greeks are not religious, we are superstitious and anarchic. Even death is less important than politics. There is a kind of old Mother Hubbard who lives on the hill there; she is much in demand at funerals because of her poetic gift. Last year when Taki the fisherman died you should have heard her singing. It would have moved a stone.

"My silver boy,

My golden one,

Softer the down on his face

Than breast of the woodcock;

Keener his mind than a snake striking.

The silver person has left us.

The golden man has gone."

'We carried him in his open box to the cemetery on the hill, and all the time this poetry was flowing out of Mother Hubbard in a continuous stream, keeping pace with her tears, for she really loved Taki.'

'Was the coffin open?' says Zarian.

'Yes. There again a point is proved.'

'Is that a religious custom of the island?'

'No. But under the Turks it was a law to prevent the smuggling of arms in coffins under the pretence of carrying corpses to the grave. In some places it has lingered on among the superstitious. So Taki's pale aquiline features were visible all the way as the ragged little procession wound up the hill. He looked as if he were about to smile. Of course no sooner was he dead and buried than Mother Hubbard, who was some vague relation, took out an injunction against his mother, to prevent her disposing of Taki's twenty olive-trees, which, she said, had been given to her as a gift. You see, there seemed to her no incongruity in making poetry for a dead man whom you love, and whose heirs you are trying to swindle. The case dragged on for months and I believe she lost it.'

As we talk we are watching out of the corner of our eyes the little party of sprayers which moves slowly down the rows of olive-trees. The foremost man holds the long canister with the tapering spout, through which he sprays a jet of arsenic and molasses, in a light cloud over each tree, to preserve the bloom against the ravages of its special pest. . . .

'It is fortunate', says the Count, 'to have a rich language. Look at my olive trees. How immeasurably they are enriched by the poetic symbolism which surrounds them—the platonic idea of the olives. The symbol for everything enriched by the domestic earth and private virtue. Then again, we use the word for those small dark moles which our women sometimes have on their faces or throats. And of course, being Greek, I find myself thinking at one and the same moment of all these facts, as well as the fact that the olive brings me in some eight hundred pounds a year on which to philosophize. Poetry and profit are not separated at all. For the Greek there is only the faintest dividing line.'

The evening light mellows very softly into its range of warm lemon tones, pressing among the close bunches of ripening grapes, and washing the tiles of the peasant houses in the valley. The turtle-doves croon softly in the arbours behind the orchard. The cicadas are dying out—station after station closing down. The two great plane-trees are already silent, and only in the meadow where the sun still plays do they keep up their singing. In the altering values of sound one becomes aware of the chink of teacups as the servant-girl clears away.

'The great god Pan', says the Count, reverting suddenly to his original theme, which has been running as an undercurrent in his thoughts all this time, 'was first announced as dead off Paxo, some miles south of us. This island must have been among the first to get the news. We have no records to tell us how the islanders received it. Yet in our modern pantheon we have a creature whose resemblance to Pan is not, I think, fortuitous. He is, as you know, called the kallikanzaros. He is the house-sprite, a little cloven-hooved satyr with pointed ears, who is responsible for turning milk sour, for leaving doors unlocked, and for causing mischief of every kind. He is sometimes placated by a saucer of milk left upon a window-sill, or a kolouri—one of those quoit-shaped peasant cakes. He also is dying out. But there is one story about him which you, my dear Zarian, will enjoy recording. It is said that on the ten days preceding Good Friday, all the kallikanzaroi in the Under-world are engaged simultaneously upon the task of sawing through the giant plane-tree whose trunk is supposed to hold up the world. Every year they almost succeed, except that the cry "Christ has arisen" saves us all, by restoring the tree and driving them up in a chattering throng into the real world—if I may call our world that. Perhaps you will be able to find classical origins for the story. I give it to you for what it is worth.'

Bats are now beginning their short strutting flights against the sky. In the east the colour is washing out of the world, leaving room for the great copper-coloured moon which will rise soon over Epirus. It is the magic hour between two unrealized states of being—the day-world expiring in its last hot tones of amber and lemon, and the night-world gathering with its ink-blue shadows and silver moonlight.

'Watch for her', says the Count, 'behind that mountain there.' The air tastes faintly of damp. 'She will be rising in a few moments.'

'I am thinking', says Zarian, 'how nothing is ever solved finally. In every age, from every angle, we are facing the same set of nat-ural phenomena, moonlight, death, religion, laughter, fear. We make idolatrous attempts to enclose them in a conceptual frame. And all the time they change under our very noses.'

'To admit that,' says the Count oracularly, 'is to admit happiness —or peace of mind, if you like. Never to imagine that any of these generalizations we make about gods or men is valid, but to cherish them because they carry in them the fallibility of our own minds. You doctor, are scandalized when I suggest that *The Tempest* might be as good a guide to Corcyra as the official one. It is because the state of being which is recorded in the character of Prospero is something which the spiritually rich or the sufficiently unhappy can draw for themselves out of this clement landscape.'

'All this is metaphysics,' says Zarian a trifle unhappily.

'All speculation that goes at all deep becomes metaphysics by its very nature; we knock up against the invisible wall which bounds the prison of our knowledge. It is only when a man has been round that wall on his hands and knees, when he is certain that there is no way out, that he is driven upon himself for a solution.'

'Then for you, Count,' says Theodore, 'the hard and fast structure of the sciences yields nothing more than a set of comparative myths, some with and some without charm?'

'I would like to pose the problem from another angle. There is a morphology of forms in which our conceptual apparatus works, and there is a censor—which is our conditioned attitude. He is the person whom I would reject, because he prevents me choosing and arranging knowledge according to my sensibility. I will give you an example. I was once asked to write a short history of sixth-century Greek sculpture. My publisher refused the work because in it I had pointed out that sixth-century sculpture reaches its peak in Maillol, an artist of whom the man had not then heard. He informed me that I could not treat history in this manner. He informed me of the fact in the exact tone of voice used by my own censor when I first happened upon a Maillol statue, standing weighed down by its connections with the Mediterranean earth. Yet an instant's observation will show one that Maillol does not belong to us in space and time, but to them; I mean to the Greeks of the sixth century.'

At this point, according to time-honoured custom, we chant in unison: 'And if you don't believe me there is a Maillol in the garden to prove it to you', at which the Count smiles his indulgent smile and nods twice. 'There is indeed,' he says.

The first bronze cutting-edge of the moon shows behind the mountain, travelling fast. 'Ah, there she is,' says Zarian.

'And here we are,' says the Count, unwilling to relinquish his subject, 'each of us collecting and arranging our common knowledge according to the form dictated to him by his temperament. In all cases it will not be the whole picture, though it will be the whole picture for you. You, Doctor, will proceed under some title like *The Natural History, Geology, Botany and Comparative Ethnology of the Island of Cofu.* You will be published by a learned society in Vienna. Your work will contain no mention of the first edition of Petrarch in the Library, or of the beautiful mother of Gorgons in the Museum. As for you, Zarian, your articles when they are collected in a book will present a ferocious and lopsided account of an enchanted island which has seduced every historical figure of note from Nero to Napoleon. You will omit the fact that communications are bad and that all Greeks are liars, and that the fleas during the summer are intolerable. It will not be a true picture—but what a picture it will be. Hordes of earnest Armenians from New York will settle here to quote your poetry and prose to each other, and I will be able to charge two drachmae for sitting in the chair which you now occupy and which will certainly outlive you.'

'And I?' I say. 'What sort of picture will I present of Prospero's Island?'

'It is difficult to say,' says the Count. 'A portrait inexact in detail, containing bright splinters of landscape, written out roughly, as if to get rid of something which was troubling the optic nerves. You are the kind of person who would go away and be frightened to return in case you were disappointed; but you would send others and question them eagerly about it. You are to be forgiven really, because you have had the best of your youth in the island. And it is only very much later that one grows the courage to return. I noticed that you did not drink of Kardaki's well the other day. I particularly noticed.'

'I do not like being bound by charms,' I say.

At this point Theodore, who has been listening with some impatience to this dissertation upon character, suggests a stroll, and soon we are walking down the avenue of cypresses together, smelling the strong tobacco from the Count's pipe.

'Ah no, Doctor,' says the old man, as if continuing aloud an argument which has been going on quietly in his mind, 'thought must be free. Let us dispense with the formalist whose only idea is to eliminate the dissonant, the discrepant. Let us marry our ideas and not have them married for us by smaller people. Only in this way will our ideas produce children—for the children of ideas are actions. Dear me,' he adds, 'I am hardly in a position to moralize. I live here quietly without children, on money which my grandfather earned. It would be useless my justifying myself to an economist by explaining that I am exercising my sensibility through loving greatly and suffering greatly in all this quietness. Don't you think?'

Insensibly his footsteps have led us across the green unkept lawns to where the nymph stands in her rotunda. Her loins fall away in their heavy inevitable lines to her shapely feet. The torso is heavy with its weight of lungs and bone. The breasts ride superbly, held by the invisible thongs of the pectorals.

'An old man's love,' says the Count. 'Look at her. There you have desire which is quite still, retained inside the mind as form and volume—like the grapes for lunch which were still warm and a little drowsy from the sun. It is the speechless potence of the old man, the most terrible kind of desire in stillness which this Mediterranean sculptor has impressed in the rock. Was he happy or unhappy, moral or amoral? He was outside the trap of the opposites. It was a mindless act of coition with the stone that made him describe her. Critics would be interested to know if it was his wife or his eldest daughter. Their speculations would lie right outside the realm in which this sixth-century Pomona stands. It is not desire as we know it—but an act of sex completed by looking at her. The weight of her. Feel how cold the stone arms are.'

The moon is up now among the trees, and the first screech of the owl rings out across the meadow.

'Ah! but I see they have lighted the candles and laid the table,' says the Count, suddenly conscious of the dew as he moves his toes in his battered felt slippers. 'And is it our function simply to stand about here making bad literature? Doctor, we are having brain cutlets in your honour this evening; and, my dear Zarian, a bottle of Mantinea red wine for you.'

Seated at the great table by the sedate light of his own candles, the Count turns to me and says: 'It is the pleasantest form of affection to be able to tease one's friends. You perhaps do not know the history of the Society of Ionian Studies and the brain cutlets?' At this Theodore shows the faintest signs of impatience, and remarking it, the Count pats him laughingly on the arm. 'The Doctor's well-known passion for brain cutlets is something of which you will have undoubtedly heard. Well, some years ago, he was asked to become President of a small informal society of local savants, who were bent on the pursuit of Ionian studies. They were a sombre and bearded collection—for the most part doctors and lawyers of the island: these being the two classes which have the least work to do. At this time our friend was pursuing some studies upon forms of idiocy at the local asylum; and he was particularly interested in the mental condition of an inmate called Giovannides, whose brain he had been coveting off and on for a number of years. In those days he used to speak about Giovannides' brain with ill-concealed cupidity, and explain what a splendid time he would have when the patient died. You see, he had been promised the brain for dissection. Now it so happened that this long-awaited event took place upon the very day when the inaugural lunch of the society was due to take place at the Doctor's house; Theodore was in a state of great excitement. He found himself unable to be patient, and spent the whole morning extracting the brain from its brain-case, remembering all the time that he must get home and prepare his speech for the Society. By midday he had succeeded in removing the brain, and, having wrapped it carefully in greaseproof paper, he had managed to reach home with it held in his arms like a precious treasure. On entering the house he realized that the day was exceptionally warm, so he entered the kitchen, where he popped the lunatic's brain in the ice-box, and retired to his study to prepare his speech. All went well. The guests arrived and were seated at table. The speech was delivered and met with restrained applause. And a steaming dish of the Doctor's favourite brain-cutlets appeared, which was greeted with delighted exclamations. As the guests were helping themselves the telephone in the corner of the room rang. It was Theodore's wife, who had rung up to apologize for having been unable to provide him with his favourite dish for lunch. There was, she said, no brain to be bought anywhere in town. An involuntary cry burst from Theodore's lips. To do him justice, it was not really of his guests that he was thinking so much as of his brain. With a muffled cry of "Giovannides' brain" he sprang to the kitchen and opened the ice-box. The brain had gone. Speechless with anxiety the good doctor returned to the banqueting-room and found that his guests were all looking either uneasy or downright ill. Where a lesser man would have carried it off without telling them anything definite, and where a greater would have wrung his hands for science, Theodore simply stood, trembling from head to foot and pointing at the dish of excellent brain-cutlets and repeating: "I get a brain and *this* is what you do. I get a brain and *this* is what you do." By this time the truth had dawned upon the Ionian Society; their dissolution was so sudden as to be amazing. The maid threw her apron over her head and burst into sobs. The inaugural lunch was a failure. But that was not the unkindest thing of all. The brain of the lunatic was at this moment safely upon Theodore's desk, in the study; the cook, who was devoted to Theodore, had spent the whole morning searching for brain, and had found some in the nick of time. The cutlets served to the Society were perfectly genuine brain cutlets. But do you think he has ever managed to persuade anyone of the truth of this? No. The Society is now referred to as the Brainfever Society, and its members are all supposed to be suffering from aberrations brought on by this meal.'

This anecdote, which we have heard perhaps a dozen times, always sinks Theodore into a profound gloom; for Zarian laughs so immoderately that he spills his wine, and has a fit of coughing until he almost rolls under the table. This is the Count's cue, and turning to him on the backwash of his laughter he says: 'But perhaps Zarian will permit me to tell you the story of his explorations into Greek wines.' At this, it is Zarian's turn to look uncomfortable, while Theodore's face is lit by a shy smile. 'You will have noticed,' says the Count, 'that Zarian champions everything

Greek except the wines. It is true they are not very good, but you would expect a few romantic notes to be blown from time to time on his trumpet. No, I might go so far as to say that he is definitely against Greek wine, and I often wonder whether the little incident of the Mantinea 1936 had anything to do with it. May I repeat the story in my own way?' he asks Zarian with elaborate courtesy. The latter runs his fingers through his mane of silver hair, braces his shoulders as one about to bear a burden, and humbly nods. It is charming to watch him ill-at-ease, picking at the tablecloth, searching for non-existent matches in the pockets of his waistcoat, or shaking his finger in his ear with an expression of simulated pain. The Count sips his wine twice, fills my glass, and continues.

'Late one night last year I received a telephone call. The voice was so full of suppressed excitement that I had difficulty in recognizing it as that of Zarian. He had, he said, something of the utmost importance to tell me. The revelation was too secret to be mentioned on the phone, but I gathered that something very frightful or very wonderful had happened to him. At that time I was in the town house, so I agreed to walk across the Esplanade and see my friend. To be frank, I thought he had simply written a poem. As we all know, when Zarian writes one of his rare poems, he telephones to all his friends and asks them to come round and have it read to them. It was not a poem or an accident. When I climbed those tottering stairs to the top floor of the St. George Hotel I found my friend sitting in a room at a table, staring with considerable rigidity at an open bottle of wine. A single candle guttered beside it on the table. Catching sight of me, he beckoned me speechlessly into the room and into a chair opposite. For a moment he said nothing but continued to stare at the bottle of wine. Then at last he spoke in accents positively strangled by excitement. "My dear Count," he said, "I have at last discovered a

Greek wine comparable to anything grown in France." He tiptoed to a cupboard and brought me a glass which he filled very gingerly, holding his breath as he did so. I sipped it. It was a very fine Beaune, ringing on the palate like a note of music. The bottle said MANTINEA 1936, and I knew that Mantinea was an ordinary table wine. I congratulated him and drank some more. Zarian was by this time walking up and down in a state of considerable excitement. "A wine for the Gods," he kept repeating. I noticed that he was in his socks. His feet, he said, hurt him. He had been walking round the town since four in the afternoon buying up all the wine of this name and date he could find. My impulse there and then was to warn him against undue optimism, but his pleasure was so warming a sight that I let him ramble on. Finally he led the way into his wife's bedroom, holding the candle high, in order to let me see the seventy or eighty bottles of the wine lying snugly upon the bed. I remember that he held his finger over his lips and spoke in whispers, for all the world as if we were in danger of waking the bottles up. It took us an hour to finish the bottle with our conversation growing more and more exalted. Zarian felt that the last link to bind him to Corcyra had been forged; always fussy about wine, he had been unable to get used to the heavy sweet products of Greece. When we had disposed of the first bottle his magnanimity lead him to tiptoe into the bedroom and come back with another. He opened it with a flourish, poured some out, and sipped. An expression of disgust came over his face. He held the wine for a moment only in his mouth before bounding to the window and spitting it out. It was obviously a faulty bottle. With a dawning look of alarm on his face he retired and fetched two more bottles. They were both full of superior vinegar. He opened a dozen. They were all the same. I left him that evening surrounded by opened bottles of Mantinea, which he was pouring away down the kitchen sink. The glorious Beaune was never repeated. And now when I offer him a glass of Mantinea—which is after all not a very bad wine as wines go—you observe the face he makes.'

Zarian, to whom the subject of wine is sacred, does not find the story in very good taste, one can see. Yet he suffers it admirably; and later upon the dazzling white terrace, sipping his cognac, he confesses that he is developing a taste for retzina. 'It is not to be drunk alone, but with meat and vegetables cooked in the peasant manner. Lamb with onions, egg-plant, potatoes, and that red sauce which you all know. Then it tastes like a divine turpentine.'

'But speaking of intoxicating drinks,' says Theodore, 'I wonder, Count, if you have remarked that arbutus berries are among the things which can also intoxicate. During the campaigns of Macedonia during the last war I noticed that on several occasions battalions of our troops became quite drunk through eating the berries of the shrub. In some cases their wits seemed turned by the habit. I often wonder whether in Xenophon the mysterious outbreak of madness among the troops could have come from the same cause.'

It is ten o'clock and the moonlight is dazzling. Across the valley I can see the shallow glare of Spiro's headlamps flash as he brings N. to me. We are off to explore the caves near Paleocastrizza and spend the night in the small hotel there. The demented honking with which Spiro always announces his approach sounds sweet and muffled across the silver trees.

Loath to disrupt the speculative calm of my three philosophers I get up and say good-bye. The Count insists on accompanying me the length of the terrace to send a message to N. Faint interior preoccupations stir behind his composed features. 'And you are coming for the vintage don't forget,' he says. 'Bring her with you. It is a time for women.' Then he adds almost apologetically, 'We do not consider them enough perhaps.' And I know all at once that his thoughts have turned to the Roman nymph standing in the rotunda with the leaves turning over around her feet. I would like to say something that was not redundant or out of place but can find no words. The very fabric of this candid and beautiful landscape forbids it. I shake his hand and walk down the long avenue to the gates where the great car stands panting with Spiro jovial behind the wheel.

The western waters of Paleocastrizza will be icy cold to-night; and under the castle of St. Angelo the silver race will be combing out its long strands. Soon there is to be a war.

A LANDMARK GONE
(1949)

SOMEWHERE BETWEEN CALABRIA AND CORFU the blue really begins. You feel the horizon beginning to stain at the rim, the sky seems to come a little nearer and into deeper focus; the sea darkens as it uncurls in troughs around the boat. You are aware not so much of a landscape coming to meet you invisibly over those blue miles of water, as of a climate. Entering Greece is like entering a dark crystal; the form of things becomes irregular, refracted. Mirages suddenly swallow islands and if you watch you can see the trembling curtain of the atmosphere. Once in the shadow of the Albanian hills you are aware of this profound change. It haunts you while you live there, this creeping refraction of light altering with the time of day, so that you can fall asleep in a valley and awake in Tibet, with all the landmarks gone.

This is perhaps why we chose Corfu to live in: the island is a sort of ante-room to Aegean Greece with its smoke-grey bare volcanic islands like turtlebacks on the water. Corfu is all Venetian green and spoiled by the sun. Its richness enervates. Its valleys are painted out boldly in heavy brush-strokes of yellow and red, the Judas trees line the dusty roads in terrific purple explosions. Everywhere you go you can lie down on grass. Even the rocky northern end is rich in mineral springs: even the bare rock here is fruitful of water.

About the town one should use the past tense. Angular Venetian architecture, arcades, colonnades, shutters—peeling shutters holding back the sunlight which bounds off the bay and strikes upwards in a terrific dazzle. You lie in bed and see the sea spangling the cracked Venetian ceilings with their scrolls and cherubs. There are other curiosities. The remains of a Venetian aristocracy living in overgrown baronial mansions deep in the country, surrounded by cypresses; a patron saint who lay (a cured mummy) in a silver casket in the church of his name, and who performed terrific miracles; festivals, dances, olive-pickings, holidays, storms, births, deaths, and magnificent murders. And outside everything beyond the charm of accidents and persons, the hallow-blue rim of the world pressing in on the outside edge of the crystal.

We took a fisherman's house built on the bare craggy northern point of the island, almost in Albania. The people were sailors and the village small. The whole landscape was metamorphic rock— great layers of laminated stone on which clung precarious symbols like the olive and cypress, myrtle and arbutus, persisting like anachronisms in this world of bareness. We built a top-storey to the house costing £43 10s, a balcony overlooking the deep curve of the bay, where we could gaze, like Jesus, on the cities, over the sloping verdant lowlands in their haze. To sit by the bare rocky border of the sea and gaze into the land of milk and honey was ideal. I had work to do; and my wife had a lot to think about.

Here we lived—though 'live' as a word takes an unfair advantage of the steady dropping away of time. Days dropped away from us like pebbles from the walls of a deep well. I wrote a good deal, burned a good deal, corrected a good deal, and went on writing.

Our skin became slowly black, and our hair coarse with salt and very bleached. We began to learn Greek—to discover the rotation of the fruits—white and red hill-cherries, prickly pears, grapes, tangerines. We marked off a section of the bare white rock, walled it in, had some soil transported, and declared it a garden. The peace of those evenings on the balcony before the lighting of the lamps was something we shall never discover again—the stillness of objects reflected in the mirror of the bay; a mirror ever so slightly swinging, its surface un-grazed by the fishes moving about its lower floors. It was the kind of hush you get in a Chinese water-colour. The darkness leaked in over it all without disturbing anything; the proportions all remaining the same but the light changing. At last the sea would rise up to meet the sky and they would merge into a single warm veil. Everywhere you smelt the sage bruised by the feet of the sheep on the mountainside.

The invisible shepherd would lie under an arbutus and start playing his pipe. Across the bay would slide the smooth, icy notes of the flute; little liquid flourishes, and sleepy quibbles. Sitting on the balcony wrapped by the airs, we would listen without speaking. Presently the moon appeared—not the white, pulpy spectre of a moon that you see in Egypt—but a Greek moon friendly, not incalculable or chilling; like the flash of swimmer's arms out in the sea. Immediately the water was transformed into a tract of silver coins; a grampus puffed and was still; the flute stopped its meditations. We walked in our bare feet through the dark rooms, feeling the cool tiles under us, and down on to the rock. In that enormous silence we walked into the water, so as not to splash, and swam out into the silver bar. The black cutter lay motionless on the glaze. We touched the deck and found the wood still warm from the sun—like a human body almost. We didn't speak, because a voice on that water sounded unearthly. We swam till we were tired and then came back to the white rock and wrapped ourselves in towels and ate grapes. Perhaps we walked for a while on the hillside in the moonlight under the cypresses.

It is astonishing how little of the past can be recaptured in words. I have been trying for a year to rebuild that white house by the water's edge in a book; the taste of the little yellow grapes—a particularity of the island—the private and forgotten cove under the red shrine of St. Arsenius where Dorothy and Veronica, two ballet-dancers, invented a water ballet by moonlight; the cool white rooms with my wife's lazy pleasant paintings of our peasant friends looking at us from every wall; the little black boat riding at anchor outside the window, its masts grazing the balcony.

The day war was declared we stood on that balcony in a green rain falling straight down out of heaven on to the glassy floor of the lagoon; we were destroying papers, drawings, packing books. We were still inside the dark crystal, as yet unconscious of our separation. We refused to read the omens.

Last April as I lay in pitch darkness on the packed deck of a caique as we nosed past Matapan towards Crete, I thought back to that balcony in Corcyra, that green rain in the shadow of the Albanian hills. I remembered it all with a regret so deep that it did not stir the emotions; seen through the transforming lens of memory the past seemed so enchanted that any regret would have been unworthy of it. We never ever speak of it any more, having escaped. Time has done its stuff, the house is in ruins, the little black cutter smashed. I think only the shrine with the three cypresses and the tiny rock pool where we bathed is still left. How can these few hastily written words ever recreate more than a fraction of it?

Oil for the Saint; Return to Corfu

(1966)

THE RETURN OF THE NATIVE—a good thing or a bad? I am not sure. On principle I have always avoided retracing my steps unless absolutely necessary. It was not, I used to think, a good thing to return to places where one had been exceptionally happy or sad, or where events had taken place that could never be repeated. People vanish, after all; buildings disappear or are transformed, and the time scale begins to nag as one revisits those famous marble staircases that one could once take at speed, three steps at a time . . . the cathedral cat-walks that caused no dizziness. . . .

The extraordinary thing is that Greece has somehow remained exempt from the flavour of such disappointments. Much has changed, yes, but more has remained obstinately and invincibly the same. The radical feel and temper of the land and its people are still what they were for me at twenty. Indeed, many of the changes bemoaned by others have only added amenities that the country sadly lacked before—the inter-island telephones for example, the new roads, the little tourist hotels. As for the people . . . Memory does not grow older by a second per thousand years in Greece. Step off the ship and everywhere you will fall upon remembered faces, be instantly recognized and embraced: and I don't mean only by friends, but by everyone who remembers you, even if his only knowledge of you is that once, nearly twenty years ago, you gave his son a lesson or let him shine your shoes. Because they remember you they possess you, and you belong to them.

But in spite of this discovery about Greece in general, I still tended to regard Corfu as a special case. I avoided it as one avoids touching a sore tooth with one's tongue. After all, this island was where I first met Greece, learned Greek, lived like a fisherman, made my home with a peasant family. Here too I had made my first convulsive attempts on literature, learned to sail, been in love. Corfu would have too much to live up to. Nevertheless I still had many links with the island and with friends who still lived there, so that it was also much less *terra incognita* than any other part of Greece. I plucked up my courage and decided to take the plunge in bright spring weather. There were no special omens or intentions; the idea of the journey had ripened, that was all.

I was up on deck at dawn to watch the first brilliant strokes of sunlight racing along the brindled waves of our wake as we coasted the Forty Saints—once our winter shooting grounds and now barred to Corfiotes by the Albanian communists. The heavy, overpowering range of mountains had only just shed its snow, for the foothills were still green and fresh. The old Venetian seamark was still in place pointing up the deeper channel, and our vessel crossed it before veering south, turning sharply—on her heel, you might say—to point her prow at the hazy Venetian city which was as yet only a smudge of soft smoke. But the north of the island had been my home and here it was, its large-boned rounded scarps of rock and closely trimmed scrub looking like a succession of nude scalps on which the hair has started to grow again. How barren it looked and how strange in the early morning light! But the real strangeness was that it was all so recognizable, down to the smallest detail. It was not so much that it 'came back to me'; I found now that, in a queer sort of way, it had never left me; I had never really forgotten it. The whole dizzy spiral of the road above Kalami and Kouloura veering away towards Kassiopi I had known like my own pocket; sweeping it now with my heavy field glasses it seemed to me that I recognized individual trees, individual sweeps of brake and arbutus. It must have been an illusion, yet it was to persist during the whole of my stay on this (now doubly) magical and precious island. I felt the salt stickiness of the rail under my elbows as I brought the glasses to bear on the sea line, sweeping slowly along the coast from Kouloura with it's bird's-nest-harbour toward Agni. I was looking of course for the white house . . . but by now surely the rains had turned it black with iron stains? No, it came swimming into my field of vision as pristine and brilliant as it always had been; moreover, there, posed like hieratic figures, were my peasant friends. Athenaios was on the grey rock outside the house, watching the sun rise as he had always done, one hand holding the diminutive cup of Turkish coffee; from the upper balcony Kerkira, his wife, hung out the coloured blanket which would signal the morning caique (the equivalent of the village bus for us northerners) that there was a passenger to be picked up from the landing stage. An octopus hung from a rusty nail. A dog scratched at fleas in the deep dust of the roadway. The daughter of the house performed some unidentifiable task with vigour. (She had been five when last I had seen her in 1948.) A little farther to the left, Niko the sailor-school-teacher had as always thrown back his green shutters to stand in a long moment of contemplation, glancing sunward and then sideways at his boat where it lay alongside the makeshift jetty. The boat was a new one, though the jetty had not changed. For a minute, caught in the spectrum of the silence, I drank in the whole scene—it was like happening upon a familiar handwriting. Then I shut away the glasses and went down to breakfast in a curious state of utterly calm excitement. The whole thing seemed to be there—quite indestructibly there. I knew that Heleni was dead and Sandos and several others; but their disappearance from the scene of the action had not succeeded in changing the fixed mythology of a glance built up over a lifetime, a taste for a dawn coffee, the cloth on the balcony. I began to wonder whether perhaps it would be I who would exhibit the greatest changes. How would I seem to them?

But now the town was approaching and here once more the early sunlight traversed to pick up the curves of the Venetian harbour, the preposterous curvilinear shapes of its belfries and balconies. We docked to the boom of the patron saint's bell—Saint Spyridon of holy memory who was still working his miracles. I felt quite weak at the knees as I stepped ashore and took one of those little horse-drawn carriages with their fixed parasols bobbing up above. The horse wore a fine new straw hat carefully pierced to allow his ears to stick through; he looked like a prize cuckold on holiday as he jogged and cantered his way up into the town.

I had forgotten how beautiful it was in the early morning sunlight—the preposterous long arcades of the French Esplanade. The deep shade of the trees, the tables, the silence.

It was too early for morning customers, and the waiters were still watering down the pavements and chasing the dust from the gravel of the Esplanade; but there were quite a few youngsters having breakfast, and among them the inevitable painter with his characteristic baggage of easel and colour box. Though the town is a series of unfinished intentions, Venetian, French, British, it remains a masterpiece; I doubt if there is any little town as elegantly beautiful in the whole of Greece. Each nation in turn projected something grandiose to beautify it—and then fell asleep. The Venetians fell asleep over the citadel, though they remembered to leave the winged lion there; the French built half the Rue de Rivoli and then discontinued it. The British elaborated the stylish Government House with stone especially imported from Malta—but did not stay long enough to enjoy its amenities fully. Yet all these motifs blend perfectly and become in some subtle fashion neither Venetian, British, French nor even Greek. They become Corfiote. Day was breaking and shutters were slowly beginning to open like flowers, like eyelids. Nothing appeared to have received even a cursory lick of whitewash in the nearly twenty years of my absence; the rains, like a master colourist, had dappled and fused and smudged and darkened the long façades. The spectrum of their colours slowly changed with the mounting sun—as it always had. I walked about the sleepy town, astonished to find that I was ravished by it all anew. I almost sat down there and then to write another Propero.

But it was dangerous to linger, for I had many friends waiting eagerly to greet me, and I wanted to cross the island without seeing anyone—to devote my first day to a return visit to the lonely house in the north which had meant so much to me. I felt it almost as a duty. Later I would return and find Marie A. and discuss the little edition of Lear's drawings we were editing together; later I would find the valiant and formidable Countess T. of the sapphire eyes who had once thrown open the hospitable gates of her country house to two gluttonous, penniless and unknown writers called Durrell and Miller. But now, by the logical order of things, it should be Kouloura and the humble peasant family with whom, through whom, I had first got to know what Greece was.

I humped my bundle of gifts and betook myself to the taxi rank, half fearful that I might be greeted by a roar from a fat dusty figure emerging from a battered blue Buick. No, but Spyro Halkiopoulos is dead. Nevertheless his roar remains behind, for a younger Spyro greeted me with it—bounding like a lion from a blue Chevrolet. I did not bother to bargain with him but told him that I wanted to go north and to be dumped at Kouloura. My fluent Greek puzzled him. He looked at me narrowly and said: 'Who are you, sir? I seem to know your face.' I replied evasively. At that moment a colleague called his name and I realized that we did know each other. He had been a boy of ten when I had seen him last; his father had taken me and my brothers fishing with the lamp and trident. But it was pleasant to live for a moment in an anonymity which would soon be stripped from me. A small island is like a small market town. Sooner or later you are recognized. In Greece, at least, the hospitality begins—an unending flow of drinks from the ouzo fountain which plays perpetually in the depths of the Greek soul. Then there is nothing to do but surrender yourself. Strong-willed men break down and cry like babies. No good. The steady flow of hospitality ends only when you are lovingly hospitalized or carried aboard a departing ship on a stretcher. I knew that to declare myself in the town of Corfu at this stage would untruss me entirely. It was not only I who would be fêted, but through me the whole Durrell family which had once inhabited these idyllic shores; I should have to eat and drink for five—my brothers, my sister, my mother; I should have to empty at least a can in each of their names. I might never reach the north at all if I allowed all this to break loose around me. . . . I tried as far as possible to look like an uncommunicative Swiss Baptist who had arrived at the wrong island by mistake.

My driver was still puzzled but disinclined to probe; he drove through the sleepy town, turning me over in his mind, so to speak. Once or twice he glanced at me in the mirror and then shook his head and sighed. No, he couldn't place me. This was all to the good, as it left me free to plunge back into my private reverie, matching the sunlit present with the past. It was as if a film of the Corfu of 1940 had suddenly been stopped in mid-frame and waited for me to come back after twenty years in order to resume playing. Nothing at all seemed to have changed, but nothing. There is, if you wish, the carcass of a new theatre, and the outer shell of a new clinic. But in the long, winding road which leads away through the cypress and lemon groves toward Ypsos there were gentlemen bartering calves against kegs of wine, there were still the sacred idiots being teased by urchins, and the whole symphony of street cries still echoed around us in hallowed cacophony. Plenty of costume, too, and real costume at that; not the detestable, government-subsidized folklore get-up of Provence. Tourists in Corfu still get an honest cameraful for their money, whatever else they may have to complain about. And talking of complaints, I must not forget the holes in the road. I'm not joking when I say that I remembered many of them from my youth—the *identical* holes. This will sound far-fetched, but four years of almost daily motoring over twenty-odd kilometres of road is enough to make you familiar with every bump. Moreover, motoring with Spyro offered an extra method of mastering and retaining a mental hole-map; he had a different swear for each type of hole. The whole family knew the holes by their swears. Once I drove from my mother's villa into town in the dark, and my passengers were able to recite all Spyro's swears like a multiplication table at the appropriate places. Well, they are all still there. In the summer, too, the same crisis still hits the Ministry of Public Works, for the King still visits Corfu to spend the dog days in his summer palace. He must not be allowed to bump his spine, they always think. An army of gnomes with teaspoons comes out one night and very deftly fills the holes with a light mix of cement and clinker—like filling cavities in teeth. This just passes the test of summer weather, but the first thunderstorms of the autumn deftly wash out the fillings and leave us once more with the original road surface—a sort of confluent smallpox effect. But by this time, of course, the King is safely back in Athens and the island can relax again for the winter. I am writing now about the macadamized section of the road only; the rest (and the network of roads left behind by the British is a pretty extensive one) could best be described as one prolonged act of God.

It will sound masochistic to say that I took pleasure in the rediscovery of the ancient hole system of the island. Nevertheless it is true.

Deftly threading our way along, we made excellent time to Ypsos, which lies along the softly curving line of creeks and inlets, chapel-crowned and cypress-stippled islets and lagoons, until with a bump the road comes up against the first scrawny shoulder of mountain rising steeply into the air beyond Nisaki. Here a sleepy policeman flagged us down and advanced to take a suspicious look at us. He recognized my driver easily enough; then he took a look at me and his face flattened out into a huge grin. 'Welcome back,' he said, thrusting a large brown paw into the car. 'I have telephoned to the police at Kouloura to tell Athenaios you are coming.' For a moment, so firm was my belief in my own anonymity, I thought that he had mistaken me for somebody else; but no, he uttered my name, and grabbing my hand pressed it to his cheek. It was like black magic. 'I am married to Kerkira's daughter,' he explained.

At this my driver also gave a yelp of mingled consternation and delight and made a grab for me over the front seat. My presents were in danger of being crushed by the force of his embrace. 'And you didn't tell me,' he said reproachfully. 'You didn't say a word. My father, God rest his soul, would never have forgiven me.'

There was nothing for it but to dismount and to be led like a sacrificial lamb to a nearby table, where already the whiskered tavern-keeper, scenting a celebration, had spread his striped cloth and unstopped his ouzo keg. Here I was, then, unmasked at last by the Greek secret service. We broke into a torrent of reminiscences, punctuating our memories with fiery gulps of the national drink. My driver was able to recount whole sections of my forgotten life on the island—shooting trips, fishing trips, feats of drinking and dancing. Some of these episodes he remembered only from his father's conversation or from hearsay, but some he had witnessed. In small islands, where people do not read very much, the powers of memory never seem to fail, and individual actions take on semi-mythological proportions. We romanced thus with pleasure and emotion for a good hour until at last the ouzo bottle had a sadly punished look. 'Never mind,' they cried, 'there is a whole barrel inside.' I stifled a groan. I was now surrounded by four other policemen, some unidentified fishermen and a neighbouring tavernkeeper whose little hotel (according to the scholarly researches of my friend Peter Bull) promises the wayfarer 'Hot and Cold Running Waiter'.

I was still curious to find out how (when my anonymity had stood the acid test of the town) I had been recognized in this remote place. The answer was so simple. It amounted to the eternal family bush telegraph of Greece. The policeman explained patiently. 'The uncle of my sister's second cousin was at the pier and saw your name on your passport. He knew you would come back here and he telephoned me. You could imagine how delighted we were after so many years. Have a drink.'

But the sun was well up now and it was time to face the horrors of the road beyond Varvati. We disentangled ourselves from our hosts with some difficulty and after many hirsute embraces we climbed the steep road and catapulted off the macadam into a series of holes large enough to bury an ox. Our average speed was reduced now to about five miles an hour; the shock absorbers whimpered like whipped dogs; dust rose in sheets. My driver swung about, manipulating the car as if we were on a trapeze, and talking with animation of the meals he planned to give me once I returned to town. But how beautiful the drive still is, despite the holes and the dust, for the road runs, now concave, now convex, above the still, hard mirror of the sea, and the silver olives slide breathlessly down in groves below one as if to plunge into it and to swim for dear life out into the blue. Albania frames the whole picture with its huge flesh-coloured scarps. As you climb you realize that the island has two faces, not one. The indolent, luxuriant lowlands with their Venetian scenery give place now to the rocky archaic north with its small bitten-out harbours and scant iron-stained soils. It might be Ithaca or Cephalonia; it might be any of the more rugged island groups that lie to the south.

It is almost forbidding in its stern, unwinking masculinity, this northern end of Corfu. Even the costume changes to chime with its mood—black kirtles and head coifs. This is an island of the sea-farer, and wherever you hit the sea and the people who make their living by it, you come upon something hard, something always in mourning, something devout and disciplined.

The faces hereabouts were older and more wrinkled, the smiles quieter, the expressions more sage and more penetrating. Yes, it was in this landscape that I learned many important lessons: the kind you cannot put into words. Even the driver had fallen silent now as we traversed these long, silent groves of ancient olive trees. Here in the north life was a struggle, not a self-indulgence. His face had become grave.

But I had already outstripped our beetlelike progress as we crashed through those silent groves. I raced ahead in my imagination, leaping from cliff head to cliff head, swerving down like a kestrel through the still air to that silent balcony where I knew Athenaios would be standing, gripping the iron balustrade which, twenty years ago, I had myself helped him set in the wet concrete. I knew that from the white house by the water's edge one can hear a car far off on that remote hillside; its noise swells and vanishes, growing gradually louder and louder as it approaches. Finally the sound flows down unimpeded as the car turns the last corner and runs—looking like a toy—along the Kouloura highroad. Yes, he would be there with his hands on the rail, his shoulders lightly hunched; he had always listened with such concentration that it gave him the stance of a blind man. Beside him in the upright chair Kerkira would be busy with her spindle or her darning. There was no time to waste for her: her hands had become almost autonomous in function. One felt that even when she slept they automatically went on working, knitting, plucking feathers, cleaning fish, sewing. At times, almost apologetically, they took a brief moment off to stifle a yawn.

Nor was I mistaken. As the car reached the corner of the mountain I saw the little tableau on the balcony across the blue water. They had heard us, but it was too far off as yet to identify the visitor. We nosed down the steep road toward sea level, winding in and out of the olive groves. The sea lay asleep below us, lime green and enticing. The little hamlet seemed asleep, for nothing stirred in the thickets by the spring; there were no voices of children singing higher up among the olives. Everybody had obviously gone to town to shop. The road ended a good hundred yards short of the old house, and so it was that I approached it at last silently, on foot, with my parcels. By this time Athenaios and his wife had moved from the balcony to the end of the olive grove, from where they could watch the approaches to the house. They stood there in the green shadow of the trees, riveted in poses of concentration, their hands clutched before them. But at my call their concentration broke like a spell and Kerkira gave a sudden wild cry like a seabird. Her husband stood his ground with a tremulous smile on his lips, his arms thrown out as if to embrace not only me but the whole sea-enchanted world about us.

'It is I.'

'It is you.'

'Yes, I.'

'At last you come back.'

One on either side, they put their arms about me and led me, a willing captive, into the house. There was so much to recount that for a moment we were all tongue-tied. But in the cool shadowy interior I saw a glimmer of white teeth as Niko the schoolmaster-fisherman rose like a great fish to embrace me. 'We've been waiting all morning,' he explained, giving me a rib-cracking embrace. 'Welcome.'

Once more the balcony over the water with its plaster stained by the winter rain; once more the little coffee cups and the glasses of kumquat, the Corfu liqueur; once more the familiar voices raised in excited talk, piling memory upon memory, trying to replace the missing fragments of that twenty-year-old tapestry. I had been halfway around the world in this time, while they had stayed here, outfacing wars and floods and family deaths, gathering white hair. Athenaios had had a small stroke two years before which had half-paralysed one shoulder, but Niko, whose white hair betrayed his sixty-odd years, was still the raw-boned Hercules of the past, tanned and sturdy, with every white tooth in his head. The women watched us laugh and talk, rejoicing obscurely in our defiance of time. The past had dealt hard with the family. Heleni, the first wife, had died of starvation during 1940— died keeping her children alive. Some years later Athenaios had married Kerkira, a little village girl who came in to help. She had blossomed now into a plump and handsome matron of a flourishing household with a new daughter of her own to boast of: a policeman's wife no less, which meant that she would one day enjoy a pension. Old albums of pictures now made their appearance, photographs yellow with age, and stained with ancient developing marks. This at least conferred upon the meeting a mild air of improbability. Who was this good-looking and rather cocksure young man who stared out at me, fishing trident in hand? What had he been so damned sure about anyway? It was hard to say. The world he lived in, like our own, had existed under the threat of sudden doom. Everybody had known it.

Deftly the women were laying the table in the shadowy inner room, clucking like chickens with delight and only pausing to replenish our glasses. The talk had turned to village matters, the familiar and immemorial landmarks of lives lived in such heroic seclusion. Niko, it is true, had once been as far as Athens on a teaching course, but the others had never been farther than the town of Corfu, ten sea miles to the south. For them words like Belgrade, Cairo, London sank into the mind like dyes, colouring these far-off places with the richness of ancient myths. They sighed and squeezed their fingers together in their laps as I spoke of them, like children hearing a fairy tale. But for my part I sank into the little world of the village with equal relief and pleasure; this was my form of romance. They could have London and Paris.

The little hamlet of Kalami with its ten families was a whole world—a total world—whose confines were all there to be enjoyed and measured. It was not limitless like the outside world. It had a formal completeness which allowed the villagers to live their lives in a kind of assured completeness—unfragmented, free from hesitation. Here the chronology too was different. Strangers had come from outside, there had been wars, deprivation and famine, but inside the spectrum they remembered the year when the children of Jani had been struck by lightning, or when Socrates severed his thumb with a knife while cleaning a fish, or when the mason lost an eye from a pinch of quicklime. This was truth; the rest belonged delightfully but uneasily to the world of fable.

When the first glad rush of conversation had spent itself, when the presents had been examined and assessed—and repaid in kisses—we sat down at the long table to eat. The women followed the old-fashioned tradition, standing behind to serve us, but not sitting down with us. From time to time, however, Kerkira would sit for a moment on a chair and sip a glass of sweet liqueur as she listened to our talk. By now I had produced my little phial of green olive oil—the delicious *Vierge* from our Provençal olives. 'How long since you have visited Saint Arsenius?' I asked Niko, and he flashed his white teeth in a smile. 'Last week,' he said. 'Why?' I held up the green French oil and said: 'I have brought a little oil for his lamp from our trees in France.' They drew their breath with pleasure and emotion—indeed with a certain pride. Who but a Greek would have thought of such a gesture? Athenaios bowed his head for a moment and when he looked up I saw that there were tears in his dark eyes. 'You have done well,' he said. 'It is not for nothing you are an adopted Greek and the godfather of Spyro.' My godson was a merchant seaman now, doing the San Francisco to Hong Kong run. Niko banged the table with pleasure. 'We will go to the saint together,' he said roundly, 'in my new boat, eh, Athenaios? This afternoon.' Everyone clapped hands and agreed delightedly.

The fare was simple and humble, a fitting reminder that here in the north prosperity was still a debatable concept. But we ate

would stand on the balcony (clad in some suitable uniform?) and confer a blessing on my admirers with their transistors. Afterward we would take the rowboat out to collect all the floating beer bottles and Ambre Solaire suntan-lotion flagons and rubber ware.

'You will sign their books,' Niko went on, 'and we will pass the time very agreeably together, you will see.'

'I shall reflect upon the matter,' I muttered vaguely. 'I don't know whether I can afford to leave my trees in France.'

'Pouf! You can go back for the harvest every year, and then return to us for the tourist season,' he assured me comfortably.

A lone green caique sputtered into view round the headland, carving the still, blue sea into curls as it crossed our line of vision. 'That will be Dimitri going to town to sell his fish.'

We finished our coffee and Niko led us down onto the white rock where his boat lay. It was a twenty-five-foot lateen-rig, sturdy but clumsy, and painted rust red. He had contrived a dashing but inappropriate housing for the front of it which gave the impression of half-decking. It was a tin form with a murky window. It would keep out the spray all right and provide some shelter in the sea, but being inappropriate to the type of boat would make her unmanoeuvrable when she was under sail.

'I know what you are thinking,' grinned Niko. 'It is very smart to look at but not very clever. We will take the cabin part off, I think.' The tin form was duly unbolted and dragged out upon the rock to make room for the three of us. We pushed off while the women of the family watched us with proud indulgence. 'Don't be too long,' cried Kerkira. Niko gave a display of sudden physical violence as he cranked the ancient engine until it fired asthmatically and sent us throbbing across the bay. It was a weird contraption, this ancient machine. Niko caught me eyeing it and said proudly: 'I know, my friend, it isn't a marine engine at all. It is really a water pump I found on an old well. I fitted the shaft and adapted it. It works well but it is very heavy.' It was indeed. If ever the boat overturned it would plummet to the bottom of the sea.

As we drew away I looked back at the familiar village and the diminishing figures of the women, who had returned to the high balcony over the water. Kerkira waved and we waved back. Here every twist of the headland, every rock and cove, was familiar. How often we had sat breathlessly for half the night gazing down into the dazzling pool of light cast by the carbide lamps, hunting for octopuses. Forgotten memories crowded in now, each one separate and vivid. One autumn night the bay was full of phosphorescence which turned our swimming bodies to fire; more than once after a winter storm we found the bay swarming with blue pipefish that could be gathered with a bucket. They behaved as though they were suffering from concussion. There on the big yellow rock by Agni, was Miller's private bathing place. He used to trot off across the headland with his towel and notebook every morning, to return only when the distant cry of 'Lunch' came to his ears across the olive groves.

Kalami disappeared now and we were in the throat of the open sea which stretched away across the calm carpet of water to where the Venetian town drowsed among its opalescent mists. Niko was talking to Atheniaos with animation. In the starvation period they had learned to eat the leaves of certain trees, which brought them out in boils. The gravedigger was too enfeebled by lack of food to pierce the rocky soil of the churchyard; the dead had begun to 'form queues' like the living, said Niko with grim humour. Nitsa dying had given a great cry and seen a vision of Greece free, once more. The smoke from the guns across the water had drifted about in the still winter air, unsubstantial as thistledown. 'Well,' said Athenaios, 'we have seen many things come to pass and yet, praise God, we are still among the living.' Niko grinned ironically and grunted. 'Not for long,' said he. 'At sixty-one it isn't for long. But so long as I can still eat and sail I don't care. Give me a few more years and I'll enjoy them.'

The sheep bells still tonked among the grassy glades above Agni; on the second headland there were fishermen at work. They were smashing up hermit crabs for bait, but they paused to wave. They were inevitably relatives of either Niko or Athenaios and by consequence were addressed in familiar fashion.

'Caught anything, you cuckolds?'

'Nothing. Where are you going, cuckolds?'

'To Saint Arsenius, cuckolds.'

'Is that the foreigner?'

'Yes.'

'Tell him welcome and wish him Godspeed.'

I thanked them and tipped a benign hat. We were heading down now for what we always regarded in the past as our own private beach. Elsewhere I have described the little shrine, the sentinel cypresses, the carved-out beach where we spent whole summers bathing naked. Once an ikon had been found floating in the sea and the faithful had taken this as a sign that Saint Arsenius was looking for a familiar place to settle. The shrine itself is hardly bigger than a large telephone booth, but the lamps are always in repair and the floor always dusted. How this is done is rather a puzzle, for the place cannot be approached by land, only by sea. Yet it has always been so. Once a year a priest comes by water with his acolytes and reads a service there.

It hadn't changed. We throttled down as we turned back the last headland like the page of a book and entered the little bay. But I am wrong; the profile of the rock has been altered somewhat by the explosion of an Italian land mine during the war. The shrine, however, had escaped unscathed. A few huge boulders had been scattered about the bathing beach, that was all. So still was the water that we did not bother to anchor. We snubbed the unfractious rock and climbed ashore, taking a line. Despite their age the two men climbed the rock as effortlessly as goats.

The door was lightly pinioned with wire, easy to undo. I entered the little chapel, after so long, with emotion. Battered by wind and sea the rotting ikon stared back at us in the musty gloom. The lamps were full but unlit. We crossed ourselves backwards, in the Orthodox way.

'Well, you old brute,' said Niko, addressing the squinting saint in terms of rough familiarity—tones one is permitted to adopt with close friends or relatives by marriage and which imply no irreverence. 'We have brought you back the foreigner at last.' I stood breathing lightly in the still, stale air of the shrine, and remembering. Athenaios grubbed about in the gloom behind the makeshift altar. He was hunting for a twist of wick. There is always a half-burned wick lying about in such places. I had found a small empty lamp among the branch of oil lamps hanging above the ikon. I unstoppered my phial of green oil and reverently tipped it into the glass bowl. 'Pour it all,' cried Niko with a sort of delighted voluptuousness, 'every drop.' The blunt fingers of Athenaios had found a small twist of wick. We set it afloat in the oil and waited for a moment to let it drink and settle. 'If it lights the first time,' Niko joked, 'it means that you are welcome and that he has no outstanding complaints against you.' I admit I felt somewhat anxious, for the saint has a beady and penetrating glare—indeed the stare of an elder Freud. And he might well have a complaint against me, for in the long years of my absence I had never sent him the smallest offering. But no. The wick flamed up and Athenaios clapped his hands softly. All of a sudden I saw the faces of my friends spring out of the gloom, touched by the yellow light; they had a chastened, ageless quality. I thought of the Byzantine faces which stare at one out of the ikons in Salonika, Athens, Ravenna—the dark eyes, the crisp curling hair, the long speculative noses. And behind this front rank, so to speak, the calm profiles of ancient Greek statues.

Niko's dark eyes twinkled with merriment. We crossed ourselves once more and embraced while Niko went on rallying the saint. 'Now you are drinking French,' he told the ikon. 'Drink then, drink deeply. Then tell us if the French oil is as good as ours.'

We stayed a while bemused, by the yellow flame of the wick as it burned on, unwavering in the still air. Outside the dark shrine with its little cone of vivid yellow light the sunlight beat down mercilessly on the rock and water. It was time to go blinking into daylight once more. Niko wound up the prayer session by calling for a blessing from Arsenius and, by his leave, for another covering blessing from his great senior, Saint Spyridon. Once more he used his ironic rallying tone, addressing them as wicked old brutes. But his eyes were grave and tender.

Suddenly I was reminded of the ancient shrines of Herakles which one could only approach backwards, uttering terrible curses. There had been one such in Lindos on Rhodes. A bit of bad language, a bit of familiarity, makes a saint feel at home with you when uttered in the right frame of mind. Standing once more upon that ragged rock face we grinned at each other and winked.

'Well, he's still there, as you see. Still on the job.' So long as Arsenius is there the Greek world will remain right side up.

There was one more visit to be made—to the little underwater cave in which we used to hide whenever a passing boat hove in sight. In here, on the shallow slip of gravel beach, we used to leave our bathing suits so that we could put them on swiftly in any case where our nakedness might give offence to the peasants. I slipped overboard into the cool water and swam into the bay. Once we had made a clay statue of Pan and set it up in the cave and I was curious to see if anything remained. No. The winter sea had long since licked out the cave. There was no trace.

We dawdled for an hour in the little bay, reminiscing. Then I spread my wet body out in the boat and Niko started up his engine with many a cajoling oath. Slowly we drew away from the Saint once more, giving him a friendly wave as we passed round the headland out of his life once more, perhaps this time for ever.

It was later than we had imagined; indeed the sun was westering steeply when at last we tied up again at the white house. 'It is a great thing,' said Niko sagely, 'to be a creator.' He used the ancient word 'demiurge' which is still current modern Greek. He seemed to have only the vaguest idea of what the concept stood for; and yet, perhaps not. After all, in the ancient world the gods walked about freely on earth and undertook many of men's duties. Why should not a 'demiurge' lend a hand with a little mild tourism and help a deserving cause? Zeus would not have blenched at the idea.

That evening the 'demiurge' held court, greeting all comers and meeting glass with lifted glass. Some were old friends, fishermen of the Forty Saints and Kassiopi; some were the grandchildren of old friends who came to press my hand and mutter warm greetings. Hands as horny as oaks, faces lined like druids, but with the fine manners of kings.

By the time we settled for supper, the moon was rising—a huge copper ball swinging up from behind the Albanian mountains, struggling free of the shimmering ground mists. It seemed to rise in one's very throat. Once more upon that silent balcony we sipped our last coffees and watched its wide shimmering path stretch across the straits. A liner slipped by with its thousand lights ablaze. But the moon outshone everything. There were stifled yawns now, for peasant folk sleep early, and I too was tired. My things had been laid out for me by Kerkira in the upper room, the old room. I dawdled a while to smoke a cigarette and watch the changing sea. A few old articles of furniture still remained—my old desk, for example, crudely painted and clumsy. The floor I had stained with my own hands once upon a time. The old fireplace which had cost us such diplomacy and anxiety had been bricked up, but I could still trace the lintel in the plaster of the wall.

I had decided that I would catch the dawn caique back to town, where other friends and other projects awaited me—alien from this small and perfectly composed world of the unsophisticated village. It was good, I thought too, to enjoy it so thoroughly without nostalgia, without false regrets. What had been lived had been thoroughly lived and thoroughly digested. Only the crumbs of old loyalties and loves remained, and they gave pleasure now, not pain. So bright was the moonlight that I could see the trees reflected in the water. A small fish broke surface under the house with the noise of a drawn cork. The flawless skin of the night sea settled again into its mirrored calm. I lay awake for a long time that night, thinking over the events of the day and watching the moonlight pouring onto the dark floor of the room. From time to time the sea gave a small sigh, like a child turning over in its sleep. Far up on the hillsides in the direction of Vigla a fox barked once and was silent. I slid slowly downhill into sleep, but so slowly that I could not discern the point at which one state superseded the other. They matched like silks.

RHODES

Upon his departure from Greece in 1941, Durrell went to Egypt. He separated from his wife, became press attaché for the British Information Office in Alexandria, and met Eve Cohen (they married in 1947). The couple left Egypt soon after Germany's defeat, and traveled to the Aegean island of Rhodes in June, 1945. Rhodes was under British Military Administration, and during his time Durrell there served as the British Public Information Officer for the surrounding region. He stayed on the island until early 1947, just before the British handed it over to Greece.

OF PARADISE TERRESTRE

(FROM REFLECTIONS ON A MARINE VENUS, 1953)

Alvarez fled; and after him the doom
Of exile was sent out; he, as report
Was bold to voice, retired himself to Rhodes

—MIDDLETON: *THE SPANISH GIPSY*

SOMEWHERE AMONG THE NOTE-BOOKS of Gideon I once found a list of diseases as yet unclassified by medical science, and among these there occurred the word *Islomania*, which was described as a rare but by no means unknown affliction of spirit. There are people, Gideon used to say, by way of explanation, who find islands somehow irresistible. The mere knowledge that they are on an island, a little world surrounded by the sea, fills them with an indescribable intoxication. These born 'islomanes', he used to add, are the direct descendants of the Atlanteans, and it is towards the lost Atlantis that their subconscious yearns throughout their island life. . . . I forget the other details. But like all Gideon's theories it was an ingenious one. I recall how bitterly it was debated by candle-light in the Villa Cleobolus until the moon went down on the debate, and until Gideon's contentions were muffled in his yawns: until Hoyle began to tap his spectacles upon the thumbnail of his left hand, which was his way of starting to say goodnight: until Mehmet Bay, in the house across the oleander-grove, banged his shutters together as a protest against the lateness of the

hour. Yet the word stuck; and though Hoyle refused its applica-
tion to any but Aegean islands, while Sand could not bring himself to look a theory so irrational in the eye, we all of us, by tacit
admission, knew ourselves to be 'islomanes'.

This book is by intention a sort of anatomy of islomania, with
all its formal defects of inconsequence and shapelessness: of conversations begun and left hanging in the air: of journeys planned
and never undertaken: of notes and studies put together against
books unwritten. . . . It is to be dedicated to the resident goddess of
a Greek island—Rhodes. I should like, if possible, to recall some
part of those golden years, whose ghosts still rise up and afflict me
whenever I catch sight of a letter with a Greek stamp on it, or
whenever, in some remote port of the world, I happen upon a
derelict tanker flying the Aegean blue-and-white.

In Rhodes the days drop as softly as fruit from trees. Some
belong to the dazzling ages of Cleobolus and the tyrants, some to
the gloomy Tiberius, some to the Crusaders. They follow each
other in scales and modes too quickly almost to be captured in the
nets of form. Only by a strict submission to the laws of inconsequence can one ever write about an island—as an islomane, that
is. And then who could ever hope to pin down, to circumscribe,
the charms of a resident Goddess? I have not attempted to cut
down below the surface of my subjects' poses. I have attempted to
illumine a single man by a single phrase, and to leave him where
he sits embedded in the slow flux of Grecian days, undisturbed by
literary artifice—as a good host should. . . . Gideon with his monocle screwed in sitting soberly before a bottle of *mastika;* Hoyle
winding his enormous watch; Mills talking; Sand sucking his pipe;
Egon Huber walking the deserted beaches hunting for scraps of
wood to carve; and the dark-eyed E, whose shadow is somehow
spread over all these—a familiar, a critic, a lover—E putting on a

flowered frock in the studio mirror with her black hair ruffled. I have tried not to disturb them in the little eternities of their island life, where somehow their spirits mingle and join that of the Marine Venus standing in her little stone cell at the Museum like a challenge from a life infinitely more remote. If I have sacrificed form it is for something better, sifting into the material now some old notes from a forgotten scrap-book, now a letter: all the quotidian stuff which might give a common reader the feeling of life lived in a historic present.

That spring afternoon of 1945 when the order to embark came through to us in Alexandria, my first glimpse of Gideon, I remember, was not reassuring. We were to be fellow-passengers aboard a military HDML—a vessel whose sleek and powerful lines suggested to my innocent eyes speedy and comfortable travel. We were promised an early morning landfall in Rhodes. In a few hours, then, I should find myself, after some four years of exile, on a Greek island once more.

Gideon stood among a cluster of engineers and seamen, abstractedly reading a book. I recall thinking to myself that he looked the personification of orthodoxy: the monocle, the clipped silver hair, the polished boots. . . . (An Indian Army regular whose knowledge of routine has placed him at the head of a sub-department devoted to sanitation or supply?) If I were to spend twenty-four hours in his company, I thought, I should undoubtedly spend them in politely deferring to judgements based on popular prejudice, or the *naif* self-regard of a regular soldier who has come to regard his regimental mess as the whole wide world. His rather obvious glass eye regarded the world from time to time with what seemed to me to be a somewhat boorish indifference—an impression which was strengthened when I saw him accept without thanks a comfortable chair and a cushion. The rest of us lay about his feet upon cushions improvised out of our kit. He was followed by a little black and white terrier, obviously very well trained.

On one point, however, my mind was soon set at rest. The panting of the great engines as they drove us storming across the oily waters of Alexandria towards the open sea made it quite clear that conversation would be an impossibility. We were each of us to be sealed up in the great throbbing privacy of sound. I cannot say I was unhappy. There was so much to think about, so much to hope for, in the idea of seeing Greece again. I thought of all the letters I had received in recent months—letters with an obituary flavour. 'You will find it completely changed' said one. 'The old life has gone forever' said another. 'Go to America' urged a third. Tomorrow I should see for myself whether the old Greek ambience had survived the war, whether it was still a reality based in the landscape and the people—or whether we had simply invented it for ourselves in the old days, living comfortably on foreign exchange, patronising reality with our fancies and making bad literature from them. Tomorrow I should know whether I must relegate my feelings about Greece to the dusty corners of memory along with so many other mad vagaries of the heart.

As we rounded the old fort I turned back to catch a last glimpse of E standing and waving to me from the corner of the esplanade before the mist began to settle and the whole scimitar-like sweep of minarets and belfries of the upper town dissolved in soft pearl and gold. Egypt and Greece—for a moment the conflicting loyalties of love and habit assailed me. But E was following me to Rhodes after an interval of weeks: and she was my only tie with Egypt. I saw her enter the old office car, and watched it move slowly off in the murk. The journey had begun!

Ten miles off Alexandria we were still carving up a solid brown trench in the waters of the open sea—waters polluted by the dense Nilotic silt—when a solitary dolphin struck surface and galloped alongside us for a moment; my heart rose at the augury, for the fish is a bringer of fair weather and luck. I leaned to follow it with my eye when, with the suddenness of an axe falling, we hit the pure Mediterranean blueness of the true Aegean: a sea with depth and tone, that swallowed and gave back the sky; a sea that belonged to the waterless islands and grey windmills, to the olive-trees and the statues. At long last we had burst through the misty curtain of atmosphere that lies forever over Mareotis.

The sun was slowly setting, lumbering down into the Under-world. My fellow-passengers had, for the greater part, fallen asleep. Gideon alone sat awake over his book, tapping away an occasional yawn with a long index finger and caressing his dog. The crew came up and distributed mugs of service tea. If you leaned to the rail now and stared down into the water you had the impression that we were flying; the flared bows of the HSL were lifted high as she drove her coarse furrow through the still sea. The snarling of the great engines wrapped us all in a deaf silence— a marvellous brutal music of vibrating steel and wood. Behind us we left great stains of oily heat upon the waters and a white cica-trice which slowly healed again. The warmth of the coarse sweet tea was delightful; it reminded one that night was falling, and that the cold was slowly settling in from the west. Presently I too lay down and drifted into a shallow sleep from which all this noise seemed to be like the placid roaring in some coloured sea-shell picked up on the warm beaches of Corfu or Delos in those happy years before the war. It was as if my longing to be back in Greece had all but exhausted itself in fulfilment. I was numbed. Forgotten scenes came into my mind, without form or coherence, yet bathed in the sunny lambency of the Greek past, and even in my sleep I felt something like the absurd disposition to tears with which I last saw the shores of Crete fade into the mists of 1941.

The storm which caught us some eighty miles off Alexandria had been described in the weather report as 'a slight squall'. It seemed nothing so negligible. Indeed the first impact suggested something like the eruption of a volcano. The HDML hit the first wave with a prodigious slap that jolted every bone in our bodies. Such weather would have been bad enough in an island *caieque*, but in a craft which could not throttle down to less than fifteen knots without making leeway, its effect was indescribable. I awoke to see the Aegean heaped up around us in glossy valleys, lit by the yellowish glare of the ship's lamps. The even snarling of the engines was now punctuated by a regular series of sobs and grunts and by the horrible grinding of the screws as they were lifted clear of purchase.

In later days Gideon was used to say (when asked how first we had met) that we had been thrown together. He enjoyed the literal as well as the figurative aspects of the phrase far more, I am sure, than either of us enjoyed the storm which first introduced us to each other. But thrown together we certainly were. At the first impact of wind and water the ship began the butting, goring motion we were to learn so well. The noise of the screws before they buried themselves in the sea once more suggested the noise of a giant grinding his teeth. Hurled into a corner, I found Gideon's head in my lap, and my legs round the neck of a soldier. We lip-read each others' apologies and disengaged as gracefully as we could—only to be flung down once more in a heap. It was impossible to stand upright; it was rather more than difficult to manage to stay in one place. Throttled down as far as she would go the HDML skidded along the surface of the sea with the waves breaking over her in a series of stabbing white concussions. We braced our feet firmly and listened to the dull whacking of the hull against the water, and the dismal sound of crockery being smashed in the galley. From this time forward we lived on all-fours, crouching like apes whenever we wished to move about the ship. Sleep became an impossibility. The terrific slap of every wave was like a punch to the solar plexus. The little dog retreated with a world-weary air to the furthest end of an empty kit-bag where it curled up and slept.

Several people began to be picturesquely sick. Gideon and I retreated in opposite corners like spiders and contemplated this weakness on the part of our fellow-passengers with a disgust so identical that we were forced to smile, catching each other's eye. I saw that he had smashed his monocle. Unbuttoning his jacket he pulled out a cigar-case containing, as far as I could judge, some twenty replacements, and inserted one.

The dawn came up as thick as glue; westward the sky had taken on the colour of oiled steel. The storm had passed over us, leaving behind it only a heavy sea propped up in an endless succession of watery slabs. The prow of the HDML still buried itself in the waves with feverish crunchings and tremblings. Some of us slept, and later by the watery beams of the early sun, were able to extend the limits of our visibility as far as a horizon dipping and swelling— but offering as yet no trace of land.

The passengers lay about upon piles of disordered kit, for all the world like corpses on pyres, waiting for torches to set them alight. As the daylight advanced a few of the hardier souls took courage and stuck out their pallid and unshaven faces to ask questions of the crew. Where were we? When would we arrive? The army showed a disinclination to discuss the question. Indeed it looked as if they knew as little as we did. We had been blown off our course. Speculation which at first seemed academic, began to be ever so slightly tinged with alarm, as we caught sight of the captain poring over a chart of the Eastern Mediterranean. The cook distributed mugs of cocoa over which the problem was discussed from every angle. Gideon, I discovered, was reading an account of Aegean travel published in the eighties of the last century by an eccentric divine, the Rev. Fanshawe Tozer, whose writings were to amuse and delight us so much afterwards. He passed me this work with the opening paragraph heavily scored by his thumbnail, and made a grimace as he did so. I took it and read: *'There is an element of excitement attending a voyage to Rhodes arising from the uncertainty which exists with regard to reaching that island.'* The Rev. Tozer then had shared many of our present misgivings in the early eighties. I hoped sincerely that this passage was not to prove an augury. It seemed a positively ominous quotation to stumble upon at this time and place.

Later we shared some mouldy rounds of sandwich and a bottle of Cyprus cognac which I had had the forethought to bring with me; and finally, inspired by the warmth of the sun and a calmer patch of weather we left the dumb-show in which our politeness had been so far continued (the wind and rain plus the noise of the engines precluding any more civilized exchange) and fell to words: single words carefully shouted across the intervening space to form sentences.

'We'll probably touch Cyprus tonight.'

'Cyprus? Surely not.'

'What will you bet?'

'It's hundreds of miles away.'

'Bah! These Army people never do anything right.'

An officer who happened to be crawling past with that peculiar air of devout forbearance that seamen affect when they are carrying unwelcome passengers, glared at Gideon. He seemed about to say something rather forcible, but my companion had already retreated behind his book. He emerged to wrinkle his nose at the retreating back.

'Mark me.' he said, 'They could land us in Beirut without turning a hair.'

It did not seem wise to continue a conversation any further along these lines. I fell into a doze and the morning passed in a series of watery sunshines punctuated by squalls and the threshings of the sea. In the late afternoon the weather brought us its omens of approaching land—two spring turtle-doves, blown off their course, no doubt. They swerved over us and were gone in the direction of Africa.

The problem of our position had not been clarified by any official pronouncement beyond the bare admission that we were off our course. Speculation still made pretty free with place-names. Dusk closed down in a series of thin, misty rainstorms, which reduced visibility to a few hundred yards; and darkness had barely followed dusk when there was a shout which turned every head in the direction of the lighted cockpit where, above the great illuminated dials of the dashboard the rubber windscreen-wipers bored circles of clarity in the pervading murk of that sottish dusk. Someone had spotted land—the merest etching of darkness upon darkness—and for an hour we thundered along a black and rocky coast, catching fitful glimpses of its capes and cliffs through the shifting packets of mist. To add to the rising emotions of optimism and relief came the pleasant sensation of a calmer sea. We began to reassemble our dispersed possessions and comb our sticky hair. I could taste the sharp brine which had dried on the unshaven stubble of my lips. Gideon traced the parting of his silver hair with something like complacence, and then examined the cavities in his teeth. He seemed to approve of what he saw.

Then he offered me his comb. 'You see,' he said, 'it will turn out to be Cyprus.'

It turned out to be Rhodes. We rounded several more headlands before an officer came aft and told us so. As if endowed with powers of human understanding Gideon's little dog (its name turned out to be Homer) emerged from its hideout and began to tidy itself up. 'That's the stuff' said its master.

Vague lights now appeared and the note of the engines mellowed and sank in tone. Dark slabs of harbour masonry wallowed and glittered against the street-lights as we nosed slowly in. All that could be seen of the famous harbour was a small area of some fifty square yards lighted by some makeshift method to guide shipping. The rest was blackness which swallowed up the cracked masonry, the steel pickets and the rusty barbed wire which covered the whole of the waterfront. Absolute blackness otherwise.

The silence that now fell with the extinguishing of the great engines was almost greater in volume than the sound to which we had accustomed ourselves for so long. People still shouted deafly at one another. Space had swollen again to its customary dimensions. We landed in the murk. The yawing and pitching of the ship had given us all a trembling muscular reflex movement of thigh and shoulder—so that we walked like old salts in a musical comedy. Our passes were collected by a tired-looking naval officer who motioned us with a vague gesture of his arm towards the outer darkness. Shouldering our packs we stumbled off towards the transit hotel down a dark street lined with rustling trees. I broke a leaf off and crumpled it in my fingers to inhale the sweet odour of eucalyptus oil. At the end of the long corridor of darkness two tall gates rose up, and behind them the once famous *Albergo della Rosa,* showing here and there a point of light, weak and diffuse. The steps seemed endless—it was like climbing into the sky. . . .

But already as I write the weariness of that late arrival begins to melt the clear outlines of the detail. I vaguely remember the vast entrance hall littered with shed equipment, the buzz of conversation from the dining-hall which served as a mess, the smashed marquetry panels of the lounge, and the timid Italians who serviced the hotel. I remember too the draughts of pure sea air that stole in from the terrace, bearing with them the scent of spring flowers, and the desire for sleep which struggled against the urge to walk into the garden and smell the darkness which stretched away across the straits to Anatolia. But it was no good: the journey had been too much for us.

We lay upon adjacent sofas in the gaunt lounge with its foggy mirrors, waiting for our rooms to be prepared by a sleepy maid with a hare-lip. I remember Gideon lying there, his monocle almost touching the floor—it had rolled out of his eye to the end of its cord: his feet clad in a pair of much-darned socks: his whole body slack and unstrung: snoring.

So we slept.

Much later we were awoken, and blind with sleep followed the clerk to our rooms. The open windows gave directly on to the sea whose melodious sighing was the perfect accompaniment to a landfall as felicitous as a Greek island: to a sleep as blankly anonymous as that which welled up around us.

I speak for myself. Some centuries later (or was it back: had one travelled backwards into sleep like history?) I woke to feel the warm early sun in my eyes, reflecting the running dazzle of water from the white roof of the room. Gideon was already standing on the balcony, clad only in a monocle and a towel, doing his exercises with the rapt devotion of a yogi, watched by his little dog.

Presently we scrambled across the garden, and still half drugged with sleep, burst into the Aegean water, clear and cold as wine. Before us across the straits the Anatolian mountains glowed, each one a precious stone. Icy though the water was we stayed awhile in it, speechless with gratitude—rubbed by the salt until our skins felt as cold and smooth as the pebbles which tesselated the shining floors of that magnificent beach.

To the memory of that first bathe I should add the memory of that first breakfast (mere bully beef and dry biscuit) eaten in the company of our fellows at the long trestle-tables which filled the once fashionable dining-room. Both were commonplaces no doubt—but translated into miracles by the feeling that, after all, we had arrived. The morning fairly danced and sparkled. Outside the hotel (whose desolate corridors, chipped marquetry, smashed fittings and marble cornices suggested nothing so much as a carnival which had ended in an earthquake)—outside, the blue race of the sea swirled round the stone lighthouse and deployed crisply across what must be one of the finest shingle beaches in the world. The sunlight freckled the foreground of things with blue and gold, while the gaunt backcloth of Caria, only tipped as yet with sunshine, seemed to be softly sifting itself through a spectrum. Utter peace.

'Heavens, I feel well,' said Gideon. We had carried our third cup of tea out on to the terrace, and were full of the warmth and well-being of that spring sunshine.

Idling there upon that terrace we first began our exploration of each other. My own task here was prosaic enough. I had been accredited to the occupying forces as an Information Officer. Gideon's own business was more obscure; he made several mumbling attempts to describe it. Finally he squared his shoulders and produced a crumpled movement order which he handed me to read. I could see nothing very strange about it. It informed me that Captain A. Gideon was proceeding to Palermo via Rhodes on duty. 'You don't see anything odd about it?' he said with a chuckle, and with a touch of fatuous if innocent pride. 'Neither did the provost-marshal.' He beamed at me and explained. He had long ago noticed that the legend 'will proceed from X to Y' on a movement order was sufficiently well-spaced to allow him to insert the word 'via' followed by the name of any little corner of the globe that he might wish to visit. He had spent a good part of the war travelling unwillingly *'from X to Y'*—but always *'via'* somewhere or other where he really wanted to go. 'It's my form of revolt,' he said coyly. 'For Godsake don't tell a soul.' I promised gravely. 'You've no idea what a difference it makes to go from one hellish place to another when you can go and spend a few days "in transit" in a place you really like.' Rhodes, I gathered from subsequent conversation, was an old love, first visited before 1914 war; more than that, Gideon was hoping to find himself a billet in the administration which would enable him to escape from an O.C. he detested in Palermo. He seemed quite confident that a few days of lobbying in Rhodes would produce something suitable. Behind the idea of a transfer, too, lay another—more deeply cherished: he intended to settle in Rhodes after demobilisation. This was interesting. We were, it seemed, both islomanes.

It was in this context that we began to share reminiscences of the pre-war world and unearth common friends. Gideon too had been a tramp in the Eastern Mediterranean before the war: had lived in Athens and Alexandria.

His figure was undergoing a transformation in my eyes. It was to suffer many others, but none so radical as this first one, from that of the average sightless soldier to the man of culture and comparatively wide reading. One element only was missing from

the picture. I supply it from subsequent experiences. I had no idea
what an old rogue he was. I was taken in by that air of benevo-
lence, of courtly gentleness. I was tempted to shake my head sadly
over the innocence of a man who imagined he could cadge himself a job after a few days in Rhodes. How wrong I was! I realised it
a month later when I glanced at a circular which named him the
newly-arrived director of—Agriculture, of all things. But none of
this could I have foreseen that spring morning as we walked
down to the harbour to pay our respects to the military rulers of
the twelve islands. I was not to foresee Gideon's numberless state
visits in his broken-down old car—visits undertaken with the
greatest urgency to consult me upon a Point of Style, or an infini-
tive that had somehow split like a string-bean in the heat of composition. Nor could I foresee how much pleasure I was to derive
'putting some style' into those fatuous concoctions titled
PROGRESS REPORT ON BEET or THE WATERCRESS OUTLOOK FOR NEXT
YEAR. We lavished the combined treasure of our not inconsider-
able intellects on those reports. To read Gideon on Beet was a new
literary experience. Everyone was pleased except the Brigadier,
who pronounced Gideon's style abominable and refused to grant
him his majority until he had read and studied Swift.

That morning however we made our first sortie into Rhodes
town, Gideon 'en pèlerinage', as he expressed it, and I very much
on duty—for I had to locate the printing-plant which was to be
the greatest part of my inheritance from the Army. Rumour had
it that the linotypes were buried somewhere in the castle and
accordingly we set off along the sparkling water-front in the direction of the Street of the Knights, Gideon talking discursively on
everything under the sun, and exclaiming with pleasure at every
new sight and sound.

Taken in by the uncritical eye of a visitor the town looked

lovely that morning despite the infernal wreckage of war—and there was plenty of it. Transcribed from a letter which remained unposted in the back of an old writing pad, these few lines give an impressionist view of Rhodes as I found it, 'Absolute chaos still reigns. The esplanade along Mandraccio, the ancient harbour, is studded with pill-boxes and long rows of iron staples from which grave Indian infantrymen are unwinding the barbed wire. Groups of German prisoners, still whey-coloured from starvation, are busy filling in the bomb-craters in the asphalt, dressed for the most part in shorts and forage-caps only. We have thousands of them on our hands. Clouds of violet smoke hang over Monte Smith from some disposal squad's morning offering to the Gods—exploded enemy mines. I have not had time to look at the medieval town as yet, but it looks fearfully disappointing from the harbour with its spattered administrative buildings and truncated statuary: the old walled town looks like a wedding-cake with all the icing chipped and cracked. A deserted market-place. An empty mosque. A very few white-faced civilians picking over garbage-tins for food. Most of the population has fled to the islands of Symi and Casos. The streets are empty of all but troops and forage-gangs of German prisoners.'

Less impressionistic, but as factually relevant to this first view of the island which I was to come to love so much, were extracts from a report which no doubt still lies mouldering somewhere among the archives of a department in Cairo, whose representative I was then. 'The position in the capital is very far from normal. Most of the population has fled leaving behind them shattered buildings and a gutted market. Those who remain have suffered from the prevailing starvation. Malnutrition cases are coming in at the rate of sixty a day. All public services are at a standstill; the buses were put out of order by the Germans, the post-office deserted, and only the little news-sheets issued by the Army Pro-paganda Executive in two languages maintains a tenuous local dis-tribution. The engineers have nearly completed their work, however, and it is hoped that the electric light plant will be func-tioning again this week. The island is stiff with mines which await the attention of the Sappers. . . .'

Civic order was indeed to be a long time coming; the restora-tion of postal services with the outside world, the establishment of newspapers, the patching up of shattered dwellings—upon all these was 'order' in its twentieth-century sense conditional. It is only if one has seen a town reduced by siege that one can get any feeling of how much our sense of community is founded in these small amenities. I was nearer, I realise, to Demetrius Polyorcites that June morning than I shall ever be again; I was near, I mean, to seeing something like the historic Rhodes as it must have been after the great siege, after the attack by Mithridates, after Cassius had gutted it; a Rhodes dispersed into a million fragments, waiting to be built up again.

Mandraccio Harbour ('The Sheepfold' of the Ancient Greeks) presented some odd contrasts; fully half of its surface was covered by wrecked boats and skiffs, huddled together, as if against fear of bombing—or perhaps blown gradually together by the force of frequent bombardments. In a clearer anchorage, under the fort of St Nicholas lay a number of island *caieques* in good repair—visitors no doubt which had been ferrying back refugees. They floated languidly in the sticky mirror of the harbour-water which was now viscid with oil from a German launch which lay on its side, its tanks squashed by a bomb, deep in the sludge. The whole length of the waterfront was picketed and wired with a thoroughness that left one in no doubt as to the original deter-mination of the enemy; stakes driven into the rocky bases of the piers trailed underwater wires, while the shallows bristled with concrete blocks and underwater defences. Shrapnel had peppered the buildings and snipped off fragments from the maudlin row of bronze Caesars with which the Italians had thought to dignify the port area.

We sat for a while upon a cracked slab of masonry and contemplated all this desolation as we listened to the innocent lapping of the water along the harbour wall. Then we pursued our way across the deserted market-place and entered the old walled town of the Crusaders, passing by the lovely and undamaged gothic tower of St Paul. At the spur of a gentle incline we turned into the famous Street of the Knights at the top of which lay the Castello—that monument to bad taste executed by the latest Italian governor. By now the hideous archness of the restoration work was becoming fully apparent. Gideon, who had seen the island under a kindlier dispensation, became plaintive and fretful. 'This will never do' he said reproachfully. But there was worse to come. The Castello, perched on the marvellous spur where once the temple of Helios stood, commanding the whole shallow spade-like tongue of land below, was in the most tasteless of traditions. Sergeant Croker led us round it, a little puzzled no doubt by our behaviour. I do not think that the most liberal of conventions would allow me to transcribe half the oaths that Gideon shed as we walked from room to garish room, from chapel to chapel, corridor to corridor; wherever you turned you were greeted with ugly statuary, tasteless hangings and tapestries, and the kind of marquetry work that suggested the lounges of passenger steamers. The sweep of Gideon's rage took in the Italian governor, the architects, the stonemasons, and the decorators who had shared in the ignoble deed. He spitted them with every thrust of his outraged forefinger. He had them dragged apart by wild horses. He pursued their ancestors back as far as the fourth century B.C. and beyond. Croker, the duty-sergeant, was a trifle annoyed; he had bothered to memorise a few items about the history of the place and was anxious to act as guide. But Gideon would not hear a word of his patter. 'My dear man,' he said testily, 'it is no good you rambling on about it. The thing is horrible. A design for a Neapolitan ice perhaps.'

'Very good, sir.'

'Anyone who thinks it's beautiful is an idiot.'

'Very good, sir.'

'And stop repeating "Very good, sir" like a parrot.'

'Yes, sir.'

Homer followed us everywhere with a sage, judicial and disapproving air. He obviously shared Gideon's views.

Yet the views from the slitted windows, and from the parapet of the roof, were superb. The town lay below us, splashed with sunshine. Swallows and martins dipped and swerved in the warm spaces of the gardens. The tangerine-laden trees of the foreground dappled the landscape with dancing points of fire. The air was charged with all the sulphurous odours of spring. The sea was calm again and blue—bluer than any metaphor could express. 'Well, I don't know,' said Gideon propping his elbows on the warm stones and wrinkling his nose to taste that tangerine-scented wind. 'If you wanted a thesis about totalitarian art, why here it is.' The duty-sergeant looked reproachfully at the back of his head; he was a north countryman with a long sandy lugubrious face and pent-up cheek. His hair grew like a mastiff's and was trained down across a pale forehead into a sort of quiff. He kept his horny thumbs strictly in line with the seams of his trousers, his shoulders square. It was obvious that he thought us a couple of frightful highbrows.

It was in one of the cellars that we at last ran my printing-presses to earth. In an atmosphere whirling with lead fumes and dense with the noise of clacking linotypes the daily news-sheets were being put to bed under the eyes of a watchful young R.A.F. officer. Here I transacted my business as briefly as possible, chatted to the compositors in order to try and assess their professional abilities, and scribbled a few notes. I learned with relief that the presses were to be moved back to their pre-war establishment; their present gloomy location in this crypt had been a measure taken against fear of bombardment. The semi-darkness here made proof-reading and layout as exacting as invisible mending.

Later the three of us walked down the hill into the old town to try and find a glass of wine. Among the loopholes and fents of the medieval town we finally discovered a little tavern called *The Helen of Troy* where we found a glass of inferior Chianti with the distinct flavour of paraffin. As a drink it was disappointing; nevertheless it must have contained some of the right ingredients, for in the corner of the tavern two Greek soldiers, very drunk, danced quietly together to the monotonous squibbling of a clarinet played by an old man in a greasy turban who lay, half asleep, upon a bundle of boxes in the corner of the shop.

We were to separate, if I remember, about our various business, but it was here, at the Helen of Troy, that we met once more at sunset—one of those fantastic Rhodian sunsets which have, since medieval times, made the island so justly famed according to the accounts of Aegean travellers. The whole *Street of the Knights* was on fire. The houses had begun to curl up at the edges, like burning paper, and with each sink of the sun upon the dark hill above us, the tones of pink and yellow curdled and ran from corner to corner, from gable to gable, until for a moment the darkening minarets of the mosques glowed into blue ignition, like the light glancing along a sheet of carbon paper. No longer susceptible to a beauty become familiar, the dark shades of the refugees moved among their bombed houses, their voices clear and shrill as they lit lamps, or disposed their tattered furniture against the evening, shrilly chaffering. Gideon was holding a glass of some rosy wine up to the red light of the sky, as if he were trying to imprison the last rays of the sunset within it. 'Where by association,' he said 'would Homer get an adjective like *rosy-fingered* from—unless he had experienced a Rhodian sunset? Look!' And indeed in that weird light his fingers, seen through the wine, trembled pink as coral against the lambent sky. 'I no longer doubt that Rhodes was Homer's birthplace,' he added gravely. I could see that he was a trifle drunk. He motioned me impressively to sit and imitate him, and for a while we examined our own fingers through our glasses before solemnly drinking a toast to Homer. ('Not you, you fool' he said to the dog.) For one moment now the whole street trembled with the unearthly light of a stage fiction, and then the darkness slid down from the hill. 'A stained-glass window shattered by a grenade.'

We walked arm in arm down those narrow unlit streets, losing our way once or twice, until we stumbled upon the squat gate of St Paul, and sneaked through its shadow into the twentieth century. A few sporadic points of light shone in the new town, but the street-lighting had not yet been restored and we walked in a deep calm darkness as the first stars began to take shape upon the evening sky. It was now, I remember, that we stumbled upon the little garden which encircles the Mosque of Murad Reis—a garden at whose heart I was later to find the Villa Cleobolus; and here we sat for a while perched upon Turkish tombstones, smoking and enjoying the darkness which had now (spring was advanced) an almost touchable smoothness, the silkiness of old velours. And here, I realise, we were very close to the spirit of old Hoyle—for later it was in this garden that he took the deepest pleasure, lying out on the star-scattered grass to smoke his cigars, or dozing away the long golden afternoons in a deck-chair. Hoyle has not put in an appearance as yet, though it is high time he was introduced, for seen across the false perspectives of memory it seems as if somehow we had already met him. Gideon, it is true, had known him years before; they were of the same generation. But his arrival in Rhodes post-dated this first week of Rhodian exploration by something like a month. He had been British Consul in Rhodes and was coming back. Apart from the printing equipment bequeathed to me by the administration there were a number of other articles which were reputed to belong to the late consul—a series of musty consular tables and code-books, together with some old tin trunks. These we had carefully stacked in the cellar which held our stocks of captured newsprint, where they were a perpetual obstruction to everyone. We were always bruising our shins on them. We had fallen into the habit of kicking the trunks viciously whenever we had any work in this particular cellar, and Hoyle became by extension in our imagination as tedious and obstructive an individual as his personal possessions were to the staff of the newspaper. It was with relief, then, that I heard of his arrival one morning. He was, they told me, even at that moment examining his jettisoned possessions in the cellar. I hastened to present myself to him, and there ensued a meeting for which he, I think, was as little prepared as I. He was standing in the cellar clad in fragments of his consular uniform, an ancient dress hat on his head, gazing with myopic disgust through the wrong end of an ancient telescope. The floor was piled ankle-deep with fantastic objects, both consular and personal. I remember a string of signal-flags, numberless cipher-keys, volumes of birth-certificates, a top-hat, a bird-cage, the remains of a consular uniform, detective stories, a sextant, a film projector, several tennis racquets, and heaven only knows what else. Hoyle looked for all the world like a startled puppy. He dropped the telescope and sheepishly removed the hat. 'Extraordinary,' he said, 'the sort of junk a grown man can collect around him.' I agreed. We introduced ourselves with a certain constraint. For my part I was dying to laugh, and Hoyle looked a trifle sheepish. He picked up a fencing foil and fell to making idle passes in the air as we talked.

Hoyle was small and rotund, with a large head and luminous eye. His manner at first suggested affectation because he had a curious slurring way of talking, and a way of varying the register of his voice from treble to bass, which gave one the impression that he was being swung back and forth in a see-saw as he talked. To this he added a mannerism which strengthened the impression—that of sawing the air with the index finger of his right hand, and marking the periods of his sentences with full stops, poked, as it were, in the air. Later I was to discover that his conversation was manufactured for him by a mind which valued exactitude above all things, and a heart which had never outgrown some of the delightful shyness of childhood. But one might easily have been deceived by his slowness of utterance into thinking that it implied slowness of thought. Quite the contrary. Ideas came so fast to Hoyle that his eyes were suddenly irradiated with light; it was the mechanism of exact expression that caused him to halt to grope for the right word, and never to be satisfied with it. Coupled with this slowness of speech was a slowness of gait which also took some time to interpret. Hoyle walked with such exaggerated slowness, with such a sleepy air, that one might have been forgiven the sin of describing him as a slothful man. Here again one would be wrong. A weak heart which needed constant care was the reason for this octogenarian's gait. But what was remarkable was the manner in which his intellect had used this physical defect for its own use. A man who cannot walk fifty yards without a rest might be forgiven if he were fretful of his infirmity. Hoyle was as equable and unruffled as a child; but since he must pause and rest after every little exertion, he had developed an eye for the minutiae of life which all of us lacked. Forced to stand for ten seconds until his heart slowed down, Hoyle would notice a particular flower growing by the road, an inscription hidden in some doorway which had escaped us, a slight architectural deviation from accepted style. Life for him was delightful in its anomalies, and no walk was possible with Hoyle without a thousand such observations which none of us could have made for ourselves. Gideon was always fond of explaining that he took a 'bird's-eye' view of life; by the same token one might describe Hoyle's eye as being microscopic in its attention to particularities. 'I wonder,' he would say, 'why the Mufti's shoes are too small? I saw him limping today.' Or 'I wonder why in Rhodes they tie up their cats with string. I saw one attached to a front door-knob this morning.'[1] Gideon used to explode with mock-exasperation at the preposterous frivolity of such observations. 'Really Hoyle,' he would say, 'I don't know where you get it all from.' Hoyle's answer never varied in tone or content. 'I was standing having one of my little rests,' he would say, 'and I distinctly noticed him limping.' Admirable Hoyle!

Among his other qualities was the gift of tongues. In the course of his long consular career he had mastered some nine languages, and the greater part of his life was spent in studying comparative

1 During the siege nearly all the cats of Rhodes were eaten by the starving, and this was later to result in a plague of rats which was only conquered by the import of cat-reinforcements from Cyprus. At this time pets who were valued were carefully tied up.

linguistics with the nine fat dictionaries he carried about with him in a tin despatch case. Gideon had an imitation of Hoyle which Hoyle himself very much enjoyed hearing. It turned upon this point, for when a conversation began in Greek or Turkish it was not long before Hoyle's eye lit with professional zeal, and he exclaimed: 'Yes, now that's an odd word, when you think of it. It very much resembles the Turkish *"duff,"* the Arabic *"fluff"* and, come to think of it, the Persian *"huff, puff* or *snuff".'* And out would come his pencil and his notebook. Whether the mountain of notes which Hoyle carried about with him all over the world will ever be refined and pruned into a thesis is another question. My own feeling is that it has become too much of a life-passion. What would Hoyle do if he had no great bundle of MSS to play with: to add to, to subtract from, to rearrange, to reconsider, to prune, to shape? He would probably die. Nor, for that matter do I ever hope to see printed his great prose anthology compiled from the writings of consuls and entitled 'A Home From Home', which contains much good material—the fruit of unhurried choice, of considered opinion ripened in the smoke of many a fine cigar; material from writers so dissimilar as Sir Richard Burton and James Elroy Flecker.

But here I shall permit myself a further digression in time from that hulk of Turkish masonry upon which Gideon and I sat together during that early nightfall: a digression from that garden-graveyard whose guardian, the Mufti, we were soon to meet. I should mention Mills, the young doctor who was later to be placed in charge of the medical service on the island. I do not remember how first we met—it was simply as if he had always been there. I do, however, remember an early occasion in our association when Gideon, for some reason best known to himself, decided that he was developing appendicitis and telephoned for him. (I was later to discover that excessive self-indulgence in food or drink always produced in my friend a form of guilty stomach-ache which lent itself to diagnosis as appendicitis.)

Mills drove about his vast parish in an absurd little Italian sports car with enormous exhaust-pipes and a bonnet held down by straps of prodigious size. He was in build short: in character voluble: in colouring blond as a kingcup. His medical equipment, loosely rolled in a piece of oilcloth that looked as if it had once held wrenches and spanners, bulged in the pocket of the blue seaman's pea-jacket which he wore when he was on duty. It would be difficult to think of anyone who seemed to be such a walking certificate for good health; it simply oozed from him, from his candid face, fresh complexion, sensitive fingers. It took him a very short time to discover little beyond an over-worked liver wrong with Gideon. 'Old man,' he said, 'you have been flogging your liver. I shall send you a bottle of castor oil and a lemon.' Gideon's face showed a mixture of feelings; relief that his malaise was not serious combined with annoyance that it did not merit sufficient attention. 'You've hardly examined me yet,' he said rather testily. Mills drank a glass of wine and regarded his subject with a steady and equable humour. 'What can I tell you that you don't know?' he said at last. 'Smoking and drinking are your two diseases. Cut them out and you'll live forever.' 'Thank you,' said Gideon stiffly, struggling into his bush-jacket. 'No trouble at all,' said Mills. He rolled his stethoscope up into the oilskin pouch, finished his wine. 'Well,' he said, 'we shall meet again': and he was gone.

Hoyle once said: 'Mills switches himself on and off like a light'—and this was an apt enough description of him, for I have never known him spend more than two minutes in one place, nor five minutes with the same patient. Yet somehow he escaped the charge of carelessness or thoughtlessness, for Mills conveyed a feeling of perception and penetration which remained with his patients long after he himself had vanished down the road in his small car, swerving about like a drunken hornet. His diagnosis of disease seemed somehow to be a criticism, not of the functioning of one specific organ, but of the whole man. Like all born healers he had realised, without formulating the idea, that disease has its roots in a faulty metaphysic, in a way of life. And the patient who took him a cyst to lance or a wheezing lung to think about, was always disturbed by the deliberate careful scrutiny of those clear blue eyes. One felt slightly ashamed of being ill in the presence of Mills. It was as if, staring at you as you stood there, he were waiting for you to justify your illness, to deliver yourself in some way of the hidden causes of it. But over and above his skill, the breadth of his intellectual curiosity and humanity were qualities which added richness and colour to our island society. He was by upbringing a Quaker. He had married a delightful Greek girl who had been his chief nurse in the U.N.R.A. unit to which he had been attached before joining the civil administration. They lived in a small flat upon the seashore, whose rooms were crowded with miscellaneous material for all the studies Mills intended to make of people and things outside the immediate limits of his own skill. Once inside the ever-open front door one stumbled over boxes full of geological specimens, of ancient pottery, of sea-shells. Every time a window opened manuscripts of essays on poetry, on sex, on biochemistry, on Elizabethan music were scattered in the air. His wife found him a delightful trial. I still hear her grumbling musical tones protesting: *'Mais voyons, chéri,'* as he proposed some new field of study—such as the guitar, or the clarinet. *'Ça, alors,'* his wife would groan. *'Soyez raisonnable.'* But Mills did not believe in reducing his enthusiasm to normal proportions; there was so much energy to be got rid of, life was so short. . . . I can hear him protesting in his fluent French and Greek. And when he had left the room to bring you his microscope slides to see, Chloe would shrug her shoulders and allow herself to smile as she said: *'Comme il est bizarre, lui. Mais dites-moi—est-ce qu'il est un vrai Anglais?'* Like all Mediterraneans she had been brought up to believe that the hall-mark of the true Englishman is an unfathomable reserve. Mills seemed more like an Italian in his bursts of enthusiasm. And listening to him sing his Greek folk-songs to the guitar she would shake her head and sigh—for surely Englishmen didn't sing in foreign languages with so much feeling? And certainly no true Englishman lost his temper, as Mills sometimes did, and threw himself with gusto into a domestic row? This, then, was Mills, and he was part of it all: indeed from points of view this is more his book than mine, since it is he who decreed the shape of it. I remember him sitting in the Villa Cleobolus one dark winter evening, roasting chestnuts before the fire, while Chloe (after her fifth attempt to make him take her home) had kicked off her shoes and gone to sleep on the sofa—I remember him repeating in his clear voice: 'I do so hope you'll write a book about the island sometime when you feel like it. I don't feel Gideon's history will ever get written somehow, nor Hoyle's study of the dialect: but it needs a book. Not history or myth—but landscape and atmosphere somehow. "A companion" is the sort of idea. You ought to try for the landscape—and even these queer months of transition from desolation to normality.' I do not remember what I answered. I realise now that he was pleading for some sort of effective monument to all the charm and grace of our stay there in Rhodes; the golden sun-washed months which only Hoyle has been left there to enjoy while the rest of us have been scattered about the earth by our several professions and that conspicuous ill-luck which, as Gideon used to say, always afflicts islomanes when they have discovered the island of their heart's desire. In the pauses of the conversation the sea roared upon the deserted beach and the wind whistled in the pines and oleanders of the garden. 'above all,' Mills is saying, as the chestnuts burst in a series of muffled explosions on their bed of soft wood-ash, 'Above all, introduce your main characters right away. Give the reader a chance to see if he likes them. It's only fair. So he can close the book if he doesn't. That's how you should begin.'

There is only one portrait I shrink from—that of the Marine Venus. If the reader should ever visit her in her little cell he would know why. The presiding genius of a place or an epoch may be named, but she may not be properly described. Yet the Venus, when she was raised that sunny morning from the damp crypt in which she had lain hidden; when the packing-case which held her had been broken open: when the pulleys finally raised her out of the darkness, slowly twisting on the end of her cable—why, which of us could fail to recognise the presiding genius of the place? ('A statue of a woman: period uncertain: found at the bottom of Rhodes harbour: damaged by sea-water.') I can still see the faces of my friends as they surrounded the dark trap-door out of which she rose so gravely into the sunlight. Hoyle and Gideon sitting astride a plank; Egon Huber, who had helped to bury her, smiling with pleasure to see her undamaged: while Mills and Sergeant Croker and a collection of barefoot urchins grunted and groaned on the ropes which were raising her.

She rose as if foamborn, turning that elegant body slowly from side to side, as if bowing to her audience. The sea-water had sucked at her for centuries till she was like some white stone jujube, with hardly a feature sharp as the burin must originally have left it. Yet such was the grace of her composition—the slender neck and breasts on that richly modelled torso, the supple line of arm and thigh—that the absence of firm outline only lent her a soft and confusing grace. Instead of sharp classical features she had been given something infinitely more adolescent, unformed. The ripeness of her body was offset by the face, not of a Greek matron, but of a young girl. We carried her, swaddled in sacking, down the Museum corridors, up a staircase, to the little room in which you will find her today. It is an ugly enough stone cabin—and chosen for her by a man who had some silly theory that she was too damaged to look beautiful except from certain angles; hence the theatrical north light which plays up the fine modelling of her back and throws those innocent features into dark relief. But in a little while your eyes will have accustomed themselves to the consuming darkness of the room, and you will be able to trace them with your finger, the cold lip and eyebrow, the stone tresses. It is as if she were made of wax: had been passed very rapidly across a flame intense enough to blunt her features, yet not materially to alter them; she has surrendered her original maturity for a rediscovered youth.

The fishermen dragged her up one afternoon in their nets. It seemed to them to be a rich catch; but it was only a heavy marble figure of a Marine Venus, tangled in weeds, and with a few startled fish leaping like silver coins about her placid white countenance with its sightless eyes.

She sits in the Museum of the island now, focused intently upon her own inner life, gravely meditating upon the works of time. So long as we are in this place we shall not be free from her; it is as if our thoughts must be forever stained by some of her own dark illumination—the preoccupation of a stone woman inherited from a past whose greatest hopes and ideals fell to ruins. Behind and through her the whole idea of Greece glows sadly, like some broken capital, like the shattered pieces of a graceful jar, like the torso of a statue to hope.

THE LITTLE SUMMER OF SAINT DEMETRIUS

(FROM *REFLECTIONS ON A MARINE VENUS, 1953)*

TOMORROW I AM TO VISIT my parish for the first time. On the great ordnance map which hangs above my desk I have traced and retraced the outlines of my islands until I know the distinctive shape of each of them. Rhodes might be a flint arrowhead: Cos a sperm whale: Leros an octopus: Patmos a seahorse: Symi an expended meteor rubbed smooth with air: Kalymnos a mussel.

Of their products, their climates and their inhabitants I already know a good deal, thanks to a brief but intensive period of study with the Army in Cairo. Even the tables of industrial statistics which fill the little army source-books seem to hold some undertones of magic for me with their cold hints of sponge, emery, currants and white cherries. Now I am to marry my theoretical knowledge to that of an eye-witness.

I have chosen the Little Summer of St Demetrius for the journey, counting upon its last fine days to enable me to travel as far as Leros and back on equable seas.

Symi

Moving northwards through this marvellous Aegean landscape lit by the intense white light of the sun, I feel the kick and plunge of the little island caieque as she aims for Cos. The mountains sweep down into the sea, planted here like the feet of petrified elephants, to revolve slowly as we pass them, as if on some great hairy turntable. On the way to Cos you come across whole hillsides littered with debris from Maillol's studio—half-finished ankles and heads, breasts and toes. Dawn had not broken when we entered the great cobweb of stone which is Symi, so I have no clear picture of it—only a series of impressions. It lies there like a black rusk upon the water—but rock so pitted and perforated by the tongues of sea thrown out by Anatolia that you would think of it as most like some black stone lung. Everywhere the sighing and blubbering of blowholes, the sound of water breathing and snuffling in that black honeycomb. On this unpromising foundation a town was built, by an idle youngster in coloured bricks. It started up the mountain but soon tired of the gradient and dissolved into a scrabble of ruined plaster and heaps of stone which nobody will use now. A human voice launched across the noise of the water and the wind from the open sea sounds small, ant-like—as if you were to scratch upon a rubber bladder with the point of a pin. 'Kalo Taxidi—a good journey to you. . . .'

Kalymnos

In Kalymnos the infant's paint-box has been at work again on the milky slopes of the mountain. Carefully, laboriously it has squared in a churchyard, a monastery, and lower down repeated the motif: a church, a monastery, a town; then, simply for the sake of appropriateness, a harbour with a shelf of bright craft at anchor, and the most brilliant, the most devastatingly brilliant houses. Never has one seen anything like it—the harbour revolving slowly round one as one comes in. Plane after stiff cubistic plane of pure colour. The mind runs up and down the web of vocabulary looking for a word which will do justice to it. In vain. Under the church the half-finished caieques stand upon a slip—huge coops of raw wood looking for all the world like the skeletons of dismembered whales.

Three little girls in crimson dresses stand arm in arm and watch us. The harbour liquefies under the keel as we throttle down and move towards the port, our engines now puffy and subdued, yet quickened like our heartbeats as we sit and watch the island. The echo of our passage—the hard *plam-plam-plam* of the exhaust—bounces gravely off the rusted iron hull of a steamer which lies on its side in the shallows, its funnels sticking up like nostrils, but all the rest of it submerged in water as clear as the purest white gin. This is Kalymnos. High up, under the walls of the Church of the Golden Hand a woman is singing, slowly, emphatically, while from the wharves across the way a man in a blue overall is hammering at a coffin. Uncanny isolation of sound and object, each dissimilar, each entire to itself. Detached from the temporal frame. A song and a hammering which exist together but never mix or muddle the hard outlines of each other.

Cos

Cos is the spoiled child of the group. You know it at once, without even going ashore. It is green, luxuriant and a little dishevelled. An island that does not bother to comb its hair. Hard by the port the famous tree of Hippocrates (to which Mills has promised himself a sentimental pilgrimage) stands, in a little arbour of greenery, like some Nubian women stricken with elephantiasis. Whole trees have burst out of it in all directions, and with no reference whatsoever to gravity or proportion. The kindly worshippers have propped, here an arm, there a thigh, with votive pillars of bricks or stone. Somehow the whole improbable structure still stands—indeed its luxuriant foliage covers a whole courtyard like a tent. The children play wonderful games among the branches. 'A stranger,' they cry, 'a stranger.' I must be the first foreign civilian they have seen for some time. We exchange oranges against sweets and discuss life in Cos. Everywhere it is the same—conversation revolves about food. They look ragged and thin but not actually starving. We climb the Prankish castle with its mounds of rubble and shattered ravelins. Once more one comes upon mounds of twisted and rusting steel—machine-gun ammunition and shells and empty petrol tins. There is no time to see the Aesculapium on this visit, as it lies some way outside the town, and the captain of the caieque is anxious to make Leros while the good weather holds. Our journeys must still be made in swept channels, as the whole sea hereabouts is mined, and I think he fears that bad weather might push us into one of these fields. . . .

Leros

In Leros one always seems to be weather-bound, according to the captain. It is a beastly island without any character, despite its rather noble Prankish castle and picturesque village. There is, however, no pastoral or agricultural land worth the name. Simply gigantic port installations now crumpled with bombing, and rotting away in the damp—prodigious jumbles of copper, steel and brass. The harbour is choked with sunk craft, and the little town has been very badly bombed. A miasmic gloom hangs over everything. God help those born here, one mutters, those who live here, and those who come here to die. The water is brackish—like the wits of its inhabitants. As far as I am concerned I am wholeheartedly on the side of the poet Phoclydes who used the name of Leros to throw mud at an enemy of his unlucky enough to be born here. An early example of literary mud-slinging! And 'Leros' still means dirt today. Yet weather-bound or not, there has been time to think, time to jot down some notes about poetry in the little black note-book E bought me, which is now stained with salt water and brandy. Major France, who presides over the officers' mess, is a delightful eccentric, an ex-commando who has spent many years of his life, in peace and war, travelling among these islands; in pre-war years he carried cargo in a small tramp-steamer belonging to himself, while during the war he exchanged his role for that of secret agent. Clad in rubber boots with soles a span thick, and armed with the most fearful assortment of cutlery the mind of man can devise, he travelled about cutting throats, piloting one of the tiny caieques belonging to the Sea Raiding Forces. Now he sits at the head of a hospitable table, covered in campaign medals as thick as confetti, and pines for the rigours of the Burma campaign.

In the smoky tavern whose frail walls quiver at each blast of rain and wind I spend half a day transacting business with the agent who is to handle distribution for me in Patmos and the other small islands. He is a little man whose appearance is one of extreme indigence, and of a cast of feature so terribly pessimistic that it is obvious one can hope for nothing in the way of efficient island distribution. While the Greeks have kept their language, only a very few can write it, and fewer still read it, he tells me. But that is not to say that they will not subscribe to a paper. No. He swigs tot after tot of burning mastika, settling his neck more deeply after each emergence into the collar of his ragged overcoat. People will buy the newspaper all right, but he cannot guarantee readers. Owing to the great shortage of wrapping paper, he says, almost *any* paper is welcome to the inhabitants of the island. They need it for wrapping fish in, or eggs. They need it for parcels and packages. So that my sales will be safeguarded by this great shortage in a way that even full literacy and the keenest interest in the affairs of the world could not achieve for me. It is one of the anomalies of war that the daily newspaper which we issue at a penny is worth twopence as wrapping paper, and already in Rhodes our receipts for scrapped issues are greater than our receipts on current sales. It puts journalism in its right perspective somehow. Meanwhile I am delighted to think of the inhabitants of these atolls subscribing faithfully to my newspaper simply in order to wrap fish in it. The agent does not smile. He is beyond that. As we part he depresses his cheeks into a sort of deathmask of a smile and says: 'At any rate you know the truth now.'

The evening comes down, smudged with rain, from a sky of dirty wool. We stand at the great bay window and watch the skirls and eddies roar into the landlocked harbour and dance like maniacs in the riggings of the caieques. A loose foresail cracks and cracks like pistol shots. Above us the shattered Prankish castle stands its ground as it has done for centuries; but each year a few more bricks are pried loose and come rumbling down the hill into the main street, a few more shreds are blown off the towers. As it gets darker the sheet-lightning starts and France tries to take a photograph of us all sitting round the table playing pontoon by its blank staring stabs. By dawn, he says, it will have blown itself out and we shall be able to start for Patmos, the last island on my visiting list, and the one I most want to see.

Patmos

Just before dawn there were one or two flashes of lightning and I woke to see the hunchback standing in the dark hall, with a telephone in one hand and a lighted candle in the other. 'Hullo,' he was calling in his cracked voice across the miles of water. 'Hullo there Patmos!' A thin crackling came back across the German field-telephone from the island, like the leaky discharge of a low electric current. The lightning flashed twice again—milky throbs of whiteness behind the dense clouds that covered Leros. 'The storm has lifted a little,' shouted the hunchback, grimacing with the effort of maintaining that tenuous contact. 'We are sending them over.'

Outside, I thought I could still hear the roaring of the sea and the whack-whack of the wind in the palm tree up the hill. The hunchback entered the room and placed the lighted candle beside me with the cup of tea. 'The sea is calm,' he said, and as if in sympathy with it, his own voice lost its harshness and became calm too. 'They will be here in a little while to take you.' For four days we had been marooned in Leros by the weather. I said nothing, drinking my tea and exploring the warm corners of the bed with my feet. He stood looking down at me for a moment, and then taking his squat pipe from his pocket, lighted it at the candle. 'Get up,' he said, and marched off in his creaking black boots to the kitchen.

I lay and watched the whiteness of the daylight slowly leak into the sky, outlining the black paw of cloud that lay across the town and shrouded the top of the castle. The air in the room smelt stale and used up. The high cracked ceiling, the odd-shaped windows above which hung the pelmets of mouldering brocade disturbed one by their associations: a Venetian etching. Lying here I felt that I was breathing in the desiccated air of another century; and the candle with its rosy pool of light added to the illusion. A room, you would say, in the house of an exiled Prime Minister in the reign of King Otto. The assassins entered by the window. In the far corner, where the wallpaper has faded, stood the sofa on which they laid him. . . .

The faithful E was awake, combing her dark head by the light of a candle and yawning. I sat and watched her dress eating some bread and butter, talking in whispers so as not to wake the others, who lay in odd corners of the old house, peacefully snoring. 'Do you think we can make it?' she asked from time to time, dreading heavy sea as much as I did. 'It's only three hours,' I said. 'It will be rough of course.'

I was wrong as it turned out. We heard the rapid imperative note of voices in the hall, and tip-toed down the cracking staircase, packs on our shoulders, to where they stood waiting for us. We left the house like thieves.

Beneath the darkness of the cloud the immediate foreground was wrapped in a dense ground-mist, raw and chilling. It was not raining, however, and the boatman grunted his satisfaction at the fact. 'The sea is calm,' he said, 'too calm.' We walked down the avenue of chestnuts together towards the town, listening to the chilling noise of torrents which had swollen with the rains. A flash of lightning showed us the main street which the storm had turned into a swirling black stream; then the darkness came down, ominous and complete—the darkness that comes with the closing of a camera's shutter. It is difficult to explain: for behind it, at the edges of the sky, the light advanced in degrees of dirty white. It was as if all one saw was the silhouette of the darkness itself.

We splashed through the narrow warrens of the port and emerged at last on the quay-side where the caieque lay, its crew stuck fast, it seemed, in attitude of complete apathy, awaiting us. The captain hung from a rope, leaning his body out at an angle, staring down at the water. The boy and the man sat, submerged in themselves at the tiller, their splayed bare feet among the twists of rope. They shook themselves as we whistled.

She was called 'Forgetfulness': a powerful little caieque built to the shallow-bosomed shape which the fisherfolk call 'Racers' because they are judged speedier than the normal deep-hulled models. The sea-raiding people had put a tank-engine in her which gave her about twelve knots. You felt the power at once as she fanned away from the stone-quay and out into the harbour, edging towards the black buoys which, the captain said, marked mine-fields. Huddled in our coats we watched the black, uninviting headland of rock paying out past us like a rapidly diminishing rope, drawing us nearer to the proper sea. Across the waters, from the direction of Turkey, the light had broken through in one place; a drop of red had leaked between the interstices of sea and sky, and was running round the rim of the horizon like the knife that slips along the rim of the oyster to let the light in with it. The red mingled with the black and turned it purple; the meniscus of the sea copied the tone: strengthened it: turned it green, and an edge of the sun shone for a second across the waste of waters and islands, hideous, like a head with one eye. Then the darkness again and the steady throb of the engines. The boy was posted at the prow. He strained through the mist and guided the helmsman with shouts and gestures.

'So we'll get to Patmos after all,' said E, unpacking the sandwiches and the little bottle of cognac.

Patmos, I thought, was more an idea than a place, more a symbol than an Island.

Yet to the boy crouching at the prow, his eyes fixed upon the mist-darkened territory ahead, it had no doubt become a name like any other, marking only a brief stony point in an oft-repeated routine, distinguished at the most by a special tavern where the wine was resinous or a house where the conversation seemed the better for a beautiful elder daughter. From time to time as he peered, he saw the shapes of islands come up on us like battleships, and with a brief wild cry—as of some trapped seabird— shook his arm to right or left, guiding us to the safety of the deeper channel. A few yards away the wet fangs of rock would emerge and

slide back into their unearthly vagueness, and the note of the pro-
peller deepen in the deeper sounding as the vellum of a drum
when the player alters its tensity. Once the mist drew back for an
instant and we saw, tinkling upon a scrubby headland, a swarm of
sheep like gold bugs, loitering among arbutus, while on a rock
commanding the prospect stood a motionless hooded figure like a
janitor. Their bells were softly dumbed out in the mist, losing
volume but not their richness.

The sun had somehow swindled us and climbed into heaven
without once shining directly upon the water. Through a cloud-
surface with a thick yellow nap like a carpet it allowed its beams to
diffuse themselves over everything with a dense coppery hue,
turning the water to lead beneath us. It increased our range of sight,
however, and with it our speed. From where he sat at the tiller the
captain made a chopping motion with his hand to indicate, in
Greek fashion, the fact that we were making better time. The boy
came aft and sat for a while to make conversation. Points of water
glistened in his beard and hair. 'Patmos,' he said, 'you will like it. All
foreigners like it. They have good fruit and water.' Then raising
himself the better to cup his hands about a box of English matches
as he lit a cigarette he added, with a touch of medieval wonder: 'And
there is a telephone. The Abbot speaks to it every day.'

'Have you ever used it?' I asked him.

'I? What for?'

The sense of blindness had now given place to a sense of
headache. The atmosphere had become warmer, but the clouds
still lay between us and the sun, which burned with a bilious
humid intensity upon the sea. The last of the islands that lined the
corridor between Leros and Patmos like ancestral totems, was
kicking in our wake. Presently we should see our objective
through the trembling curtain of the mist.

The captain handed over the tiller and came forward to the prow; hanging outwards he stared long and intently towards the vapourized horizon, and then came aft to consult a watch—not without a touch of pride, for it looked like German booty. We had been going two hours.

'In the channel it is often rough,' said the old man. 'Praise God, it is all right. But tonight there will be more storm.'

We informed him that we had determined to return to Leros that night, and he nodded once or twice in a protective manner as he puffed his cigarette. 'And if you can't,' he said, 'there is no need to worry. There is the telephone.'

Our attention was caught by a cry from the boy who had returned to the prow. Away to the northward the mist had shifted and beyond it, gleaming in a single pencil of sunlight was a white cape—lifted like the wing of an albatross upon the very place where sky and sea met. For an instant this snowy apparition paused, and then the beam moved slowly along the mass to pick out a turret, a battlement, the cupola of a chapel. 'The monastery,' said the captain. 'Patmos.'

We stood for a long time now watching the lights playing upon the island, now touching up a dazzling pane of glass in the monastery, now extinguishing the whole seascape to the tones of a black and white drawing. The sun was trying to find a way through the clouds.

'In another half hour,' said the old captain, as if he were trying to instil patience into himself. 'In another half hour we shall be there.'

'Come,' said E, 'we should eat now.'

We had neither of us had much appetite before, but now with the still straits before us and the island in sight, we turned with real hunger to the cognac and the sandwiches. The boy boiled a kettle of water and I saw with some surprise that the whole crew had developed the habit of drinking British Army Tea, brewed sweet and strong—surely the most disgusting drink ever invented. This was a legacy of the sea-raiding days no doubt, as was the expertness of wrist with which the captain opened a tin of bully beef.

We finished eating just as the caieque fanned into the little harbour of Patmos, free from cloud at that moment, and blazing like a diamond among the hillocks.

'Welcome,' cried the figures on the quay as we tied up, and at once we felt grateful to be back in the traditional type of Greek island after the rather spurious Italianate atmosphere of Rhodes. They were all there in that little whitewashed port; you could see at a glance the representatives of the six or seven types which have furnished Greek islands since the beginning of history. The old sea-captain with his knotted hands and shaggy whiskers, the village schoolmaster in his dignity and European clothes, the mad boy who plays the violin outside the tavern door—the island poet whose wits, says tradition, have been turned by the Nereids. Their clear eyes and lovely brown skins proclaimed them islanders, born in this clear blue air; and the pleasure and warmth with which they cried 'Welcome'—and uttered among themselves the sacred word 'Strangers'—proved them as Greek as one could wish. We declined in rapid succession, a donkey, a bunch of flowers, and a conversation about how old we were, where we had come from, and what our business was. The tavern-keeper swept us a disappointed bow from the door of the tavern in the shadowy interior of which the familiar Homeric group sat round a table playing cards. We walked through the narrow main street between the smiling faces of the women, past the old date palm tree—last of many palms which earned for Patmos the name of Palmosa among the Venetians—and addressed ourselves to the bare hill whose brown rocks were still wet with the rain and noisy with overflowing torrents.

Before us, balanced against a cloud, stood the monastery, its odd arrangement of machicolated turrets and belfries reminding one of a medieval castle—such as one only sees in Russian films. The great gate stood open. One expected to see a troop of Tartar horsemen swing out of it suddenly, waving their lances and hide bucklers, uttering shrill cries; but nothing passed through the door save some small children singing an island song in tiny cracked voices, perfectly reproduced by the blue atmosphere despite the distance.

Halfway up we met a shepherd, sitting on the stone parapet crook in hand, talking to his daughter, and occasionally uttering barbaric whoops at his flock. We sat down and rested beside him, for the going was steep and hard. In exchange for the piece of bread he shyly offered us we took his photograph, while he showed a hospitable annoyance with the Patmos weather for not favouring our visit more conclusively. The ominous wrack of cloud still stretched away to the east and west of the island; while everything lay, enchanted by sunlight, in an oasis of midsummer. Even the bees in the little white hives by the monastery were duped by it.

'Are they expecting you?' asked the shepherd.

'We telephoned to the Abbot.'

'Then you will eat well,' he said comfortingly; the monastery lay about a quarter of an hour off, along the great sill of red-brown stone. The smaller monastery of St John, where the Apocalypse was written, lay beneath us with its cave of the illumination and musty banners. The three ruined windmills glimmered on the ultimate crags.

'We'll be going,' I said.

'God be with you,' he responded, reluctantly, for conversation with strangers is a rare pleasure among islanders who have known each other from childhood. 'God be with you,' repeated his daughter, enchanted by her own grownupness.

We entered the great gate and found ourselves immediately in a warren of cobbled streets, each just wide enough for the passage of a loaded mule, and thrown down upon each other in a sort of labyrinth. We followed them up stairways, down alleys, round corners, doubling back upon ourselves at different levels until we found the great door of the monastery. It also stood ajar. From every nook now the prospect began to shine out, the brilliant bay and the further seas, set in the green and grey.

In the courtyard the hush was intense. The faces on the painted wooden screens glowed softly. Then from the gloom of the chapel came the thin scribbling noise of Byzantine Greek, lifted in prayer. Another voice began a humming twanging response. 'There's a service going on,' said E. Several voices now attacked the silence as if heard through a comb and paper. The faint chink of censers, the faintest whiff of incense leaked out of the darkness. I eased the heavy pack off my back and coughed twice. Immediately a servant came out of the recess under the staircase and told me my name, showing no surprise when I did not disagree. 'At once,' he said in a low, urgent voice, 'at once.' He sprang into the dark chapel like a diver into a pool and re-emerged holding the Abbot by the hand. We began our greetings, seasoning them with apologies for the interruption. The Abbot smiled in his beard and waved the latter away. 'Come,' he cried with a spontaneous good-nature, 'we have nearly finished. Come with us.' And led us by the hand into the little darkness where by now the very anna livia plurabelle of a service was going on.

They looked for all the world like benign tree-bears which had burrowed into the trunk of an old tree for honey. The deacon was humming and yawing from a muscle-bound byzantine evangel which he held against his chest. The Abbot subsided into his place, and we each fitted ourselves into those uncomfortable pews where you hang by the elbows like a bat. It was an admirable introduction, for while the utterances and responses rose and fell in the darkness, I was able to rest and let my eyes wander over the rich altar-screen with its ornaments and paintings. The only light came in through a foggy piece of glass in the dome. The darkness was restful, and I found myself inclined to doze, as the monks trotted backwards and forwards to various points of the darkness, shouting and twanging out of various books, or swinging the censers and spinning round upon themselves with predetermined smartness. One had a sense of infinite remoteness—these voices rising, it seemed, from the bottom of the sea, muffled by the mushroom-shaped dome of the monastery, muffled by the darkness, by the dense gloom.

Presently the service came to an end; facing the altar one of the deacons lifted his mouth and blew out a candle; and at once we were among friends. Six large priests, with luxurious curling beards and expressive hands. 'Praise be to God,' the Abbot said, 'at last some English we can talk to.' Later he doubtless revised his opinion of my lame Greek. But E chimed in, and under her interest and delight everybody came alight, falling naturally into that generous full-bodied loquacious amiability which is so truly Greek, as we streamed out once more into the courtyard to have the painted wood screens explained to us, and the intricacies of the corridors exhibited. In a little dark magazine behind the altar we were shown the treasures of the monastery—richly embroidered copes and stoles, a dozen different kinds of pyx, diamond-studded bindings for books.

By now the weariness of our journey was upon us, and we

asked leave to rest; but this was not to be. There was the whole rambling architecture of the place to see; and then there was the fatal bait of the camera which I carried slung from my shoulder. I could see several pairs of dark eyes fixed meditatively upon it, and several pairs of dark hands beginning with an anticipatory combing-out of beards, the adjustment of black stove-pipe hats. Presently we should have to take everyone's picture.

The monastery of St John was itself as much a treasure as any of its heavily priced treasures in silk or ivory or vellum; it was a wilderness of chimneys, cupolas, belfries, turrets and dazzling white walks. Connecting battlements complement each other so you can walk from the eastern side where the island lies and study the shapes of other islands, faint as a wash drawing on the smooth surface of the sky. Leros, Icaria, Amorgos, Samos. The clouds had turned them down like wicks, but there they lay stubbornly insisting on their identity against the darkness of the horizon. 'Bad weather,' said the Abbot, learning that we intended to start back that afternoon. 'You should have stayed for a month with us.' This gave him a chance to show us the commodious quarters for guests, eight lovely whitewashed rooms, with angle-windows looking out on to the sea. I would have liked to stay for the rest of my life, but did not wish to seem fulsome in expressing so a thought which must have sprung to so many minds. 'Are you not lonely?' said E to the Abbot. The old man repeated the word once or twice, looking from one to the other of us, holding it, as it were, so far away from himself as possible, the better to see the concept which it represented. He did not answer directly. A few drops of rain fell loudly on the terrace. The rent in the cloud-scape was rapidly closing once more. Below us the harbour with its viridian borders and the pearly tones of the hill beyond, began to dissolve and fade, as the thunder opened up in the west. He led us into the library and showed us the famous manuscripts, writhing painted bestiaries and ancient scripts, pressing our shrinking fingers to the thick vellum to feel its weight and quality. When we had exhausted these treasures he allowed us to photograph him leaning in the narrow window-sill, conscious of the elegance of his beard and beautiful hands. Outside a rain of thistles had begun to descend blotting out all perspectives, and turning the whole monastery in a moment from dazzling white to soaking neutral grey. The rain stood for a moment in great drops on the lips of the bell and then ran down to the courtyard, seeking the already swollen gutters. 'We shall never get away tonight,' I muttered.

In the refectory, whose windows were lit by yellow stabs of lightning, we watched the storm slowly wheeling the clouds into formation. The islands had vanished. Strange manoeuvres were going on in the dark sky beyond which the sun still shone. We ran from window to window calling to each other to look. Through holes in the cloud long shafts of yellow light played down on the leaden sea like searchlights, circling slowly, or running the whole length of the horizon before going out. Such tense needles of light as one saw piercing the gloom of those old oil-engravings to the shilling Bible, on which the dove descended as upon a scaling ladder.

An old woman had laid out supper for three, and presently the Abbot joined us to pour out the heavy red wine into the glasses and serve us portions of the delicious chicken with lemon-rice. He seemed obscurely troubled and looked up nervously as each heartbeat of lightning lit up his bearded face. For a while we attempted a desultory conversation which could compete with the storm. Drops of water climbed down the windows. Somewhere a shutter banged again.

'It was you who telephoned?' asked the old man.

'Yes, from Leros. Major F's servant spoke to you."

He nodded twice with something like impatience and ate another mouthful of chicken. 'So many people ring up and say they are coming,' he said. 'Some do. Others never seem to arrive.' He issued some impatient orders over his shoulder to the aged woman and began to tell us of the war. The monastery was forced to play the role of philanthropic neutral to three nations. A smile lit up his face as he told us how three separate units, Italian, German and English, had been sheltering in the monastery at the same time. 'Two of the three might have shot us,' he said. 'What could we do? An Italian signal section on the top floor, a wounded German officer whose life I saved in the granary, and six British commandos in the cellar which was their H.Q.'

It had been as difficult and dangerous a time as any he cared to remember. Naturally they were pro-British—but a monastery is a monastery. 'We could not leave the German to die outside on the hill. As for the Italians . . .' He shrugged his shoulders.

Suddenly he turned round and said: 'And this man Anthony— why did he not come with you from Leros?' We looked at each other. 'An English Major who also rang up.' To the best of our knowledge there had been no one else in Leros intending to make the crossing; had there been he would certainly have had to ask the permission of Major F, our host. We should certainly have known. 'That's what I mean,' said the Abbot in a distressed tone. 'People are always ringing up.'

The storm had travelled over the peak and was now thrashing the palm tree in the valley. We finished the excellent chicken, and the Abbot led us slowly from room to room of the monastery, down winding corridors, up and down stairs. This was where the brothers lived. This was a reception room. This was where the conclave met to discuss ecclesiastical problems, or those connected with the administration of the monastery. In one of these large echoing rooms stood the German field-telephone, a replica of the one at the mess in Leros—an ugly bakelite box with a handle and a small receiver. As the Abbot looked at it I saw an expression of disgust and anger cross his face. 'This is the telephone,' he said. The rain was pouring in at an open window, stirring the dust on the floor, and shaking the heavy red hangings by the dias. I closed the window, and we went down the corridors in single file. As we emerged upon the penultimate balcony overlooking the court-yard we heard the sound of voices. Looking over, I could see the soaked figure of our captain standing in the great door with a piece of sacking over his head. In half an hour, he shouted up at us, there would be a lull in the storm. If we chose to take advan-tage of it we could be back in Leros by dinner time. If not . . .

'We have not spoken of St John,' said the Abbot. 'Of his won-derful book. You must see his church. Stay with us.' His tone changed to one of hospitable coaxing. It was very difficult to explain that, if we missed the motor-launch which was due to start for Rhodes at dawn the next day we should be stranded for a week over schedule—delightful as the idea seemed. He was sad. He had intended an exposition of the Apocalypse.

However, he helped us pack our belongings, and one by one the brothers came out of the various rooms to shake our hands and bid us goodbye. 'Come again,' they cried, 'come and stay with us. We are on the telephone, you know. You can always ring up and say you are coming. Just come any time, and stay with us as long as you like.'

We passed out through the great doorway into a blinding drizzle that thinned off as we neared the harbour; the little caieque was standing off with her engine going. It had all been timed to a second. With hardly a moment to say a breathless goodbye to the friendly loafers in the tavern we were aboard, and drawing free of the harbour towards a sea that looked foully disturbed, with whitecaps flicking the horizon.

Darkness fell before we had cleared the rough straits but we were making good time. The caieque rode superbly, her round canoe-shaped nose chopping down the head-sea. By seven, the black shapes of rocks gleamed wetly at us from either bow, and we slackened speed. Leros hung against the sky, a part of the darkness and yet separable from it if one looked carefully enough; but the middle distance was blotted out by skirls of rain. One could taste the dry salt on one's lips, feel its powdery dryness upon the throat and ear. Soon we crossed the bar and the few dim lights of the harbour bulged greasily at us. It was still raining as we disembarked and crossed the wet deserted streets towards the mess. The rain rattled like shot among the chestnuts.

In the dark hall we stood for a moment, peeling off our clothes and shouting for the hunchback, who came from the kitchen at last, bringing with him a great bar of light and the gleam of an oven.

Upstairs, the two officers were finishing dinner. It was good to sink into one of the luxurious armchairs with which the German commander of Leros had furnished his mess and sip a drink while the baths were heated up. We gave an account of our trip to our host and thanked him suitably for the use of his caieque. As we were talking the telephone in the hall began to ring. 'The damned thing,' said the young officer running downstairs to answer it. 'It's been out of order all day.' In a moment he returned and said: 'It's the Abbot. Wants to know if you are safe. Would you like to go down and do your stuff?' I picked my way down to the dark hall and picked up the ugly little receiver. Damp crepitations echoed inside the earpiece. 'Hullo,' I called, and for a moment I heard, as if in a sea-shell, nothing but the sibilance of sea-water lashing those stony promontories, boiling among the shapes of volcanic stones, among the deserted quays of Patmos harbour.

'Hullo'. The Abbot's voice emerged from a criss-cross of scratchings and whirrings, as if from some old prewar gramophone disc. 'Your Beatitude,' I said, giving him, for good measure, what was really a patriarch's due. 'We arrived safely, thank you.' And I added compliments suitable for the occasion. The young officer came downstairs and stood beside me as I spoke, putting a cigarette between my lips and lighting it. 'After you,' he said. The Abbot sounded squeaky and alarmed. No doubt he was unused to telephones. 'This man, Major Anthony,' I said, 'who is he? The old boy wants to know whether to prepare food for him or what.' The officer took the phone from me and began a bantering conversation with the island. 'No such person, Abbot,' he said. 'Your imagination again. No. You won't be disturbed for some time now.'

Together we walked upstairs to the lighted room where the cards had been laid out upon the table and where a sleepy E was already beginning to put her things in order against packing. Tomorrow, at dawn, the naval launch would take us back to Rhodes. Much later, when I was already in bed, listening to the whacking of the palm tree up the hill, the young officer came to say goodnight standing at the open door with a candle in his hand. We should not see him before we left. 'Is the Abbot often mistaken about visitors who ring up?' I asked on a sudden impulse.

'It's just one of those things,' he answered indifferently. 'Beastly things, these German phones.' Then he added: 'It's curious. The Abbot always seems to be getting phone calls from this Anthony chap. I wonder who he could have been—if at all, I mean. . . . Well, goodnight.' I wondered, too. Lying in bed, tasting the luxury of the sleep which was moving toward me across the noises of the house, and the deep hushing of the wind and the rain, I suddenly thought to myself that perhaps this was a ghost which for some reason or other was destined forever to long for Patmos (which is after all a symbol of something for which we all keep a place in our hearts).

On the way home, another storm is brewing. Heading for the harbour we pass a poor wretch in a leaky boat, half-naked, setting out lobster pots. He does not even turn to watch us as our wash sets him bouncing. Through those patched rags I see the lean muscles of his arm tighten as he struggles for purchase in that crazy cockle-shell. Yet he does not even turn to curse us—and in a flash I see the Greece I love again: the naked poverty that brings joy without humiliation, the chastity and fine manners of the islanders, the schisms and treacheries of the townsmen, the thrift and jealousy of the small-holders. I see the taverns with their laurel wreaths, the lambs turning on the spit at Easter, the bearded heroes, the shattered marble statues. Eastward now lies Anatolia, its sunburnt mountains brooding under the eagles where the shepherd treads all day among myrtle and arbutus stabbed scarlet with berries. Some day I shall find the right way of dealing with it in words. . . .

THE THREE LOST CITIES

(FROM *REFLECTIONS ON A MARINE VENUS*, 1953)

THE FUNCTION OF HISTORY in all this is a small but precise one: as in some renaissance painting where the hermit occupies the foreground, seated in his drab ochre-coloured cell, but where, over his shoulder, set like a jewel in the rock, his only window gives on to a limitless panorama of smiling country, exact and glittering in its perspectives, symbol of the enamel landscape on which he has turned his back. So here I would like our own idle history of conversations to open like a sally-port, and throw into relief the many-coloured background of the island's own history. Only in this way can one nourish the other, so that the landscape may be evoked from both, before the eyes of a reader who is not free to touch the living grass of Cameirus with his own hands, or to feel the waves of sunlight beating upon the rocks of Lindos. What, now, of the three ancient cities which once dominated the politics and government of the island before the foundation of Rhodes, the capital? Of Ialysos alas! little remains, but their situation has preserved the two others, while the hundred or so miles of modern motor-road which encircles the island places them within easy reach of the present capital, their child. They lie, too at roughly the same distance from the tip of Rhodes, one upon the northern shore, the other upon the southern. While they are easily reached by road, however, that is not the best way to see them.

I am thinking now of that fine August afternoon when Gideon and I set out on foot to explore the ancient cities, fortified by the knowledge that a long week-end lay before us. Our plan of march was an ingenious one, for we had arranged that Hoyle and Mills should run out by car and meet us at the end of each day's march to share the pleasures of camping out. Time and distance did not permit us to walk the whole way, so we planned to walk to Cameirus in two stages and thence to travel by car over the eastern end of the island to Lindos where we would spend our last night.

Leaving the town we chose the upper road because, if I remember rightly, there was some site whose location Gideon wanted to identify among the rock tombs which cluster round the nape of Monte Smith; but the sun was hot, and the steep hill was enough to set him puffing and blowing by the time we reached the crest overlooking Rhodes. Below us the sea sat perfectly still, cold as jelly; the old grey fort, its walls stitched and cobbled, resembled the pelt of an aged elephant. Neohori (Newtown) by contrast glittered softly in its plaster walls and red roofs. (At one time, says an ancient writer, it was known to the vulgar as Keratohori or Cuckoldville owing to the questionable morals of its inhabitants.) We sat for a while in one of those little rock-tombs where the temperature of the stone, as Gideon observed, made one think that the occupant had just left it for a stroll by the sea; and then, shouldering our packs, climbed up past the last villas and the dismantled battery where dark-skinned Indians lay about in the grass chattering, and took the high road which runs over the crown of the hill and along the glittering cliffs. It was cool here and windy. Westward along the shingle beaches around Trianda the sea was laying down its successive washes of prussian blue and violet, and thinning them out as they touched sand to green and citrons and the innocent yellows you can see on the ripening skins of tangerines. Here too we sat to get our breath and to watch, directly below us, the traffic moving along the main road. Mills emerged suddenly at the wheel of his car, bowling along to some urgent appointment, trailing a puff of dust behind him like a cherub's cloud, and skilfully negotiating the long caravans of mules moving in the opposite direction, carrying produce for the Rhodes market. Here, too, then my companion's attention was taken up for a while with the professional appraisal of some sheep. Since his appointment as agricultural officer, he had developed a ridiculously proprietary air whenever any livestock came within his field of vision. 'Now, that's a fine cow,' he would say, or 'There. How's that for a sheep? Fattened up by the Gideon method.' So now, while I sat under a pine-tree and drank some wine, he took himself off to discuss a flock of sheep with a ragged shepherd-boy who was guarding them. He came back looking rather gloomy and took a savage pull at the wine-bottle. 'Their bowels are out of order,' he said at last. 'I hope to God it's not contagious enteritis.'

We set off across the plain with some caution, for the ever-present danger of mines was a constant preoccupation, and no detailed map of existing mine-fields had been published. Indeed the Italians during the earlier part of the war had mislaid their own defence plans, so that when the Germans moved into Rhodes they were forced to re-mine many areas. Maps of the latter fortunately were in our hands. But there were still large mined areas of the island unaccounted for, and Gideon had more than once been in danger of his life as he was forced to tip-toe on to an apparently 'live' field to rescue Homer, his dog, whose curiosity was always leading him into undesirable places. A maze of dry paths led us across the valley, through silvery groves of olives, and pastures richly scented with thyme and myrtle bruised by the hooves of goats. The little cottages here were encircled with walls of hibiscus and oleander, and we stopped once or twice to knock at a strange door and ask if the area was mined. But nobody seemed to be sure. One old lady in a red handkerchief assured us that there were no mine-fields here, but that on the other side of the main road 'among the archaics' there was a large field. Gideon groaned. 'This incredible talent the Germans have,' he said, 'for choosing valuable antiquities as gun-sites—such vandalism.' But it is really only Teutonic military logic. What commander could choose a better defensive position than an acropolis?

We were fortunate in not having to carry provisions, for a message had been sent to Peter, the warden of Phileremo, to expect us; and from what little I knew of Peter's habits and temperament—he combined the trades of poacher, guide and family man with perfect harmony—what I knew of him led me to expect nothing less than a whole lamb on the spit. I told Gideon so. 'Lamb?' he said irritably. 'He mustn't kill lambs. We've forbidden that by proclamation.' 'Wait till you taste it—the sage and garlic, Gideon, the sauce.' Gideon cannot resist licking his lips, but he wags his head reproachfully at the idea and strikes an olive-tree in passing with the flat of his hand—as if to chastise the forbidden thought.

The village of Trianda stands on the level ground at the end of the fine valley which bears its name; the houses stand off the main road which passes through it, for the most part hidden in groves of olive, fig and orange. They are the summer-houses of the wealthier Rhodians, and the ambition of every man of men is to have a little house at Trianda where he can sit in the cool shade of his own fig-tree during August and September, when Rhodes is hot. It was here, I am reminded, that Lady Hester Stanhope lived during her short and dramatic stay in the island—in one of these small blind-looking Turkish houses with its barred windows and shadowy interior, with its grove of orange and cherry-trees shutting out the view of the sea: it was here that she took to trousers— or the Turkish equivalent of trousers.* Here we set our backs to

---

* I am wrong. It was at Lindos or perhaps Malona.

the sea and the village, and our faces to the bulk of Phileremo, the flat-topped mountain which was Ialysos once, and which has offered a first-class defensive site to a hundred armies, Greek, Prankish, Roman, Turkish, German. It is little wonder that no traces of the ancient Acropolis remain. To our right in the valley, as we reach the first upward curve of the road, we see the 'archaics' which the old woman spoke of; a series of trenches and parapets cut in the red soil of the valley to form a square.

How much is archaeology and how much military workings we are unable to gauge until we break the back of the mountain ahead of us, following the sinuous road which now leads through a dense forest of young pine. Here on a shoulder of hill Gideon called a truce to the pace I was setting and we sat for a while to look down over the valley which now lay spread beneath us, its squares and oblongs of cultivation picked out in russet browns and green until the whole prospect looked like some fine old tweed plaid, much darned. The sun was sinking behind Tilos, and the mountains across the way had become wine-dark and bony. A light wind siphoned up the water in the shallows beyond the town and kicked up spray around a caieque heading south. Trianda drowses among its silver-grey olive-trees. Directly beneath we can see the slight tump of excavated ground where the city of Ialysos once stood, and can even discern among its scarred furrows traces of ancient wall. Of the minefield, however, there is no discernible trace from this range. Westward the torn gun-emplacement of Mount Paradiso (an almost exact replica of Phileremo) flares for a moment as the sun picks up fragments of glass and metal to play upon. We shall, I calculate, have about half an hour of light in which to potter about the ruins on the crown of the hill. We turn away from the prospect and climb the long steep road to the summit. The air has become colder, and spicy from the pine-forest which surrounds us. From time to time we shout Peter's name aloud, and the echo of our voices plays back upon us from several sides at once. But there is no answering call. He must be up at the monastery, waiting for us.

But then his laugh came out of nowhere and startled us. It was as if the trees laughed. Homer barked. We turned about, looking now here, now there, like characters in *The Tempest*, while Peter's tittering laughter sped from tree to tree, from rock to rock. Finally he had pity on us, and climbed down from the branches where he had been hiding. Brushing the dust and bark from the battle-dress of which he was so proud he came towards us, a short stocky man, with yellowish eyes, a snub nose, and an irresistibly comic expression on his round face. 'Did you think I was a *kaous*?' he asked. We shook hands and he expressed himself honoured to meet Gideon of whom he had many favours to ask. Together the three of us left the road and followed a narrow turning path to the summit, walking deep in anemones across the shadowy glades and mossy brakes which crown Phileremo. 'First,' said Peter, 'I shall explain all the archaics to you without any charge, and then we will go to my house where I have a splendid dinner for you.' Gideon grunts.

'I suppose you have a sheep?' he said in an off-hand way, torn between duty and a hunger which Timocreon would have sympathised with.

'A sheep?' Peter sounds outraged. 'For six people, not including my family? I have two sheep.'

The others are supposed to be coming on to join us later in the evening, and to be bringing blankets and mattresses for Gideon and me.

There is precious little to explain about Phileremo today; the monastery has been thoroughly bombed, and the image of the Virgin, which was the object of so much veneration in the time of the Crusaders, has long since vanished. Once more, however, we found ourselves walking among shattered field-guns and a metal harvest of cannon-shells, for Phileremo had been the site of fierce action between Italian and German troops shortly after the fall of Italy. The Italians, though they outnumbered the Germans by six to one, and held the crown of the hill, only lasted out a week of Stuka bombardment. They left behind them mounds of live ammunition and a small pyramid of tin helmets. The little monastery is a ruin. In the garden a few fragments of Byzantine and Hellenic stone lie forlornly about. But the view is incomparable from the little monk's walk, tree-lined and shady, which has been contrived to cross the summit from end to end. From here you can stare down landwards at the gutted aerodrome of Maritza, now dotted with abandoned aircraft, some wingless, which lie about among the fields like charred moths under a lamp. Beyond that green bowl the hills rise again and lead away to the green-spires of Monte Profeta.

'In old times,' says Peter, 'the image of the Panaghia was the patron saint of the island. In moments of trouble it was carried in a solemn procession to Rhodes, and all round the town. Even before the last siege of the Turks they did this, but it had no effect.'

'Where do you get your information from?' asks Gideon.

'There is an old monk in the village who told me.'

'How does he know?'

'Books,' said Peter, 'he has many books. Before, there were many relics in the island, but now none.' He is right there; Torr has preserved a list of them which for sheer variety takes some beating. I quote: 'Chief among the many relics preserved at Rhodes were the right hand of John the Baptist: one of the three bronze crosses made by the Empress Helena from the basin in which Christ washed the Apostles' feet: a cross made from the

True Cross: a fragment of the Crown of Thorns, which budded yearly on Good Friday: and one of the thirty pieces of silver; wax impressions of which, if made by the priest in Passion Week, were efficacious in travail of child-birth and in peril by sea.'

While Gideon and I went to make a further exploration of the hillside, Peter sat down under a tree to wait for the rest of the party. As we returned we heard voices among the trees. Mills, to the alarm of his wife, was already busy collecting souvenirs from among the cannon-shells that littered the paths. Hoyle sat in Sand's old German car, quizzing the view through his glasses, while Sand himself and E were climbing the staircase to the monastery tower with Peter. After a good deal of ferocious banter from Hoyle and Mills, Gideon was permitted to announce himself more than ready for dinner, and the cavalcade started off down the hill to Peter's house, Hoyle taking his little rests every fifty yards with the punctuality of a Swiss clock, and Mills singing at the top of his voice.

The house of Peter the guide lies off the main road some two hundred yards before it breaks up through the pine-forest and reaches the crown of the hill. It is built in a cutting sheer against the mountainside. Its forecourt is shaded by an enormous plane-tree, while a stream runs thickly out of the side of the hill, so that the air under the great tree is a perpetual mixture of shadow and spray. To the noise of cold running water the children shout and play all day, the seven cages of canaries slowly swing in the arbour under the terrace, while their occupants chirp to the note of the water. To live so close to a powerful stream is as good as living by the sea; the noise of it—black water squirting down upon stone—provides a background, a momentum for one's life. The air vibrates and wavers round one as if from the hum of a great dynamo. Even when you enter the house, and the noise of the water is stilled, you have, as if within the canals of the middle ear, a deep echo.

Peter's house boasted a precarious balcony overlooking the valley—an extremely dangerous-looking wooden arrangement built along the first floor. The feeling of height, the great expanse of country below one, and the fear that at any moment one might fall through those crazy planks of wood into the valley, gave a strange character to that first dinner-party in Phileremo. Hoyle said that he felt he was up in a balloon. Peter's own feeling for metaphor was not far behind Hoyle's as he added proudly: 'Sitting here you know what the bird feels when you hang its cage in a tree.'

The house abounded in livestock and small black-eyed children. Visitors to the table included a tiny and immaculate lamb, with a coat as soft as moss, and an eye like a live coal. It drank wine from a saucer with the utmost concentration, its chevril ears crumpled upon its flat and woolly skull. Two tortoises walked about with a blameless clockwork air; and Gideon was kept busy buying up cicadas from the smaller children and setting them free. The peasant children have a nasty habit of catching a cicada and tying it to a piece of string. It makes an admirable bull-roarer, for if you swing it round and round your head it lets out a dull creaking sort of protest. Needless to say this is a habit which Gideon dislikes intensely, and no sooner does he see a cicada trussed up in this way but he must buy it and set it free. 'Let me see,' I remember him saying, 'Six children, six cicadas at five lirettas a head. . . . Philanthropy is an expensive game, Hoyle. Don't have anything to do with it.' But Hoyle, who was carving the lamb with an infectious air of approval, was too occupied to give much thought to this animadversion. 'I was afraid,' he said, 'it was going to be a *leetle* bit tough but,' putting a segment in his mouth, 'praise be to our Lady of Phileremo, it isn't.' It wasn't.

Lamps had been lit by now and perched on nails. They cast a frail radiance over the balcony so that, seen from the ground-floor, where Peter's wife was still busy cooking a dish of octopus in a metal cauldron, the balcony looked like some lighted ship sailing upon a canal perhaps, or the unruffled waters of some great lake. A comparison I thought poetical enough to express to Mills, who had come down with me to inspect the octopus. 'Yes,' he said, standing beside me and gazing up at the scene. 'And Gideon is lifting his glass to his mouth with the regularity of a Varsity oarsman, rowing.' Gideon, indeed, had become as ruddy as a lamp himself. He glowed. His monocle was misty with good cheer. The fourth bottle of wine had brought its customary loosening of tongues. The octopus when it appeared looking like a boiled motor-tyre was greeted with shouts of applause. Gideon proposed a toast to it. The octopus was in no condition to reply to these courtesies. It lay bubbling in a rich red sauce flavoured with garlic and peppercorns. Hoyle once more constituted himself taster and repeated 'I was afraid it was going to be a *leetle* bit tough but,' putting a piece of the sucker in his mouth, 'praise be it isn't.' It wasn't.

Mills slipped down to the car and brought up his guitar. The wooden house proved an extraordinary sound-box, mellowing the note of the strings, and making it louder, more resonant and authoritative. Voices too had a curious ebbing volume over that blue valley with its darkened border of sea. We sang for the most part the traditional Greek folk-songs, tasting once more their extraordinary purity of line, and the marriage of words and music in dance-measure which is their supreme quality. Later Peter felt emboldened enough to sing us some of his Anatolian songs, with their sharp quarter-tones and strange lapses from key to key. In order to achieve this kind of singing you must put your head back and let the voice become pliant, soft, almost undirected. Peter's

voice bubbled in his throat like rose-water in the bowl of a nar-
guileh as he followed the windings of these old melodies with their
intricate cross-references of rhythm and accent. It is the singing of
a bird, apparently haphazard and undisciplined, but demanding
far greater voice-control than European singing does. The songs,
too, though they resembled those of Crete and of Macedonia, had
a hint of something else in them—the flavour of Arabia, of Persia.
Their melancholy was not wild and savage as the Greek mountain
melancholy is: it was softer, more quaintly flavoured.

Gideon by now was asleep with his head upon the table. Hoyle,
whose capacity was normally a minim of wine per meal, had
poured himself a whole glass and was sunk, I could see, in his own
memories of the East, the songs he had heard in Beirut and
Damascus before the last war. E sat with her black eyes fixed upon
the singer's face following every supple turning, every sour
change of tone and key. By her side Chloe petted the lamb and
tried to interest it in a slice of octopus. Mills and Sand were
cracking walnuts in the palms of their hands, expressing an over-
exaggerated solicitude whenever the noise seemed to border upon
rudeness to Peter. But the singer himself was lost. He held the
guitar lightly between his knees, his blunt fingers folded about it
with the repose that comes from long familiarity: and as I hold
this picture for a moment in my mind I see him singing with his
black eyes fixed on the darkness of the valley below us, his sleeves
rolled back, his collar open, and the sound of his voice wobbling
in his throat like a second pulse.

From there to the roaring of cars, the loud good-nights, and
the yellow swathes of headlight cutting the pines, and diminishing with the noise of engines in the valley—from there the
transition is immediate. Yet it must have been late. We were left
with the roaring of the mountain spring and first whoop of owls.

We settled down to sleep in flea-bags on the balcony, Gideon and I. 'We must be up at cock-crow,' he cried once, indistinctly, in the voice of one leading a charge against hopeless odds—and then fell asleep with his head buried upon his arm. I blew out the lights and lay for a long time, listening to the wind stirring the pines, and the faint noise of cars crossing the valley below us. The children were long since in bed, and only Peter sat upon the deserted balcony, drinking a last glass of mastika before turning in.

On the landward side of Phileremo, no doubt, the early moon had risen above the horizon and set. Meanwhile without ceasing the stream flowed on from the heart of the mountain, its water ringing steadily upon the stone still of the fountain before it disappeared among the mosses and cresses of its underground track again. But already our ears had become so accustomed to it that we should not have recognised the silence that might follow if it should suddenly stop.

It was already dawn when I awoke. Gideon had rolled out of his flea-bag and was lying on his back snoring like a clockwork toy, his face smoothed out and juvenile, the round circle of his eye scored out by his eyeglass gleaming white as a scar.

In order to reach the privy at the back of the house one had to pass through a ground-floor room whose furniture would have delighted a surrealist. There, standing upon the earthen floor, without any attempt at premeditated arrangement, I saw a sewing-machine, several Louis Quinze pieces, a Sheraton sideboard, desk, a typewriter, and a very handsome grand piano. The piano had been whitewashed. The reason for this accumulation of treasures is a simple one; during the period of acute starvation in Rhodes the peasants refused to trade their vegetables for money because they were afraid of fluctuations in value, or even of the Italian liretta being recalled in exchange for some valueless occupation currency.

They would accept articles of value, however, in exchange for vegetables; so it was that one saw caravans of carts setting off from the town every morning for the interior loaded with furniture, pictures, typewriters, plates, linen, etc. In the remote villages these objects were freely exchanged, and now the peasant houses are crammed with them. And the whitewashed piano? Peter's explanation has a certain nobility about it. 'Of course we whitewashed it,' he said. 'You know as well as I do that black is the colour of mourning. We did not wish to attract a death to the house. So we painted the piano white.'

The air was sweet with the damps of night as we set off, and we walked steadily until we reached Kremasto, where we explored the church with its holy well and immense cypresses; and where the vicar, who looked like a dispossessed earwig, conducted us from ikon to ikon with great circumstance and a wealth of pointless detail. Afterwards we took a glass of sticky liqueur with him in the sunlit courtyard whose floor was paved in pure white sea-pebbles, dusted spotless by the brooms of two old women who seemed to be nuns. Kremasto is the scene of the greatest festival of the year, held on Assumption Day, and on the ninth day after that date, in honour of the Panaghia. Here, as in Tenos, the holy ikon performs its yearly miracle of healing, and here come crowds of foreign visitors from Turkey and the islands round about. Along four sides of the monastery are the cells in which they are accommodated during the festival. Despite the prevailing dislocation of traffic with the mainland a good crowd of suppliants is expected, says the old man. During the war years everything was at a standstill, the narrow straits were mined, everyone was starving. Now . . . peace is here. He leaned forward and took one of Gideon's hands, pressing it warmly between his own. 'England has brought us white bread,' he said, nodding that rusty old head on his shoulders.

We moved off in good order down the sunny main street of the town which was lined with barrows full of bright vegetables, for Kremasto is the nearest market-town to Rhodes, and it is here that the peasant unloads his stocks if he does not feel like travelling to the capital in search of a buyer. Needless to say, keeping a vegetable stall is one of those occupations which do not take up all one's time; there is plenty of time to drink, to gossip and play cards—and these seem to be the major occupations of the stall-owners, who sit in the little cafés lining the main street and while away the hours in this manner. Here we bought some apples, not without difficulty, for the owner of the stall was engaged in a game of backgammon and sent us a message with a friend to say that he was indisposed; he was sitting in full view at the time, his big coarse face bent over the board, his coffee cup beside him. We entered the café and after a long argument prevailed upon him to serve us. He did so with hauteur.

We made good time in the direction of Villa Neuova along the broad motor-road for it was early as yet. Gideon chatted amicably as we walked, pausing from time to time to cross the hedge and peer anxiously into the features of a goat or a cow. By the early afternoon we had reached a hollow in a hillside beyond the town of Villa Neuova where a number of sources broke from the mossy banks of a hill and created a shady pleasaunce—I do not know how else to describe it—encircled by some tall plane-trees, forming a sort of pavilion around the little whitewashed tavern where we proposed to halt and eat. The sunshine was, by this time, fierce enough to have turned Gideon's thoughts in the direction of a siesta. There was no food to be had beyond a boiled egg or two, so we were glad of what we had brought with us. There was, however, plenty of good red wine, served in generous tin cans which had originally been intended as measures for oil.

The tavern-keeper was a tiny emaciated man in the last stages of consumption. He served us deftly and quietly, and paused with pride to indicate the superb view from the little earth-terrace upon which we sat. It was indeed worth looking at—that sloping foreground of mulberry-trees, thinning away to the bold blue of sea and the violet-cloud of mountains opposite. But it was not a view that one 'saw' in the strict sense; it radiated over one, dancing in that brown heat, pouring into the eyes and spreading within the five senses—as light enters the pin-hole of a camera's lens but floods the whole gelatine surface of the negative; so that we sat in a kind of dark inebriation, tasting the sweat and wine mixing in our mouths, and breathing in the whole landscape with every breath we drew like a perfume.

The wine was ice-cold, for the pitcher had been hanging down the well all morning on the end of a rope. Our host came timidly to the table and sat down with us to watch us eat and to ask the inevitable questions. He accepted some bread and lamb with a dignified air, stretching out his thin talons in a way that reminded one of something fastidious and small—a cat, perhaps: and this impression was strengthened by his thin black moustache which grew limply enough, but whose ends were waxed and turned up like a cat's whiskers. He was called Panayotis Porphyrogennis. 'But,' he added modestly, 'they call me Pipi here.'

You have guessed it? The inevitable happened. Gideon, animated by his own excellent conversation and the weather, drank more than three glasses of wine, which turned him the colour of brickdust, and sapped his stamina as a walker. There was nothing for it but take a short nap on the mossy bank under the planes until the sun had westered a bit. This we did, and it was not until four that we mustered up enough energy to strike the road again. 'We shall never make Cameirus,' groaned Gideon, as he stumped along. 'We shall be picked up by Mills and he will jeer at me, I know it. He always swore we should never reach Cameirus if we found a tavern on the way.'

We did however manage to get a tidy way across the Kalavarda valley with its long flat grape-orchards, and its hundreds of metal windmills imported by the Italians to draw up water from the artesian wells. Despite the fact that each of these rather crude contrivances bore the legend MADE IN CHICAGO they looked very poetical in the greenish afternoon light, slowly turning their metal flukes in the north-wind. The roads were shaded too and everywhere there sounded the noise of water flowing out along the irrigation channels on to the parched red soil. Storks had built their crazy muddled nests in some of the water-wheels and we heard their cracked voices as we passed, mingled with the bubbling of water, and the swish of wind in the silver-grey olives that stretched away in clumps towards the receding hills.

We passed through one or two dirty and dilapidated villages— Gideon religiously averting his face whenever we were confronted with the word 'Kapheneion' written on a wall or lettered out on some crude signpost. By the time Mills' little hornet of a car came whizzing up we had good enough reason to be pleased with ourselves, for we had covered a good part of the way to Kalavarda. To Gideon's surprise and relief Mills was full of admiration for our prowess. He had collected the mattresses and flea-bags and proposed to go on ahead to Cameirus. As there was no room for us in that tiny car—which barely accommodated Chloe and himself on two seats shaped like egg-cups—he roared off again along the dusty road, and left us sitting in a dry river-bed among a clump of vivid oleanders to wait for Hoyle and E. Gideon was much relieved at Mills' respect for his day's walk, and felt disposed to boast a bit, and he was still in this vein when Hoyle's old German Mercedes came into sight. Hoyle, however, seemed surprised to see us so soon. 'What?' he said, 'I thought you people told me you were going to walk?' He commented briefly on Gideon's partiality to tavern life, adding dark asides about the lower nature of man, until Gideon was quite out of humour, and pretended that a sprained ankle had prevented him from walking as far as he might have done.

We climbed into the car, and swept down the long straight road into Kalavarda. Here the country changed abruptly, very much as it does when one enters the valley of Epidaurus, and the change was like a premonition, a quickening of something inside one which only the sight of Cameirus itself could satisfy. The hills were low here, and the road ran along the sea-shore. A sense of something definite and pre-arranged, as in the landscapes contrived by those ancient Chinese gardeners for the rulers of old China. Or, as Hoyle put it, 'Limestone formations, with a thinnish topcrust of green. Look here, Gideon, holm-oak and juniper.' Gideon was still disposed to be testy. 'My dear Hoyle, that's not holm-oak, it's barbed wire from a gun-post.' At last we came to a fountain set in a circle of young plane trees, and here we found Chloe washing great bunches of grapes against dinner, while Mills, who had run his car off the road under the pines, was lovingly tinkering about in its entrails with the air of a surgeon performing a delicate operation.

Leaving them to fill the water-jar, we climbed the tree-lined way which leads up the hill to Cameirus, the car groaning and panting in second gear at the steepness of the slope. Beyond the swaying tips of the pines somewhere lay the city, and in ancient times this gracious tree-lined approach to it from the little harbour of Mylantia was made more lovely by the population of statues that stood beside the road to welcome the newcomer. Now the fleshy scalp of the hillside showed the ugly workings of anti-tank gun sites. This had been part of the defensive system manned by the Italians. We deduced this from their refuse which always contained a high percentage of empty hair-oil bottles and discarded clothing. The road wound higher and still higher, passing the ugly cemetery for German troops (pitched with such vandalistic accuracy slap in the glade below the town) and breasting the green hummock which cuts Cameirus from the world.

You arrive in the centre of the ancient town almost before you know it; it is as sudden as a descent from a balloon. The whole thing assembles itself before your eyes like a picture thrown upon a cinema-screen. It lies there in the honey-gold afternoon light listening to the melodious ringing of water in its own cisterns, and the faint whipping of wind in the noble pines which crown the amphitheatre. The light here has a peculiar density as if the blue of the sea had stained it with some of its own troubled dyes. The long sloping main-street is littered with chipped inscriptions. One can make out the names of city fathers long since dead, of priests and suppliants; they rise in a long progress up the chalky pathways of the town to the red earth wall beyond which the archaeologist has not trespassed, to the rather over-poetic votive column which, one can guess without being told, is part of the most recent Italian restoration work. Nevertheless Cameirus is beautiful in a way that persuades mere ugliness to conform to its grace of air and situation; even the curator's Nissen hut, now crammed with verminous filth, smashed bottles, shed equipment, and bandages—even this cannot intrude upon the singing beauty of this ancient town uncovered by the spade of the archaeologist. If such a city, you find yourself thinking, if such a landscape-out-of-time was not able to strike the right chord in the human heart by its appeals to clemency, truth, and intellectual order of life, what chance have we with our unburied cities to do so? And when you see the grave-stones from the little necropolis of Cameirus stacked up in our museums (it is inevitable that the treasures of towns like these are hoarded up in Museums) it is the so-often repeated single word—the anonymous $Χαῖρε$—which attracts you by its simple, obsessive message to the living. It is not the names of the rich or the worthy, not the votive reliefs and the sepulchral epigrams, but this single word, 'Be Happy', 'Be Happy', serving both as a farewell and admonition, that goes to your heart with the whole impact of the Greek style of mind, the Greek orientation to life and death: so that you are shamed into regarding your life, and realising with bitterness how little you have fulfilled of the principle behind a thought so simple yet so pregnant, and how even your native vocabulary lacks a word whose brevity and grace could paint upon the darkness of death the fading colours of such gaiety, love and truth as $Χαῖρε$ does upon these modest gravestones.

The party was not nearly as riotous as the one we had enjoyed the previous night. Cameirus, glimmering whitely below us, was perhaps the reason. Its silence and its utter self-possession forced themselves between our sentences like the blade of a knife, separating thought from contemplation, and filling one with self-consciousness by their volume. So it was that for the most part we ate silently, staring out from the dim circle of wavering yellow light to where the late moon had quicksilvered the marbles of the old town, and picked up the three small promontories which jutted into the sea below Cameirus, one of which contained, in ancient times, a temple to Pan. But if our conversation was desultory it reflected in no way upon the humour of the company; Gideon had recovered from his fit of pique—a bottle and a half of white Kastellaneia had seen to that. Hoyle himself was disposed to be complimentary about our walk; he was always slow to reach what he himself called 'a considered opinion', and perhaps by now he had realised that Gideon's annoyance at his teasing was genuine and not simulated.

Mills and I walked about the ancient town for a while before turning in. The moon was all but gone, yet the light brimmed the whole amphitheatre, casting a surface of glittering aluminium over the white houses, and blocking in great masses of shadow on the seaward side. Despite the light frost, and the thick nap of dew which had fallen over everything, we were only mildly cold; a few moments of walking about, and we found ourselves warm again. In the silence we could hear the water gurgling somewhere down there, below the earth.* An owl whistled once, twice, and we heard its creaking flight from one tree to another, like the rustle of a linen skirt. I suddenly remembered other moments of time spent in this landscape, time printed upon silence with all its real colours up: the faint burring of honey-bees in Agamemnon's tomb: one glittering spring day, the noise of snow melting among the meadows at Nemea: a bird singing stiffly at noon like a voice on stilts from the bushes where we had slept: the crash of a falling orange in an island: all isolated moments existing in a peculiar dense medium of their own which was like time but not of it. Each moment to itself entire, populating a whole continuum of feeling. Coming over the ridge into Sparta, bursting through a cloud to see the lime-green Eurotas gushing into the valley carrying with it a multitude of tinkling spots of ice. . . . And these separate moments, quite loose, not stitched together except by their parentage in the same quality of feeling, suddenly added themselves to this quiet

---

* The bat-infested underground water-conduits of Cameirus I never had the courage to explore until one memorable day when Paddy and Xan and the Corn Goddess shamed me into following them down its dark tunnels.

second of time spent with Mills, sitting in the frail moonlight of Cameirus, tracing an inscription on a votive stone, feeling the chisel's edge hard through the moss, spelling out Χαῖρε. 'Be Happy', 'Be Happy.' Then the owl whistled once again from a different quarter, and someone struck a match up there under the trees. We rose by mutual consent and walked back up the long main-street of the town.

Next morning I awoke with a start to see Mills on his knees pumping the Primus stove. The sun had risen, but was still behind the hill. Its warmth, however, penetrated the crust of the island, warming the statues back to life, drying the dew from the houses of Cameirus, and offering us the auguries for another lovely day. A green lizard had crawled up to a favourite stone, and was warming itself in the indirect light of the sun. Its satin throat quivered as if with song.

Today we intended to complete the circuit of the island, and spend the night at Lindos—a journey which would put us within striking distance of Rhodes for the morning following; when we were due back at our respective establishments. We started off together, but the sedateness of Hoyle's driving soon wore out Mills' patience, he passed us on a corner and disappeared across the valley in a cloud of dust. 'It'll be a case of physician heal thyself one of these days,' remarked Hoyle sadly. His own driving technique, while accurate enough, would perhaps have been more suited to a landau. It was as if he had carried over his tendency to have 'little rests' into his driving—or else as if he had infected the engine of the Mercedes with some of his own heart-trouble. At any rate, when a new idea struck him, it was his habit to slam on the brakes, stop the car, and sit awhile to consider it from every angle.

The sun was up now. I sat behind with E while Hoyle and

Gideon shared the front. We ate grapes and watched the valley unroll itself before us. Hoyle and Gideon were still deep in the subject of vampires, I remember, a subject which sounded more than ever fantastic in that clear air. The road from Cameirus runs along the flat sea-line, dotted with beaches. Shallow hills like green tumuli stretch away landwards, studded with bushes of myrtle and thyme—a haunt for the red-legged partridges and the rock-dove. The road is a bad one, so that we were quite surprised to catch Mills up by the time we reached the little harbour of Cameiro Skala. As we lumbered up across the plain we saw why he had stopped. Three yellow fishing-boats had just put in and were piling up their catch. In the middle of a chaffering crowd of Symiot fishermen Mills was standing, blond and stocky, bargaining for half a dozen red mullet. Gideon's resourceful eye had already noticed a tavern by the roadside, and here we waited for the deal to be closed, drinking a mastika that tasted like horse-embrocation and listening to the squibbling of a clarinet played by a fisherboy. Here, too, we met the inevitable American Greek who made the inevitable comparison between Detroit and this 'lousy country', and complimented us on speaking our mother-tongue as well as we did. Gideon flew into a temper with him: 'You stinking empty-headed son-of-a-bitch,' he said, with an excellent imitation of a New York accent, 'why the hell do you come back here and poison the air of your mother-country with your cheap snarls and your passion for Coca Cola?' The man recoiled as if he had received a push in the chest. Hoyle clicked his tongue against his teeth. 'Really Gideon,' he said. 'An officer and a gentleman simply *doesn't*, you know.' Gideon adjusted his eyeglass. 'Perhaps he doesn't,' he said mildly. 'But I do, old man. I definitely do. The cheek of these people.' Mills by this time had concluded his business and stowed the fish in the tool-box of his car. We set off pursued by the cries of 'Good journey' 'Come back soon'. Greeks adore partings.

The road winds steeply uphill, past the old Prankish fort called Castello today, and then turns abruptly inland: and rising out of the cluster of hills before us, we saw the frowning crags of Atabyron, the chief mountain of the island. Its massifs of shining black towered up into the sky from a green vegetation-line marking the site of Embona. Atabyron in that lucid morning air looked more like some invention of man than a natural phenomenon, it was as if some prodigious rough model for a statue had been abandoned here. The wind and rain had eroded it. The winter snows had polished its slippery black surface until it glinted with a bluish light, as charcoal does. It lay with all the massive pregnancy of a liner at anchor among the lesser hills, and as we climbed towards it the air became thinner, and bluer, while the mountain-villages glittered in its rareness like clusters of lump-sugar.

Up there on the final crag, from which one could faintly see the mountains of Crete, had once stood the little temple to Zeus where the great sacred bull had uttered its oracles. There is evidence to suggest that the sacred bull cult had not concerned itself with the worship of a live animal but with a gigantic bronze representation of it, in which the bodies of human beings had been placed, to roast over a fire. Their cries and groans, it is suggested, may have been taken for prophecies.

Tasting the blue refinements of that air, and watching the geological structure change to granite, we felt the first pangs of hunger steal upon us, though we were far from our objective— Monolithos. We stopped in an orange-grove outside Embona and nibbled some bread and fruit, while Gideon cracked a bottle of wine. He had got into the habit of 'fining' himself for little errors of taste or judgement. 'Damn,' he would say, 'I fine myself two glasses of red.' Or else 'I simply can't let that pass without fining myself a glass of white.' Needless to say he derived a certain pleasure from this odd method of self-punishment. Now he fined himself for his rudeness to the American Greek of Cameiro Skala while Hoyle watched him with all the weight of his unexpressed distaste apparent in his expression. 'Your liver will have to pay up in the end,' he remarked sourly.

We passed the road to Embona and turned right, to circle the great charred butt of Atabyron, whose stony ramps of black rock made it seem more than ever medieval—like some old black-letter bible rotting away in a Museum. . . . Gideon showed some disposition to try and climb it but we shouted him down. Monolithos lay ahead, and we pushed on across this razor-back landscape of rock and thistle, punctuated everywhere by springs gushing out of the side of the mountain, and giant walnut-trees, Artamiti . . . Saint Isidore (whoever he may be). The air was thickly scented with pines now, for we were descending gradually.

To reach Monolithos you must crash over the brow of a hill and think that you are falling into the sea. Miraculously, however, you see that the dirt road continues, and the great hump of rock stabs at you, rising out of the sea like a pointing finger. You crawl down almost to sea-level before you reach the pine-glade lying at the foot of the castle. 'How Mills ever got down here without breaking his neck I don't know,' mutters Hoyle as he eases the big Mercedes into the hollow with circumspection. But Mills is sitting in a cleft of stone at the very top of the castle, tossing pine-cones into the sea, and singing at the top of his voice.

There was everything to be said for singing. In that dry clement sunlight we climbed the grassy staircases to the summit. Every-where there were tiny dells dense with anemone and daisies.

Chloe had flung herself down between two knuckles of rock, and when she sat up to welcome us we saw that she was covered with bright yellow pollen. The summit of Monolithos is like some great sculptured lion's paw; between the claws thick mossy carpets have grown up, fed by some underground spring, no doubt, and here you may lie down in beds of flowers for all the world as if you were still in the lowland glades around Rodini. It was in one of these that we had lunch and talked, idly watching the kestrels dip in the blue gulfs beneath us, and the little coloured lizards scrabble about among the crannies of the rock.

Afterwards Mills and I went off together and climbed the tower of the Byzantine chapel to see if one could spit directly into the sea from this vantage-point. Mills was of a distinctly competitive turn of mind. He was always thinking up feats of this kind to test his native skill. Spitting over bridges, playing ducks-and-drakes upon a calm sea, diving for pennies—there was nothing that he would not do for the sheer pleasure of doing something active and, if possible, slightly irresponsible. In the intervals of spitting over the cliff he said: 'I say, have you ever looked at Gideon's monocle? I picked it up yesterday while he was asleep, to see how weak his eye was. Do you know what?'

'No. What?'

'It's made of ordinary glass.'

'But what's the point of that?' Mills sighed and dusted his blue pea-jacket with his hands. 'Humanity is so constructed that when it wants to hide something it is forced to accentuate it, to throw it into relief: I doubt if you'd notice Gideon's glass eye at all if the poor old thing hadn't drawn attention to it by wearing that mon-ocle.' I had not noticed any signs of shyness about Gideon, I must say, and the idea came as rather a surprise to me. 'But Gideon could carry a couple of glass eyes and a pair of wooden legs with ease,' I exclaimed. 'He bluffs his way through life like a tenth century man-at-arms.' Mills jumped down from the rock and began picking flowers. 'Have you never heard Gideon's own definition of an Englishman?' he asked. 'It fits him perfectly. An Englishman may be defined as a soft-centred creature with a tough and horny shell, through which two sensitive antennae (humour and prejudice) explore the world around him.'

The journey down into the flat and featureless valley to Cattavia was uneventful. Gideon discovered Hoyle's copy of the Abbé Cutlet in a pocket of the car and regaled us with quotations in an exaggeratedly correct French accent. 'Après Lindos, Cattavia,' he intoned, 'paysage plus riant.' It wasn't really 'riant'—simply a stretch of alluvial marshland, poorly cultivated, and lying at the back of the eroded mountain we had crossed. After an hour or so we hit the nondescript, flattish, amorphous coastal belt, with a few villages fast asleep in their flea-tormented isolation. Here sunlight was a drug.

Nearing Lindos, however, it all changed abruptly and rose up into a gnarled rock-hewn landscape—a coast bitten out in huge mouthfuls of metamorphic rock, gleaming dully with mica, and shot through with the colours of iron and trap. It was as if a storm at sea had suddenly been solidified and compressed into these frowning capes and fastnesses of coloured rock. The sea boomed upon the sand of the long beaches, while everywhere the rusty wire and the skull with its legend 'Achtung Minen' spoke Prussian to us. To the east tiny figures knelt in a frieze along the thundering coastline, as if engaged in some obscure rite. They were lifting mines. Even from this great range one could see the tense preoccupation that convulsed them, kneeling there within the sound of the sea, burrowing in the sand with their nervous fingers. Later at a bend in the coast-road we saw the little island where Lady Hester Stanhope was washed up. It is called 'the biscuit'* on the charts today.

Doubling back a quarter of a mile before Calato you come upon Lindos through a narrow gulley of rock. It is as if you had been leaning against a door leading to a poem when suddenly it swung open letting you stumble directly into the heart of it. The road bores through a blank wall of rock and turns sharply to the right, running down an inclined plane. Lindos with its harbour lies below you—as if at the bottom of a pie-dish. The configurations of the promontory upon which the town is built suggest something like the talons of the crab. The little harbour is all but land-locked and the blue of it drenches you like spray. The beach-shallows are picked out in lime-green and yellow, against the reddish, deckle-edged surfaces of stone. In the air above it rides the acropolis. It does not insist. It can afford not to presume, so certain of the impact which it must make on everyone who comes upon it through the gulley in the rock. Is not Lindos the official beauty-spot of Rhodes? The contrast with Cameirus is remarkable—for where Cameirus is refined, turned in upon itself in sunny contemplation, Lindos is bold, strident. Cameirus has all the stillness of an amphora in a Museum, with its frieze of dancers caught in a timeless dancing; Lindos, under the sweetness of its decoration, is like a trumpet-call, beaten out in gold-leaf and vibrating across the blue airs of time.

The little modern town which lies at the foot of the acropolis is perhaps a quarter of the size of ancient Lindos. Its beauty is of a scrupulous Aegean order, and perfect in its kind. The narrow streets which rise and fall like music are paved with clean sea-pebbles, and criss-crossed with little inter-communicating alleys.

* Paximadi.

Their width is enough to accommodate two mules abreast, but no car can enter them. Everything is painted white, a dazzling glitter of plaster and white-wash, so that if you half closed your eyes you might imagine that Lindos reflected back the snowy reflections of a passing cloud.

We had intended to sleep on the summit of the acropolis, but the women declared that they would prefer beds, so we accordingly did what all travellers in Greece must sooner or later learn to do if they explore areas where there are no hotels. In the sunny tavern of Lindos we asked for the mayor of the town, and when he arrived, introduced ourselves and set him down to drink a glass of wine with us. He was eager enough to help, and without much difficulty managed to find rooms for us. The nature of Greek hospitality is such that no traveller who flings himself upon the mercies of a village 'demarchos' will ever go bedless.

The sun was low, but there was still time to admire the little Greek church, inspect samples of the famous Lindos ware in some private villas, and admire the four or five Crusader houses which were still standing, and in excellent repair. All the latter were inhabited by Greek families who offered us cups of coffee and the polite possibility of a political discussion. Mills did his 'Florence Nightingale act' as he called it, and visited the sick. By the time he came back to the tavern we had sorted the baggage and prepared such food as we had to carry up the acropolis. The sun was westering rapidly as we walked up the winding paths of the Acropolis behind Markos, the guardian of the site. He was a slow-spoken, lazy-looking man, with a fine head set well back on broad shoulders: his broken nose gave him a slanting quizzical expression. He had been a commercial traveller and regretted that we spoke Greek, for he would dearly have loved to conduct the party in French, which he said he knew well. He was as breathless as we were, however, by the time we reached the carved rock-relief of the ship which marks the entry to the fort, and which had been executed in ancient times as a trophy—perhaps even to celebrate the long Thallassoocratia of the Rhodians, which endured some twenty-three years of naval competition about 900 B.C. Markos sat him down on a stone and waited for his breath to come back as he rubbed his hands along the stone bows of the vessel. He accepted a cigarette from Mills who had completed the ascent at record speed, and who betrayed no signs of strain. 'You're too healthy,' said Gideon.

Hoyle had been left miles behind, resting on a convenient rock and staring down into that blue circle of sea whose outer end is marked by a stone tomb rising out of the sea which, say some authorities, is where Cleobolus is buried. I walked back to accompany him. As we toiled up the hill, he chatted knowledgeably about Athene Lindia who had been worshipped in Ancient Lindos with 'flameless sacrifices'. It was at the remains of the temple of Athene that we found the others. They were lying on their stomachs and gazing down six hundred feet into the eye of the sea— that peacock-green twilight eye, glimmering with caverns and deeps where only enough light penetrated to print the diffuse markings of rock and seaweed. Markos, the guide, was in full flight. 'This is Athene Lindia's temple. There.' He picked up a pebble and threw it. 'There the temple of Zeus Policus.' Nobody, I am sorry to say, was listening to him. Down there on that darkening water lay a tiny fishing-boat like a model. 'Listen,' said E. In the silence, like the voice of an insect, came the thin strains of a fisherman singing. The sound slanted up at us through the canyons of coloured rock. We stared down it, watching the curdled greens and reds of the seaweed wavering under it. From this height we could see fish moving under the boat which were invisible to fishermen, travelling in little phosphorescent sparks of light. 'Athene Lindia' I was repeating to myself, like an incantation. Somewhere there had been a grove of sacred olives dedicated to her. Pindar's great ode on Diagoras of Ialysos had been graven on tablets and placed in the temple. In the height of her glory strangers had sent her offerings from Syria and Egypt.

The sun had been sucked down into the sea; dazzling spokes of silver spread out for a moment on the blue, as if from some great lighthouse. Then the uniform dusk. 'Cleobolus was a remarkable old thing,' Hoyle was saying, for the stream of classical evocations which had seemed to dwindle away had suddenly come to life again. The fisherman was out of sight, his singing out of sound. 'Tell us about him, Markos.' Markos took a deep breath and fired out his knowledge in demotic. 'He travelled in Egypt, was very beautiful, and wrote thousands of lovely acrostics, distichs, and other verse. He was one of the Wise Men, and a close personal friend of Solon. He lived to be seventy years old. His famous epigram "Nothing in excess" is one which the Greeks have treasured to this day.'

'But haven't lived up to,' said Gideon dryly. Markos avoided his eye and pretended that he had not heard the interruption. 'He was, with Pythagoras, one of the first to admit women into the circle of knowledge,' he said amiably baring his teeth at E. 'His daughter Cleobulina was also a writer and left many beautiful poems.'

It was getting chilly. We made a leisurely circuit of the battlements, peering down into the little inlet where, says popular tradition, St Paul was shipwrecked on one of his many voyages. Out at sea the light was fading upon four little islands which Markos pointed out to us: the fourth was a mere shaving of rock awash when the sea was rough. 'Look,' said the guide, 'those islands they call Tetrapolis.'

'Who does?'

'Everybody. The people of Lindos. In ancient times, they say, four cities were there, and all of them sank in a great earthquake.' Gideon was getting restive. He preferred sharper lines of demarcation between legend and attested fact. 'Who says this?' he demanded—and to do him justice you will not find the story of Tetrapolis in any of the authenticated histories.

'Since before my grandfather they say so.'

'But who says so?'

Markos became a trifle impatient. He waved his arm like a wand over the dusky village beneath us. 'Everyone,' he said with a trace of sulkiness. 'Is it true?' said Gideon. Markos nodded vigorously. 'Once,' he said, 'the truth was proved to me by sponge-divers. Every summer they worked this coast and every day I drank with them in the tavern. They had seen columns of marble and statues under the sea when they dived for sponges. Once they gave me some coins which they had brought up and I sold them to a German for bread.'

We slept well that night at the tavern, and next morning did the run to Rhodes in good style, wheeling up through the rock-face where the road turns at right angles to run down to the green plains by Calato. The jagged ruin of Pheraclyea lay on the coast to our right, but Gideon had assured us from an earlier visit that nothing remained of the fort but rubble, and that extensive mine-fields thereabouts made it hazardous for tourists.

We lumbered through Malona and past the sunburnt farms which the Italian government had subsidised and settled with Sienese farmers—one of the richest agricultural areas in Rhodes. Here Gideon stopped for a brief chat with his Italian overseer. Many of the families had stayed on to wait for a passage to Italy, and they still worked the fields as they had always done, singing and smiling.

The road curls around the shaft of the mountain called Tsambika and through a pass, so that the entry to this second valley is nearly as sudden as the entry upon Lindos.

But at last we ran out along the final spine of the island and saw, at a turn of the road, the spires and turrets of the capital come into view. Here there was time for a final cup of coffee before separating about our various business. We took it under an olive-tree, on dry grass already waking up to the drumming of cicadas.

My heart sinks as I think of the mass of proofs, of correspondence, of files, which await me.

Mills starts up his car and gets into it slowly. 'We have a little while yet,' he says. 'Before they scatter us all over the world.'

The dust rises on the road as the cavalcade sets off.

CYPRUS

After leaving Rhodes in 1947, Durrell continued his work in the diplomatic service, spending a year in Argentina (he was bored and unable to write) and four years in Yugoslavia (not much better). He was then offered a choice between Russia and Turkey—and instead chose to leave the service and move (with his second wife, Eve Cohen) to the island of Cyprus, which the British had annexed in 1914. The couple arrived on the island in early 1952, and Durrell—delighted to be back in the Mediterranean—set to work on his famous series of novels, *The Alexandria Quartet.* He was soon embroiled in Cyprus's politics. Mainland Greeks and Cypriots alike were demanding union between Greece and Cyprus, but the British (as well as the island's Turkish population and Turkey's government) were strongly opposed. Durrell bought a house on the island and spent two years writing and teaching at a local school. He made many friends among the Greek Cypriots, only to loose most of them when he became British director of public information on the island. His marriage to Eve Cohen fell apart, and he became involved with Claude-Marie Vincendon. The new couple left Cyprus in the late summer of 1956, amid growing violence and anti-British feeling. Durrell finished *Bitter Lemons* in England—"Pudding Island," as he called it—far from his adopted lands of the Mediterranean.

How to Buy a House

(FROM *BITTER LEMONS*, 1957)

> 'Last of all came the Greeks and inquired of the Lord for their gift.
> ' "What gift would you like?" said the Lord.
> ' "We would like the gift of Power," said the Greeks.
> 'The Lord replied: "Ah, my poor Greeks, you have come too late. All the gifts have been distributed. There is practically nothing left. The gift of Power has been given to the Turks, the Bulgarians the gift of Labour; the Jews of Calculation, the French of Trickery and the English of Foolishness."
> 'The Greeks waxed very angry at this and shouted "By what intrigue have we been overlooked?"
> ' "Very well," said the Lord. "Since you insist, you too shall have a present and not remain empty-handed—may Intrigue be your lot," said the Lord.'
>
> —BULGARIAN FOLK-TALE

SABRI TAHIR'S OFFICE IN THE TURKISH QUARTER of Kyrenia bore a sun-blistered legend describing him as a valuer and estate agent, but his activities had proliferated since the board was painted and he was clearly many things besides. The centre of the cobweb was a dark cool godown perched strategically upon a junction of streets, facing the little Turkish shrine of some saint or warrior whose identity had vanished from the record, but whose stone tomb was still an object of veneration and pilgrimage for the faithful. It stood under a dusty and desiccated pepper tree, and one could always find an *ex voto* or two hanging beside it.

Beyond was a featureless empty field of nettles in which stood a couple of shacks full of disembodied pieces of machinery and huge heaps of uncut carob and olive, mingled with old railway sleepers and the carcasses of buses which always turned up here at the end of the trail, as if to some Elephants' Graveyard, to be turned into fuel. Sabri's Empire was still in an embryonic stage, though it was quite clear that he was speculating wisely. A circular saw moaned and gnashed all day in one of the shacks under the ministrations of two handsome Turkish youths with green headbands and dilapidated clothes; a machine for making cement blocks performed its slow but punctual evacuations, accompanied by a seductive crunch.

Sabri could watch all these diverse activities from the darkness of his shop where he sat for the greater part of the day before a Turkish coffee, unmoved, unmoving, but watchful. His desk was in the far corner against the wall, and to reach it one traversed a *terrain vague* which resembled the basement of Maple's, so crowded was it with armchairs, desks, prams, cooking-stoves, heaters, and all the impedimenta of gracious living.

The man himself was perhaps forty years of age, sturdily built, and with a fine head on his shoulders. He had the sleepy good looks—a rare smile with perfect teeth, thoughtful brown eyes— which one sees sometimes in Turkish travel posters. But what was truly Turkish about him was the physical repose with which he confronted the world. No Greek can sit still without fidgeting, tapping a foot or a pencil, jerking a knee, or making popping noises with his tongue. The Turk has a monolithic poise, an air of reptilian concentration and silence. It is with just such an air that a chameleon can sit, hour after hour, upon a shrub, staring unwinkingly at the world, living apparently in that state of suspended judgement which is summed up by the Arabic word *kayf.* I have seen Sabri loading logs, shouting at peasants, even running down a street; but never has he conveyed the slightest feeling of energy being expended. His actions and words had the smoothness of inevitability; they flowed from him like honey from a spoon.

On that first morning when I stepped into the shadows of his shop, the headquarters of the empire, he was sitting dreamily at his desk mending a faulty cigarette-lighter. His good-morning was civil, though preoccupied and indifferent; but as I approached he paused for one instant to snap finger and thumb and a chair materialized from the shadows behind him. I sat down. He abandoned his task and sat silent and unwinking before me. 'Mr. Sabri,' I said, 'I need your help. I have been making inquiries in Kyrenia and on all sides I am told that you are the most untrustworthy man of business in the place—in fact, the biggest rogue.'

He did not find the idea offensive so much as merely interesting. His shrewd eye sharpened a trifle, however, and he lowered his head to scan me more gravely. I went on. 'Now knowing the Levant as I do, I know that a reputation for being a rogue means one thing and one thing only. It means that one is *cleverer* than other people.' I accompanied this with the appropriate gesture— for cleverness in the hand-language is indicated by placing the forefinger of the right hand slowly and portentously upon the temple: tapping slightly, as one might tap a breakfast-egg. (Incidentally, one has to be careful, as if one turns the finger in the manner of turning a bolt in a thread, the significance is quite different: it means to be 'soft in the head' or to 'have a screw loose'.) I tapped my skull softly. '*Cleverer* than other people,' I repeated. 'So clever that the stupid are envious of one.'

He did not assent or dissent from the proposition. He simply sat and considered me as one might a piece of machinery if one were uncertain of its use. But the expression in his eyes shifted slightly in a manner suggesting the faintest, most tenuous admiration. 'I am here,' I went on, convinced by this time that his English was good, for he had followed me unerringly so far, to judge by his face, 'I am here as a comparatively poor man to ask you a favour, not to make you a business proposition. There is no money to be made out of me. But I want you to let me use your brains and experience. I'm trying to find a cheap village house in which to settle for a year or two—perhaps forever if I like it enough here. I can see now that I was not wrong; far from being a rogue you are obviously a Turkish gentleman, and I feel I can confide myself entirely to your care—if you will accept such a thing. I have nothing to offer except gratitude and friendship. I ask you as a Turkish gentleman to assist me.'

Sabri's colour had changed slowly throughout this harangue and when I ended he was blushing warmly. I could see that I had scored a diplomatic stroke in throwing myself completely upon the iron law of hospitality which underpins all relations in the Levant. More than this, I think the magic word 'gentleman' turned the trick in my favour for it accorded him an unaccustomed place in the consideration of strangers which he certainly merited, and which he thenceforward lived up to in his dealings with me. By a single tactful speech I had made a true friend.

He leaned forward at his desk, smiling now, and patted my hand gently, confidingly: 'But of course, my dear,' he said, 'of course.'

Then he suddenly threw up his chin and barked an order. A barefoot youth materialized from the shadows bearing Coca Cola on a tray, apparently ordered by some invisible gesture a while before. 'Drink,' he said quietly, 'and tell me what house you want.'

'A village house, not a modern villa.'

'How far away?'

'Not far. Among these hills.'

'Old houses need doing up.'

'If I can buy one cheaply I shall do it up.'

'How much can you spend?'

'Four hundred pounds.'

He looked grave at this and this was understandable, for the price of land had been soaring since the war, and indeed continued to soar until the time of my departure from the island when building plots in the centre of Nicosia cost roughly the same as those in Washington. 'My dear,' he said thoughtfully, and stroked his moustache. 'My dear.' Outside the darkness of his shop the spring sunshine glistened on trees loaded with cold tangerines; a cold wind touched the fronds of the palm-trees, quick with the taste of snow from the Taurus mountains across the water. 'My dear,' repeated Sabri thoughtfully. 'Of course if you lived very far away it would be quite easy, but do you wish to be within reach of the capital?' I nodded. 'If I run out of money then I shall have to work, and there is nothing to be found out of Nicosia.' He nodded. 'Somewhere not too far from Kyrenia you want an arty old house.' That summed it up perfectly. Sabri took a thoughtful turn or two among the shadows and stubbed out his cigarette on the box. 'Honestly, my dear,' he said, 'it will be a matter of luck. I do hear of things, but it is a matter of luck. And it is very difficult to find one person to deal with. You are at once in a bloody family, my dear.' I did not then know what he meant. I was soon to learn.

'Do not be disappointed if you hear nothing from me for a while. What you ask is not easy, but I think I can do it. I will be working on it even if I am silent. Do you understand, my dear?' His handshake was warm.

I had hardly reached the main street on my way back to Panos' house when Renos the boot-black came out of a side street and took my arm. He was a tiny little wisp of a man with the sort of eyes one finds sewn on to rag dolls. 'My friend,' he said, 'you have been to see Sabri.' This is the favourite Mediterranean game, a tireless spying upon the movements of friends and acquaintances, and is common to all communities which do not read, whose whole life is built up by oral tradition and common gossip. 'Yes,' I said.

'Phew.' He went through a pantomime in the hand language, burning his fingers on hot coals and blowing upon them. This meant 'You will be stung.' I shrugged my shoulders. 'What to do?' I said cheerfully. 'Aie aie,' said Renos, laying one hand to his cheek and rocking his head commiseratingly as if he had toothache. But he said no more.

By the time I got home Panos himself had been informed of my visit—doubtless by bush telegraph. 'You have been to see Sabri,' he said as I crossed the brilliant courtyard of the church and joined him on his balcony over the bewitching blueness of the spring sea. 'About a house?' I nodded. 'You have done well,' he said. 'Indeed I was going to suggest it.'

'Clito says he is a rogue.'

'Nonsense. His dealings with me have been perfectly honourable. He is a pretty sharp business man, of course, which is not usual among Turks who are always half asleep. But he is no more of a rogue than anyone else. In fact, Clito himself is a rogue, if it comes to that. He overcharged me for this bottle of Commanderia. Incidentally did you tell Sabri how much money you have?'

'No, I told him less than I actually had.'

Panos chuckled admiringly. 'I see you understand business in these parts. Everything gets gossiped about, so that whatever price you would be prepared to pay would soon be known to everyone. You did right to put it low.'

I accepted a glass of sweet Commanderia and a pickled pimento from the coloured china plate; the two children were doing a puzzle in the sunshine. The beadle crashed at the church bell in a sudden desultory burst of mania and then left the silence to echo round us in wing-beats of aftersound.

'I hear,' said Panos when the vibrations had died away, 'that your brother was killed at Thermopylae during the war.'

'To be absolutely honest with you,' I said, 'I made the whole thing up in order to . . .'

'Tease Frangos!'

'Yes. I was afraid there would be a fight.'

'Excellent. Capital.' Panos was delighted by the subtlety of my imagination. He struck his knee delightedly as he laughed. 'Capital,' he repeated. 'It is clear that as rogues go you are as bad as any of us.' It was a compliment to be thus included in the rogues' gallery of Kyrenia.

That evening it was I who recited the geography lesson while Panos stood behind me, nodding approvingly as I picked out the salient points of the Kyrenia range with a forefinger, travelling gently over the blue spines of the hills from the point where Myrtou lay invisible among its hazy farms and vineyards to where Akanthou (equally invisible) drowsed among its fields of yellow-green barley. In truth, by now I had memorized the lesson so well that the very names of the places I had yet to visit communicated a sharp visual image of them. I could see the lemon-groves of Lapithos and feel the dense cool air of its orchards: hear the sullen thunder of the headspring as it gushed into the valley from the mountain's summit. The great double-combed crown of Hilarion stood almost directly behind us with its castle taking the last lion-gold rays of the evening upon its tawny flanks. Over the saddle below it ran the main road to Nicosia, piercing the range at its lowest point. East of us loomed other peaks whose sulky magnificence echoed each other, mingling like the notes of a musical chord: Buffavento, seat of the winds, with the silent and graceful Gothic abbey of Bellapaix below it in the foothills; Pendedactyl whose five-fingered peak recalled the fingerprints of the hero

Dighenis; fading all of them, and inclining slowly eastward into the mist like the proud sails of some Venetian argosy, to where Cape Andreas drowsed in spindrift at the end of the long stone handle of the Karpass. The place names chimed as one spoke them like a carillon, Greek Babylas and Myrtou, Turkish Kasaphani, Crusader Templos. . . . The mixture was a heady one.

'Very good,' said Panos at last, with a sigh of real pleasure. 'You really do know it. But now you must visit it.' I had intended to ere this, but my preoccupations about a house had quite consumed me, while problems of correspondence and the transport of luggage, money, etc. had made my mind too turbid for use. I had left it all lying there, so to speak, multiplying itself in my imagination, until I should be ready to go out and meet it. Apart from a few short excursions around Kyrenia in search of spring flowers and mushrooms I had been nowhere; indeed had done nothing except bathe and write letters. Life in an island, however rich, is circumscribed, and one does well to portion out one's experiences, for sooner or later one arrives at a point where all is known and staled by repetition. Taken leisurely, with all one's time at one's disposal Cyprus could, I calculate, afford one a minimum of two years reckoned in terms of novelty; hoarded as I intended to hoard it, it might last anything up to a decade.

That is why I wished to experience it through its people rather than its landscape, to enjoy the sensation of sharing a common life with the humble villagers of the place; and later to expand my field of investigation to its history—the lamp which illumines national character—in order to offer my live subjects a frame against which to set themselves. Alas! I was not to have time.

The month or so of spring weather with its promise of summer to follow proved fraudulent. One day we woke to a sky covered in ugly festoons of black cloud and saw drift upon drift of silver needles like arrows falling upon the ramparts of Kyrenia castle. Thunder clamoured and rolled, and the grape-blue semi-darkness of the sea was bitten out in magnesium flashes as the lightning clawed at us from Turkey like a family of dragons. The stone floors turned damp and cold, the gutters brimmed and mumbled all day as they poured a cascade of rain into the street. Below us the sea dashed huge waves across the front where not a week ago we had been sitting in shorts and sandals, drinking coffee and *ouzo*, and making plans for the summer. It was a thrilling change, for one could feel the luxuriant grass fattening under the olives, and the spring flowers unwrapping their delicate petals on the anemone-starred slopes below Clepini.

It was hardly a propitious moment for Sabri to arrive, but arrive he did one black afternoon, wearing as his only protection a spotted handkerchief over his head against the elements. He burst through Panos' front door between thunder-flashes like an apparition from the underworld, gasping: 'My dear.' His suit was liberally streaked with rain. 'I have something for you to see—but *please*' (in anguish almost) 'don't blame me if it is not suitable. I haven't seen it myself yet. But it *may* be . . .' He accepted a glass of wine in chilled fingers. 'It is in the village of Bellapaix, but too far from the road. Anyway, will you come? I have a taxi. The owner is a rogue of course. I can guarantee *nothing*.'

I could see that he was most anxious that I should not judge his professional skill by what might turn out to be a mistake. Together we galloped across the rain-echoing courtyard and down the long flight of stairs by the church to where Jamal and his ancient taxi waited. The handles were off all the doors and there ensued a brief knockabout scene from a Turkish shadow-play among the three of us which finally resulted in our breaking into the vehicle at a weak point in its defences. (Jamal had to crawl through the boot, and half-way through the back seat, in order to unlatch for us.) Then we were off through a landscape blurred with rain and the total absence of windscreen wipers. Jamal drove with his head out of the window for the sake of safety. Outside, the rain-blackened span of mountains glittered fitfully in the lightning-flashes.

Just outside Kyrenia a road turned to the right and led away across a verdant strip of olive and carob land towards the foothills where Bellapaix stood in rain and mist. 'Nevertheless,' said Sabri thoughtfully, 'it is a good day, for nobody will be out of doors. The café will be empty. We won't cause the gossips, my dear.' He meant, I suppose, that in any argument over prices the influence of the village wiseacres would seriously affect the owner's views. A sale needed privacy; if the village coffee shop undertook a general debate on a transaction there was no knowing what might happen.

I was prepared for something beautiful, and I already knew that the ruined monastery of Bellapaix was one of the loveliest Gothic survivals in the Levant, but I was not prepared for the breath-taking congruence of the little village which surrounded and cradled it against the side of the mountain. Fronting the last rise, the road begins to wind through a landscape dense with orange and lemon trees, and noisy with running water. Almond and peach-blossom graze the road, as improbably precise as the décor to a Japanese play. The village comes down to the road for the last hundred yards or so with its grey old-fashioned houses with arched vaults and carved doors set in old-fashioned mouldings. Then abruptly one turns through an arc of 150 degrees under the Tree of Idleness and comes to a stop in the main square under the shadow of the Abbey itself. Young cypresses bent back against the sky as they took the wind; the broad flower beds were full of magnificent roses among the almond trees. Yet it all lay deserted in the rain.

The owner of the house was waiting for us in a doorway with a sack over his head. He was a rather dejected-looking man whom I had already noticed maundering about the streets of Kyrenia. He was a cobbler by trade. He did not seem very exuberant—perhaps it was the weather—but almost without a word spoken led us up the boulder-strewn main street, slipping and stumbling amongst the wet stones. Irrigation channels everywhere had burst their banks and Sabri, still clad in his handkerchief, gazed gloomily about him as he picked his way among the compost heaps where the chickens browsed. 'It's no good, my dear,' he said after we had covered about a hundred yards without arriving at the house. 'You could never get up here.' But still the guide led on, and curiosity made us follow him. The road had now become very steep indeed and resembled the bed of a torrent; down the centre poured a cascade of water. 'My God,' groaned Sabri, 'it is a trout-stream, my dear.' It certainly seemed like one. The three of us crept upwards, walking wherever possible on the facing-stones of the irrigation channel. 'I am terribly sorry,' said Sabri. 'You will have a cold and blame me.'

The atmosphere of the village was quite enthralling; its architecture was in the purest peasant tradition—domed Turkish privies in courtyards fanning out from great arched doors with peasant mouldings still bearing the faint traces of a Venetian influence; old Turkish screen-windows for ventilation. It had the purity and authenticity of a Cretan hamlet. And everywhere grew roses, and the pale clouds of almond and peach blossom; on the balconies grew herbs in window-boxes made from old petrol tins; and crowning every courtyard like a messenger from my Indian childhood spread the luxuriant green fan of banana-leaves, rattling like parchment in the wind. From behind the closed door of the tavern came the mournful whining of a mandolin.

At the top of the slope where the village vanished and gave place to the scrubby outworks of the mountain behind, stood an old irrigation tank, and here our guide disappeared round a corner, drawing from his breast an iron key the size of a man's forearm. We scrambled after him and came upon the house, a large box-like house in the Turkish-Cypriot mode, with huge carved doors made for some forgotten race of giants and their oxen. 'Very arty, my dear,' said Sabri, noting the fine old windows with their carved screens, 'but what a place'; and then he kicked the wall in an expert way so that the plaster fell off and revealed the mysteries of its construction to his practised eye. 'Mud brick with straw.' It was obviously most unsatisfactory. 'Never mind,' I said, stirred by a vague ulterior premonition which I could not put exactly into words. 'Never mind. Let's look now we're here.'

The owner swung himself almost off the ground in an effort to turn the great key in the lock which was one of the old pistol-spring type such as one sees sometimes in medieval English houses. We hung on to his shoulders and added our strength to his until it turned screeching in the lock and the great door fell open. We entered, while the owner shot the great bolts which held the other half of the door in position and propped both open with a faggot. Here his interest died, for he stayed religiously by the door, still shrouded in his sack, showing no apparent interest in our reactions. The hall was gloomy and silent—but remarkably dry considering the day. I stood for a while listening to my own heart beating and gazing about me. The four tall double doors were splendid with their old-fashioned panels and the two windows which gave internally on to the hall were fretted with wooden slats of a faintly Turkish design. The whole proportion and disposition of things here was of a thrilling promise; even Sabri glowed at the woodwork which was indeed of splendid make and in good condition.

The floor, which was of earth, was as dry as if tiled. Obviously the walls of the house offered good insulation—but then earth brick usually does if it is laid thickly enough. The wind moaned in the clump of banana trees, and at intervals I could still hear the whimper of the mandolin.

Sabri, who had by now recovered his breath, began to take a more detailed view of things, while I, still obscured by premonitions of a familiarity which I could not articulate, walked to the end of the hall to watch the rain raiding among the pomegranates. The garden was hardly larger than twenty square yards, but crammed with trees standing shoulder to shoulder at such close quarters that their greenery formed an almost unbroken roof. There were too many—some would have to go: I caught myself up with a start. It was early for me to begin behaving like the house's owner. Abstractedly I counted them again: six tangerines, four bitter lemons, two pomegranates, two mulberry trees and a tall leaning walnut. Though there were houses on both sides they were completely hidden by greenery. This part of the village with its steep slope was built up in tiers, balcony upon balcony, with the trees climbing up between. Here and there through the green one caught a glint of the sea, or a corner of the Abbey silhouetted against it.

My reverie was interrupted by a moan and I feared for a moment that Sabri had immolated himself in one of the rooms upon the discovery of some dreadful fact about the woodwork. But no. A heifer was the cause of the noise. It stood, plaintively chewing something in the front room, tethered to a ring in the wall. Sabri clicked his tongue disapprovingly and shut the door. 'A bloody cow, my dear,' he smiled with all the townsman's indulgence towards the peasant's quirks. 'Inside of the house.' There were two other rather fine rooms with a connecting door of old workmanship, and a couple of carved cupboards. Then came a landslide. 'Don't open it!' shouted the owner and flew to the help of the gallant Sabri who was wrestling with a door behind which apparently struggled some huge animal—a camel perhaps or an elephant? 'I forgot to tell you,' panted the owner as we all three set our shoulders to the panels. The room was stacked breast-high with grain which had poured out upon Sabri as he opened the door. Together we got it shut but not before the observant Sabri had noticed how dry the grain was in its store. 'This place is dry,' he panted grudgingly. 'So much I can say.'

But this was not all; we were about to leave when the owner suddenly recollected that there was more to see and pointed a quavering finger at the ceiling in the manner of Saint John in the icons. 'One more room,' he said, and we now took a narrow outside staircase where the rain still drizzled, and climbed out upon a balcony where we both stood speechless. The view was indescribable. Below us, the village curved away in diminishing perspective to the green headland upon which the Abbey stood, its fretted head silhouetted against the Taurus range. Through the great arches gleamed the grey-gold fields of cherries and oranges and the delicate spine of Kasaphani's mosque. From this high point we were actually looking down upon Bellapaix, and beyond it, five miles away, upon Kyrenia whose castle looked absurdly like a toy. Even Sabri was somewhat awed by the view. Immediately behind, the mountain climbed into blue space, topped by the ragged outcrop and mouldering turrets of Buffavento. 'My God,' I said feebly. 'What a position.'

The balcony itself was simply a flat platform of earth with no balustrade. Up here in one corner of it was a rather lofty and elegant room, built on a bias, and empty of everything save a pair of shoes and a pile of tangerines. We returned to the balcony with its terrific panorama. The storm had begun to lift now and sun was struggling feebly to get out; the whole eastern prospect was suffused with the light which hovers over El Greco's Toledo.

'But the balcony itself,' said Sabri with genuine regret, 'my dear, it will need concrete.' 'Why?' He smiled at me. 'I must tell you how the peasant house is built—the roof. Come down.' We descended the narrow outside stair together, while he produced a notebook and pencil. 'First the beams are laid,' he said indicating the long series of magnificent beams, and at the same time scribbling in his book. 'Then some reed mats. Then packets of osiers to fill the airspace, or perhaps dried seaweed. Then Carmi earth, then gravel. Finally it all leaks and you spend the whole winter trying to stop the leaks.'

'But this house doesn't,' I said.

'Some do sooner than others.'

I pointed to the mason's signature upon the graven iron plaque which adorned the main door. It bore the conventional Orthodox cross embossed on it with the letters IE XR N (Jesus Christ Conquers) and the date 1897. Underneath, on the lower half of the plate, in the space reserved to record subsequent building or alteration was written only one date (9th September 1940), when presumably some restoration work had been undertaken. 'Yes, I know, my dear,' said Sabri patiently. 'But if you buy this house you will have to rebuild the balcony. You are my friend, and so I shall insist for your own good.'

We debated this in low tones on the way down the hill. Though the rain had slackened the village street was empty save for the little corner shop, a grocery store, where a thickset young man sat alone, amid sacks of potatoes and dry packets of spaghetti, playing patience on a table. He shouted good afternoon.

In the main square Jamal sat uneasily under the Tree of Idleness beneath an open umbrella, drinking coffee. I was about to engage the owner of the house in discussion as to the sort of price he had in mind for such a fine old relic when Sabri motioned me to silence. The coffee-house was gradually filling up with people and faces were turning curiously towards us. 'You will need time to think,' he said. 'And I have told him you don't want to buy it at all, at any price. This will make the necessary despondence, my dear.'

'But I'd like to have an idea of the price.'

'My dear, he has no idea *himself*. Perhaps five hundred pounds, perhaps twenty pounds, perhaps ten shillings. He is completely vacant of ideas. In the bargaining everything will get cleared. But we must take time. In Cyprus time is everything.'

I rode regretfully down the green winding ways to Kyrenia thinking deeply about the house which seemed more desirable in retrospect than it had in actual fact. Meanwhile Sabri talked to me in knowledgeable fashion about the drawbacks to buying out there. 'You simply have not considered such problems,' he said, 'as water, for example. Have you?'

I had not, and I felt deeply ashamed of the fact. 'Give me two days,' said Sabri, 'and I will find out about the land and water-rights of the property. Then we will ask the man and his wife for the big price-conversation at my office. By God, you will see how tricky we are in Cyprus. And if you buy the house I will send you to a friend of mine to do the rebuilding. He is a rogue, of course, but just the man. I only ask, give me time.'

That night when I told Panos that I had seen what might prove to be a suitable house for me at Bellapaix he was delighted, for he had lived there for several years, teaching at the local school. 'They are the laziest people in the world,' he said, 'and the best-natured in Cyprus. And you have honey, and also in the valley behind the house nightingales, my friend.'

He did not mention silk, almonds and apricots: oranges, pomegranates, quince. . . . Perhaps he did not wish to influence me too deeply.

Sabri meanwhile retired into silence and contemplation for nearly a week after this; I imagined him sharpening himself for the coming contest of wills by long silent fasts—broken perhaps by a glass of sherbet—or perhaps even prayer for long stretches. The skies turned blue and hard again, and the orange-trees in the Bishopric put out their gleaming suns. The season was lengthening once more into summer, one felt; was stretching itself, the days beginning to unfold more slowly, the twilights to linger. Once more the little harbour filled up with its crowds of chaffering fishermen darning their nets, and of yachtsmen dawdling over caulked seams and a final coat of paint.

Then at last the summons came; I was to present myself at Safari's office the next morning at eight. Panos brought me the message, smiling at my obvious anxiety, and telling me that Sabri was rather despondent because it now appeared that the house was owned not by the cobbler but by his wife. It had been her dowry, and she herself was going to conduct the sale. 'With women,' said my friend, 'it is always a Calvary to argue. A Golgotha.' Nevertheless Sabri had decided to go forward with the business. The intervening space of time had been valuable, however, because he had come into possession of a piece of vital information about the water supply. Water is so scarce in Cyprus that it is sold in parcels. You buy an hour here and an hour there from the owner of a spring—needless to say no quantity measure exists.

The trouble lies here: that water-rights form part of property-titles of citizens and are divided up on the death of the owner among his dependants. This is true also of land and indeed of trees. Families being what they are, it is common for a single spring to be owned by upwards of thirty people, or a single tree to be shared out among a dozen members of a family. The whole problem, then, is one of obtaining common consent—usually one has to pay for the signatures of thirty people in order to achieve any agreement which is binding. Otherwise one dissident nephew and niece can veto the whole transaction. In the case of some trees, for example, one man may own the produce of the tree, another the ground on which it stands, a third the actual timber. As may be imagined the most elementary litigation assumes gigantic proportions—which explains why there are so many lawyers in Cyprus.

Now Sabri had got wind of the fact that the Government was planning to install the piped water supply to the village which had been promised for so long; moreover that the plans were already being drawn up. The architect of the Public Works happened to be a friend of his so he casually dropped into his office and asked to see where the various water-points were to be placed. It was a stroke of genius, for he saw with delight that there was to be a public water-point outside the very front door of the old house. This more than offset the gloomy intelligence that the only water the cobbler owned was about an hour a month from the main spring—perhaps sixty gallons: whereas the average water consumption of an ordinary family is about forty gallons a *day*. This was a trump card, for the cobbler's water belonged in equal part to the rest of his wife's family—all eighteen of them, including the idiot boy Pipi whose signature was always difficult to obtain on a legal document. . . .

I found my friend, freshly shaven and spruce, seated in the

gloom of his office, surrounded by prams, and absolutely motion-less. Before him on the blotter lay the great key of the house, which he poked from time to time in a reproachful way. He put his finger to his lips with a conspiratorial air and motioned me to a chair. 'They are all here, my dear,' he hissed, 'getting ready.' He pointed to the café across the road where the cobbler had gath-ered his family. They looked more like seconds. They sat on a semicircle of chairs, sipping coffee and arguing in low voices; a number of beards waggled, a number of heads nodded. They looked like a rugger scrum in an American film receiving last-minute instructions from their captain. Soon they would fall upon us like a ton of bricks and gouge us. I began to feel rather alarmed. 'Now, whatever happens,' said Sabri in a low voice, tremulous with emotion, 'do not surprise. You must never sur-prise. And you don't want the house at all, see?'

I repeated the words like a catechism. 'I don't want the house. I absolutely don't want the house.' Yet in my mind's eye I could see those great doors ('God,' Sabri had said, 'this is fine wood. From Anatolia. In the old days they floated the great timbers over the water behind boats. This is Anatolian timber, it will last for ever'). Yes, I could see those doors under a glossy coat of blue paint. . . .'I don't want the house,' I repeated under my breath, feverishly trying to put myself into the appropriate frame of mind.

'Tell them we are ready,' said Sabri to the shadows and a bare-footed youth flitted across the road to where our adversaries had gathered. They hummed like bees, and the cobbler's wife detached herself from the circle—or tried to, for many a hand clutched at her frock, detaining her for a last-minute consideration which was hissed at her secretively by the family elders. At last she wrenched herself free and walked boldly across the road, entering Sabri's shrine with a loud 'Good morning' spoken very confidently.

She was a formidable old faggot, with a handsome self-indulgent face, and a big erratic body. She wore the white headdress and dark skirt of the village woman, and her breasts were gathered into the traditional baggy bodice with a drawstring at the waist, which made it look like a loosely furled sail. She stood before us looking very composed as she gave us good morning. Sabri cleared his throat, and picking up the great key very delicately between finger and thumb—as if it were of the utmost fragility—put it down again on the edge of the desk nearest her with the air of a conjurer making his opening dispositions. 'We are speaking about your house,' he said softly, in a voice ever so faintly curdled with menace. 'Do you know that all the wood is . . .' he suddenly shouted the last word with such force that I nearly fell off my chair, 'rotten!' And picking up the key he banged it down to emphasize the point.

The woman threw up her head with contempt and taking up the key also banged it down in her turn exclaiming: 'It is not.'

'It *is*.' Sabri banged the key.

'It is *not*.' She banged it back.

'It is.' A bang.

'It is *not*.' A counter-bang.

All this was not on a very high intellectual level, and made me rather ill at ease. I also feared that the key itself would be banged out of shape so that finally none of us would be able to get into the house. But these were the opening chords, so to speak, the pre-liminary statement of theme.

The woman now took the key and held it up as if she were swearing by it. 'The house is a good house,' she cried. Then she put it back on the desk. Sabri took it up thoughtfully, blew into the end of it as if it were a six-shooter, aimed it and peered along it as if along a barrel. Then he put it down and fell into an abstraction.

'And suppose we wanted the house,' he said, 'which we don't, what would you ask for it?'

'Eight hundred pounds.'

Sabri gave a long and stagy laugh, wiping away imaginary tears and repeating 'Eight hundred pounds' as if it were the best joke in the world. He laughed at me and I laughed at him, a dreadful false laugh. He slapped his knee. I rolled about in my chair as if on the verge of acute gastritis. We laughed until we were exhausted. Then we grew serious again. Sabri was still fresh as a daisy, I could see that. He had put himself into the patient contemplative state of mind of a chess player.

'Take the key and go,' he snapped suddenly, and handing it to her, swirled round in his swivel chair to present her with his back; then as suddenly he completed the circuit and swivelled round again. 'What!' he said with surprise. 'You haven't gone.' In truth there had hardly been time for the woman to go. But she was somewhat slow-witted, though obstinate as a mule: that was clear. 'Right,' she now said in a ringing tone, and picking up the key put it into her bosom and turned about. She walked off stage in a somewhat lingering fashion. 'Take no notice,' whispered Sabri and busied himself with his papers.

The woman stopped irresolutely outside the shop, and was here joined by her husband who began to talk to her in a low cringing voice, pleading with her. He took her by the sleeve and led her unwillingly back into the shop where we sat pointedly reading letters. 'Ah! It's you,' said Sabri with well-simulated surprise. 'She wishes to discuss some more,' explained the cobbler in a weak conciliatory voice. Sabri sighed.

'What is there to speak of? She takes me for a fool.' Then he suddenly turned to her and bellowed, 'Two hundred pounds and not a piastre more.'

It was her turn to have a paroxysm of false laughter, but this was rather spoiled by her husband who started plucking at her sleeve as if he were persuading her to be sensible. Sabri was not slow to notice this. 'You tell her,' he said to the man. 'You are a man and these things are clear to you. She is only a woman and does not see the truth. Tell her what it is worth.'

The cobbler, who quite clearly lacked spirit, turned once more to his wife and was about to say something to her, but in a sudden swoop she produced the key and raised it above her head as if she intended to bring it down on his hairless dome. He backed away rapidly. 'Fool,' she growled. 'Can't you see they are making a fool of you? Let me handle this.' She made another pass at him with the key and he tiptoed off to join the rest of her relations in the coffee-shop opposite, completely crushed. She now turned to me and extended a wheedling hand, saying in Greek, 'Ah come along there, you an Englishman, striking a hard bargain with a woman. . . .' But I had given no indication of speaking Greek so that it was easy to pretend not to understand her. She turned back to Sabri, staring balefully, and banging the key down once more shouted 'Six hundred,' while Sabri in the same breath bellowed 'Two hundred.' The noise was deafening.

They panted and glared at each other for a long moment of silence like boxers in a clinch waiting for the referee to part them. It was the perfect moment for Sabri to get in a quick one below the belt. 'Anyway, your house is mortgaged,' he hissed, and she reeled under the punch. 'Sixty pounds and three piastres,' he added, screwing the glove a little to try to draw blood. She held her groin as if in very truth he had landed her a blow in it. Sabri followed up swiftly: 'I offer you two hundred pounds plus the mortgage.'

She let out a yell. 'No. Never,' and banged the key. 'Yes, I say,' bellowed Sabri giving a counter-bang. She grabbed the key (by now it had become, as it were, the very symbol of our contention. The house was forgotten. We were trying to buy this old rusty key which looked like something fitter for Saint Peter's key-ring than my own). She grabbed the key, I say, and put it to her breast like a child as she said: 'Never in this life.' She rocked it back and forth, suckled it, and put it down again.

Sabri now became masterful and put it in his pocket. At this she let out a yell and advanced on him shouting: 'You give me back my key and I shall leave you with the curses of all the saints upon you.' Sabri stood up like a showman and held the key high above his head, out of her reach, repeating inexorably: 'Two hundred. Two hundred. Two hundred.' She snapped and strained like a hooked fish, exclaiming all the time: 'Saint Catherine defend me. No. No.' Then quite suddenly they both stopped, he replaced the key on the desk and sat down, while she subsided like a pan of boiling milk when it is lifted off the fire. 'I shall consult,' she said briefly in another voice and leaving the key where it was she took herself off across the road to where her seconds waited with towels and sponges. The first round was a draw, though Sabri had made one or two good points.

'What happens now?' I said, and he chuckled. 'Just time for a coffee. I think, you know, my dear,' he added, 'that we will have to pay another hundred. I feel it.' He was like a countryman who can tell what the weather will be like from small signs invisible to the ordinary townsman. It was an enthralling spectacle, this long-drawn-out pantomime, and I was now prepared for the negotiations to go on for a week. 'They don't know about the water,' said Sabri. 'They will let us have the house cheap and then try and sting us for the water-rights. We must pretend to forget about the water and buy the house cheaper. Do you see?' I saw the full splendour of his plan as it unfolded before us. 'But,' he said, 'everything must be done today, now, for if she goes back to the village and makes the gossips nothing will be consummated.' It seemed to me that she was already making the gossips in the café opposite, for a furious altercation had broken out. She was accusing her husband of something and he was replying waspishly and waving his arms.

After a while Sabri whispered: 'Here she comes again,' and here she came, rolling along with sails spread and full of the cargo of her misfortunes. She had changed her course. She now gave us a long list of her family troubles, hoping to soften us up; but by now I felt as if my teeth had been sharpened into points. It was clear that she was weakening. It was a matter of time before we could start winding her in. It was, in fact, the psychological moment to let out the line, and this Sabri Tahir now did by offering her another hundred ('a whole hundred,' he repeated juicily in a honey-eyed voice) if she would clinch the deal there and then. 'Your husband is a fool,' he added, 'and your family ignorant. You will never find a buyer if you do not take this gentleman. Look at him. Already he is weakening. He will go elsewhere. Just look at his face.' I tried to compose my face in a suitable manner to play my full part in the pantomime. She stared at me in the manner of a hungry peasant assessing a turnip and suddenly sat herself down for the first time, bursting as she did so into heartrending sobs. Sabri was delighted and gave me a wink.

She drew her wimple round her face and went into convulsions, repeating audibly: 'O Jesus, what are they doing to me? Destruction has overtaken my house and my line. My issue has been murdered, my good name dragged in the dust.' Sabri was in a high good humour by this time. He leaned forward and began to talk to her in the voice of Mephistopheles himself, filling the interstices between her sentences with his insinuations. I could hear him droning on 'Mortgage . . . two hundred . . . husband a fool . . . never get such an opportunity.' Meanwhile she rocked and moaned like an Arab, thoroughly enjoying herself. From time to time she cast a furtive glance at our faces to see how we were taking it; she could not have drawn much consolation from Sabri's for he was full of a triumphant concentration now; in the looming shadows he reminded me of some great killer shark— the flash of a white belly as it turned over on its back to take her. 'We have not spoken of the water as yet,' he said, and among her diminishing sobs she was still able to gasp out, 'That will be another hundred.'

'We are speaking only of the house,' insisted Sabri, and at this a look of cunning came over her face. 'Afterwards we will speak of the water.' The tone in which he said this indicated subtly that he had now moved over on to her side. The foreigner, who spoke no Greek, could not possibly understand that without water-rights the house itself was useless. She shot a glance at me and then looked back at him, the look of cunning being replaced by a look almost of triumph. Had Sabri, in fact, changed sides? Was he perhaps also planning to make a killing, and once the house was bought . . . She smiled now and stopped sobbing.

'All this can only be done immediately,' said Sabri quietly. 'Look. We will go to the widow and get the mortgage paper. We will pay her mortgage before you at the Land Registry. Then we will pay you before witnesses for the house.' Then he added in a low voice: 'After that the gentleman will discuss the water. Have you the papers?'

We were moving rather too swiftly for her. Conflicting feelings beset her; ignorance and doubt flitted across her face. An occasional involuntary sob shook her—like pre-ignition in an overheated engine which has already been switched off. 'My grandfather has the title-deeds.'

'Get them,' said Sabri curtly.

She rose, still deeply preoccupied, and went back across the street where a furious argument broke out among her seconds. The white-bearded old man waved a stick and perorated. Her husband spread his hands and waggled them. Sabri watched all this with a critical eye. 'There is only one danger—she must not get back to the village.' How right he was; for if her relations could make all this noise about the deed of sale, what could the village coffee-shop not do? Such little concentration as she could muster would be totally scattered by conflicting counsels. The whole thing would probably end in a riot followed by an island-wide strike. . . .

I gazed admiringly at my friend. What a diplomat he would make! 'Here she comes again,' he said in a low voice, and here she came to place the roll of title-deeds on the table beside the key. Sabri did not look at them. 'Have you discussed?' he said sternly. She groaned. 'My grandfather will not let me do it. He says you are making a fool of me.' Sabri snorted wildly.

'Is the house yours?'

'Yes, sir.'

'Do you want the money?'

'Yes.'

'Do you want it today?'

'Yes.'

My friend leaned back in his chair and gazed up at the cobwebs in the roof. 'Think of it,' he said, his voice full of the poetry of commerce. 'This gentleman will cut you a chekky. You will go to the Bank. There they will look with respect at it, for it will bear his name. They will open the safe. . . .' His voice trembled and she gazed thirstily at him, entranced by the story-book voice he had put on. 'They will take from it notes, thick notes, as thick as a honeycomb, as thick as salami' (here they both involuntarily licked their lips and I myself began to feel hungry at the thought of so much edible money). 'One . . . two . . . three,' counted Sabri in his mesmeric voice full of animal magnetism. 'Twenty . . . sixty . . . a hundred' gradually getting louder and louder until he ended at 'three hundred.' Throughout this recital she behaved like a chicken with her beak upon a chalk line. As he ended she gave a sigh of rapture and shook herself, as if to throw off the spell. 'The mortgage will have been paid. The widow Anthi will be full of joy and respect for you. You and your husband will have *three hundred pounds*.' He blew out his breath and mopped his head with a red handkerchief. 'All you have to do is to agree. Or take your key.'

He handed her the key and once more swivelled round, to remain facing the wall for a full ten seconds before completing the circle.

'Well?' he said. She was hovering on the edge of tears again. 'And my grandfather?' she asked tremulously. Sabri spread his hands. 'What can I do about your grandfather? Bury him?' he asked indignantly. 'But act quickly, for the gentleman is going.' At a signal from him I rose and stretched and said, 'Well I think I . . .' like the curate in the Leacock story.

'Quick. Quick. Speak or he will be gone,' said Sabri. A look of intense agony came over her face. 'O Saint Matthew and Saint Luke,' she exclaimed aloud, tortured beyond endurance by her doubts. It seemed a queer moment to take refuge in her religion, but obviously the decision weighed heavily upon her. 'O Luke, O Mark,' she rasped, with one hand extended towards me to prevent me from leaving.

Sabri was now like a great psychologist who divines that a difficult transference is at hand. 'She will come,' he whispered to me, and putting his fingers to his mouth blew a shrill blast which alerted everybody. At once with a rumble Jamal, who had apparently been lurking down a side street in his car, grated to the door in a cloud of dust. 'Lay hold of her,' Sabri said and grabbed the woman by the left elbow. Following instructions I grabbed the other arm. She did not actually resist but she definitely rested on her oars and it was something of an effort to roll her across the floor to the taxi. Apparently speed was necessary in this *coup de main* for he shouted: 'Get her inside' and put his shoulder to her back as we propelled her into the back of the car and climbed in on top of her.

She now began to moan and scream as if she were being abducted—doubtless for the benefit of the grandfather—and to make dumb appeals for help through the windows. Her supporters poured out into the road, headed by a nonagenarian waving a plate and her husband who also seemed in tears. 'Stop.' 'You can't do that,' they cried, alerting the whole street. Two children screamed: 'They are taking Mummy away,' and burst into tears.

'Don't pay any attention,' said Sabri now, looking like Napoleon on the eve of Wagram. 'Drive, Jamal, drive.' We set off with a roar, scattering pedestrians who were making their way to the scene of the drama, convinced perhaps that a shot-gun wedding was in progress. 'Where are we going?' I said.

'Lapithos—the widow Anthi,' said Sabri curtly. 'Drive, Jamal, drive.'

As we turned the corner I noticed with horror that the cobbler and his family had stopped another taxi and were piling into it with every intention of following us. The whole thing was turning into a film sequence. 'Don't worry,' said Sabri, 'the second taxi is Jamal's brother and he will have a puncture. I have thought of everything.'

In the brilliant sunshine we rumbled down the Lapithos road. The woman looked about her with interest, pointing out familiar landmarks with great good-humour. She had completely recovered her composure now and smiled upon us both. It was obviously some time since she had had a car-ride and she enjoyed every moment of it.

We burst into the house of the widow Anthi like a bomb and demanded the mortgage papers; but the widow herself was out and they were locked in a cupboard. More drama. Finally Sabri and the cobbler's wife forced the door of the cupboard with a flat-iron and we straggled back into the sunshine and climbed aboard again. There was no sign of the second taxi as we set off among the fragrant lemon-groves towards Kyrenia, but we soon came upon them all clustered about a derelict taxi with a puncture. A huge shout went up as they saw us, and some attempt was made to block the road but Jamal, who had entered into the spirit of the thing, now increased speed and we bore down upon them. I was alarmed about the safety of the grandfather, for he stood in the middle of the road waving his stick until the very last moment, and I feared he would not jump out of the way in time. I closed my eyes and breathed deeply through my nose: so did Sabri, for Jamal had only one eye and was unused to speeds greater than twenty miles an hour. But all was well. The old man must have been fairly spry for when I turned round to look out of the back window of the car I saw him spread-eagled in the ditch, but quite all right if one could judge by the language he was using.

The clerks in the Registry Office were a bit shaken by our appearance for by this time the cobbler's wife had decided to start crying again. I cannot for the life of me imagine why—there was nobody left to impress; perhaps she wanted to extract every ounce of drama from the situation. Then we found she could not write—Grandfather was the only one who could write, and she must wait for him. 'My God, if he comes, all is lost again, my dear,' said Sabri. We had to forcibly secure her thumbprint to the article of sale, which sounds easy, but in fact ended by us all being liberally coated with fingerprint ink.

She only subsided into normality when the ratified papers were handed to Sabri; and when I made out her cheque she positively beamed and somewhat to my surprise insisted on shaking hands with me, saying as she did so, 'You are a good man, may you be blessed in the house.'

It was in the most amiable manner that the three of us now sauntered out into the sunlight under the pepper trees. On the main road a dusty taxi had drawn up and was steadily disgorging the disgruntled remains of the defeated army. Catching sight of her they shouted vociferously and advanced in open order, waving sticks and gesticulating. The cobbler's wife gave a shriek and fell into her grandfather's arms, sobbing as if overtaken by irremediable tragedy. The old man, somewhat tousled by his expedition, and with grass in his eyebrows, growled protectively at her and thundered: 'Have you done it?' She sobbed louder and nodded, as if overcome. The air was rent with execrations, but Sabri was quite unmoved. All this was purely gratuitous drama and could be taken lightly. With an expressive gesture he ordered Coca-Cola all round which a small boy brought from a barrow. This had the double effect of soothing them and at the same time standing as a symbolic drink upon the closing of a bargain— shrewdly calculated as were all his strokes. They cursed us weakly as they seized the bottles but they drank thirstily. Indeed the drive to Lapithos is a somewhat dusty one.

'Anyway,' said the cobbler at last when they had all simmered down a bit, 'we still have the water-rights. We have not yet discussed those with the gentleman.' But the gentleman was feeling somewhat exhausted by now, and replete with all the new sensations of ownership. I possessed a house! Sabri nodded quietly. 'Later on,' he said, waving an expressive hand to Jamal, who was also drinking a well-earned Coca-Cola under a pepper tree. 'Now we will rest.' The family now saw us off with the greatest good humour, as if I were a bridegroom, leaning into the taxi to shake my hand and mutter blessings. 'It was a canonical price,' said the old greybeard, as a parting blessing. One could not say fairer than that.

'And now,' said Sabri, 'I will take you to a special place of mine to taste the *meltemi* wind—what is the time? Yes, in half an hour.'

High upon the bastions of Kyrenia castle was a narrow balcony which served the police officers as a mess. Sabri, I discovered later, was a sergeant in the specials. Here, gazing across the radiant harbour-bar towards the Caramanian mountains, we sat ourselves down in solitude and space like a couple of emperors while a bewildering succession of cold beers found their way out on to the table-cloth, backed up by various saucers full of delicious Cypriot comestibles. And here Safari's wind punctually arrived— the faintest breath of coolness, stirring across the waters of the harbour, ruffling them. 'You see?' he said quietly, raising his cheek to it like a sail. He was obviously endowed with that wonderful Moslem quality which is called *kayf*—the contemplation which comes of silence and ease. It is not meditation or reverie, which presupposes a conscious mind relaxing: it is something deeper, a fathomless repose of the will which does not even pose to itself the question: 'Am I happy or unhappy?'

He had been jotting on a slip of paper and now he handed it to me, saying: 'Now your troubles begin, for you will have to alter the house. Here, I have costed it for you. A bathroom will cost you so much. The balcony, at so much a cubic foot, should cost you so much. If you sell the beams—they fetch three pounds each, and there are eighty—you should have so much in hand. This is only for your private information, as a check, my dear.' He lit a cigarette and smiled gently. 'Now the man you want to build for you is Andreas Kallergis. He is good and honest—though of course he is a rogue like me! But he will do you a solid job—for much can go wrong, you know. You will find the cost of cement brick there, and rendering per cubic metre.'

I tried to express my gratitude but he waved his hand. 'My dear Durrell,' he said, 'when one is warm to me I am warm to him back. You are my friend now and I shall never change even if you do.'

We drank deeply and in silence. 'I was sent to you by a Greek,' I said, 'and now the Turk sends me back to a Greek.'

He laughed aloud. 'Cyprus is small,' he said, 'and we are all friends, though very different. This is Cyprus, my dear.'

It seemed in that warm honey-gold afternoon a delectable island in which to spend some years of one's life.

THE TREE OF IDLENESS

(FROM BITTER LEMONS)

'Perched on a mountain-side, her terraces looking down into the gardens of Cerinia, and across the waters of Adana towards the glens and pastures of the Bulghar Dagh, her situation is no less lovely and secluded than herself. Her name is Peace. Nestling in woods, high above the port, her Anglo-Norman builders called her Peace—convent of Peace—Cloîture de la Paix; a beautiful and soothing name, which the intruding Cypriotes corrupted into Delapays, and their Venetian masters into Bellapaese. Here during many ages, gallant Western men and pious Western women found their rest.'

—BRITISH CYPRUS BY W. HEPWORTH DIXON, 1887

ANDREAS KALLERGIS PROVED TO be a sort of Shock-headed Peter from a story-book. He lived with his pretty wife in a tumble-down little house among the orange groves below the Bishopric. Though he spoke very fair English he was delighted by my evident desire to speak Greek, and it was in his little car that I made my next visit to what was to become 'my' village, sweeping up through the bland green foothills in true spring sunshine towards where the grave hulk of the Abbey lay, like some great ship at anchor. He too was something of a diplomat and coached me in those little points of protocol which are essential if one intends to make the right sort of impression.

Together we called upon the Bellapaix *muktar* whose house actually formed part of the Abbey and who waited for us on a balcony hung high above the smiling groves which stretch toward Kasaphani. He was a thick-set, handsome man in his late forties, slow in manner, with a deep true voice and a magnificent smile. He stood, impressively booted and belted for the shoot upon which he was about to embark (he was a passionate hunter), lovingly handling a gun while his handsome dark wife dispensed the traditional sweet jam and spring water which welcomes the stranger to every Greek house. He noticed my admiring glance and handed the weapon to me saying: 'A twelve-bore by Purdy. I bought it from an Englishman. I waited a year for it.' We turned it upon the kestrels and turtle-doves which flickered down below us over the plain, trying it for balance and admiring it, as he questioned me quietly and discreetly about my intentions. He had already heard of the sale of the house. ('Two things spread quickly: gossip and a forest fire'—Cypriot proverb.) I told him what was in my mind and he smiled approvingly with calm self-possession. 'You'll find the people very quiet and kindly,' he said in his deep voice, 'And since you speak Greek you know that a little politeness goes a long way; but I must warn you, if you intend to try and work, not to sit under the Tree of Idleness. You have heard of it? Its shadow incapacitates one for serious work. By tradition the inhabitants of Bellapaix are regarded as the laziest in the island. They are all landed men, coffee-drinkers and card-players. That is why they live to such ages. Nobody ever seems to die here. Ask Mr Honey the gravedigger. Lack of clients has almost driven him into a decline. . . .'

Still talking in this humorous, sardonic vein he led us through the thick grove of orange-trees to Dmitri's café, which stands outside the great barbican, and here in the sunlight I had a first glimpse of my villagers. Most of the young men and women were in the fields and Dmitri's clients were mostly grandfathers wearing the traditional baggy trousers and white cotton shirts. Gnarled as oak-trees, bent almost double by age and—who knows?—professional idleness, they were a splendid group, grey-bearded, shaggy-haired, gentle of voice and manner.

They gave us a polite good day in voices of varying gruffness, and it seemed to me from the number of crooks and sticks which had collected like a snowdrift in the corner of the tavern that many of them must have deserted their flocks for a mid-morning coffee. We did not sit under the Tree of Idleness, though the temptation was strong, but gathered about a table set for us under the fine plane-tree which spans the terrace of the café, and here (as if to introduce me fittingly to Cypriot life) the *muktar* ordered a small bottle of amber-coloured brandy and some black olives of a size which betokened comestibles specially prepared against a feast-day. I had already noticed with disappointment that the Cypriot olive is a small and flavourless cousin of the Italian and Greek olive, and I was surprised at the size and richness of the plateful which the good Dmitri set for us. There is only one place in Greece which produces such an olive—and I scored a triumph in pronouncing its name, Kalamata. I earned a respectful glance from the *muktar* for this observation which showed me to be a person of experience and discrimination, and Andreas smiled warmly upon me, making it clear that I had won my spurs by it.

I had been casting covetous eyes upon the Abbey, which I was dying to explore—indeed I was already beginning to feel somehow a part-owner in it—when a short sturdy man clad in the uniform of an antiquity-warden emerged from among the flowering roses and joined us with a smile of welcome. He had the round good-natured face of a Friar Tuck and a brightly quizzical eye, and he addressed me in excellent pointed English. 'Your brother,' he told me briefly, 'died at Thermopylae. You must have a drink with me, and see *my* private property.' This was a shaft aimed at the *muktar*. 'It is a good deal more impressive than *his* house. Look at it!'

Indeed the Abbey cloisters with their heavily loaded orange-trees and brilliant flower-gardens were a study in contrasts—the grave contemplative calm of Gothic pricked everywhere, as silence is by music, by the Mediterranean luxuriance of yellow fruit and glittering green leaves. 'Somewhere to walk,' said Kollis, for that was the newcomer's name, 'to think, whenever you please, to be quiet among the lemon-trees.'

The *muktar* must have read my mind for he suddenly said: 'Wouldn't you like to visit it? Go along with Kollis, it won't take long. Andreas and I will wait here and talk.'

We entered the broad gate of the outer barbican in sympathetic silence, Kollis smiling to himself as if he surmised my own surprise and pleasure. Indeed Bellapaix on that radiant spring morning looked like a back-drop for *Comus*. The great church-doors stood open upon the rich shadowy interior with its one coloured window which stained the flags with a splash as of spilt wine. Footsteps and voices echoing in the musty interior. We paused to buy a farthing dip before examining the icons in the little chancel. 'The church is still in use,' explained my guide, 'and that gives the whole ruin life. It's something more than just an antiquity. It is the village church, *my* church—and indeed your own since you are coming to live here.' Outside in the courtyard lay the familiar branches of green laurel which would later make incense for the villagers. On the breathless silence of the cool air came the small sounds of the village which later I could identify exactly, attaching to each the name of a friend: Michaelis' bees burring among the blossoms, Andreas' pigeons murmuring; the sharp knocking and planing from Loizus' little carpentry shop; the rumble of an olive-drum being rolled along the street by Anthemos to where a bus waited; the high clear voice of Lalou singing to the dirge of the spindle.... They existed for me as sounds without orchestration or meaning, not more human than the whistle of swifts below the Abbey, or the distant whirr of a motor-car spinning down the white ribbon of road below.

The full magnificence of the Abbey's position is not clear until one enters the inner cloister, through a superb gate decorated with marble coats of arms, and walks to the very edge of the high bluff on which it stands, the refectory windows framing the plain below with its flowering groves and curling palm-trees. We looked at each other, smiling. Kollis was too wise to waste words on it, realizing perhaps how impossible it would be to do justice to the whole prospect. He told me nothing about it, and I wished to know nothing; we simply walked in quiet, bemused friendship among those slender chipped traceries and tall-shanked columns, among the armorial shields of forgotten knights and the blazing orange-trees, until we came into the shadow of the great refectory with its high roofs where the swallows were building, their soft agitations echoing in the silence like breathing, our own breathing, captured and magnified in the trembling silence with an unearthly fidelity. I found myself repeating in my mind, without conscious thought, but irresistibly—echoes in a sea-shell—some lines from *Comus,* built as this place had been built, as a testimony to the powers of contemplation which rule our inner lives. Bellapaix, even in ruins, was a testimony to those who had tried, however imperfectly, to grasp and retain their grip on the inner substance of the imagination, which resides in thought, in contemplation, in the Peace which had formed part of its original name, and which in my spelling I have always tried to retain. The Abbey de la Paix, corrupted by the Venetians into Bella Paise. . . . It was to take me nearly a year to gain currency for the spelling Bellapaix, which is as near as one can get today to its original.

But no such thought was in my mind that first spring morning as I walked in those deserted cloisters, touching the rosy stones of the old Abbey with an idle hand, noticing the blaze of flowers from the beds which Kollis tended so lovingly—and here and there, bursting from a clump of fallen masonry, cracking the rock triumphantly, the very plumes of yellow fennel which the good Mrs Lewis had obser-vantly noticed, adding with all the delight of the amateur botanist: 'It is the Narthex of Prometheus. It likes old ruins best, growing there more freely than on the natural rock. In the hollow tube of its long dry cane, which remains stiffly standing when the flowers and leaves have perished, Aeschylus says Prometheus brought down the fire from heaven, and thus speaks Prometheus bound:

> I bear the yoke who stole
> The fount of fire and in a reed *(narthex)* enclosed
> Transferred to men the precious gift which hath
> Become the mistress of all arts and crafts.'

In that silence the light airs of the plain climbed up to us, full of the small sound of birds as they stooped and dived in the blue gulf below. Somewhere near at hand came the rustle and dribble of spring-water feeding the flowers.

'If this were all, it would be enough,' said Kollis, 'but let us go up.' He led the way up a crumbling staircase to where the roofs fanned away in galleries, and from which new panoramas opened to the east and west. As we ascended, Kyrenia came into view again and the whole fretted coast like lacework. I had begun to feel guilty of an act of fearful temerity in trying to settle in so fantastic a place. Could one ever do any work with such scenery to wonder at? And this fantastic mixture of the Gothic north and the gentle alluring Levantine plains spreading out from the Kyrenia range soft as a lion's paw. . . . How did Lady Hester come to miss this Abbey?

We walked out of the great arch once more into the little square where the others sat waiting for us. The group had now been swelled by one or two fine-looking old gentlemen who were quite obviously consumed with curiosity about the new foreigner. They were massive and booted mountaineers with craggy faces and splendid sweeping moustaches. One of them, Morais, owned the house directly above mine, where he lived alone with his young daughter. He addressed a few rough questions to the *muktar*, accompanied by a keen and by no means friendly glance or two at me, before stumping off up the street leading a pony laden with sacks. 'You may have words with him,' said the *muktar* quietly. 'He's not a bad chap—but, well—many of them feel strongly about Enosis these days. But take it calmly.'

Of the friendliness of the other two men there could be no doubt. Andreas Menas was as brown as a nut, with the liveliest and kindest eyes one could hope to see; he was in his late fifties but in every movement betrayed an agility and ease of movement which suggested a body kept young by unremitting physical work. His handshake was warm and innocent. He was my next-door neighbour but one. He at least belied the indolence attributed to the villagers by popular superstition, for when he came to work on the house he never left his job before dusk had fallen, and he was always there on the dot in the morning. And this, despite the fact that every Sunday he took his morning coffee under the fatal tree! Michaelis was big and moustached like a pirate or a Keystone cop; his massive strength, like that of a rooted tree, showed in every movement which threw out the line of a bicep against his rough sailor's jersey. But it was strength without guile—his shy slow smile spoke of good fellowship and spontaneity. He came of a long line of gentle topers who had filled the air of village taverns with the noise of singing and laughter, and as a story-teller he was incomparable. During the lunch hour, while we worked on the house, he would take his food and can of wine to the shade of a lemon-tree and tell stories which held the other workmen enthralled. Indeed so successful was he that work itself began to fall off until I put a veto on his gift. Thereafter he would sit with a somewhat reproachful air under the tree and tease the workmen who always besought him for stories: 'Ah, Michaelis, tell us a story, do. Just a short one.'

'And the boss?' he would say, his eyes glittering with mischief, as he looked across at me. 'The boss hears,' I would say. 'In half an hour we work.'

'Tell us a short one,' they would plead.

'Ask the boss,' he would say, 'and I'll tell you of the comedy of the Englishman who came to our village to buy a house and of the wicked widow who cast eyes upon him. . . .'

Laughter. 'Tell us. Tell us,' they pleaded; and indeed my own pleasure and instruction demanded that we should hear him out, so that sometimes I found myself pleading too. 'That's a fine state of affairs,' he would rumble. 'First the boss stops me telling stories. Then he himself wants a story. And he a writer of stories!'

It was Michaelis who now stood massively smiling, with one arm resting on the shoulder of Anthemos, the grocer, whose little shop stood at the foot of the hill and from whom I would have to obtain food and fuel. He was a portly youth full of quaint humours. 'Sir, I am hoping to grow fat on you. My shop needs a Noble Buyer like yourself. Otherwise how shall I marry next year?'

'What of your wife's dowry?' I said, and got my laugh. 'His wife's dowry is already consumed,' said Andreas. They were all still entranced by the novelty of my Greek—a fact which never ceased to puzzle me. Indeed, throughout my stay in Cyprus, wherever I went, the fact that I spoke Greek was regarded as a phenomenon. It thrilled people. Why, I don't know. There were a number of Government officials who knew the language better than I. But always a conversation in Greek created a stir, until I felt like a Talking Mongoose.

When formal introductions had been completed the whole company drifted with me up the hill, talking and laughing, to visit the house. I was pleased to learn from them that the price I had paid for it was a reasonable one. The cobbler was regarded as rather a fool, however, for not asking twice the sum and sticking to it. News of the water supply had gone round now, and the *muktar* agreed that a water-point outside my door would enable me to pipe off as much as I needed for domestic use. That would certainly increase the value of the house. And later when the electric light came, as it had already come to Lapithos . . . another increase.

All this was warming news, as warming as the cries of 'Welcome' which came to me from the old carved porches and windows fronting the stony path up to the house. There was a spontaneous guileless joy about them—so that all my doubts vanished at once, and I was only afraid that the old house itself would not come up to expectations. I had put the huge key in the breast-pocket of my coat and now I produced it amidst acclamations. Andreas seized it from me and, agile as a monkey, vanished ahead of us to open the doors and set everything to rights for the contractor's examination. My rucksack was grabbed from me and heaved on to Michaelis' great shoulder. Andreas Kallergis took my book and bottle of wine. I had the feeling that if I wasn't careful they would pick me up and carry me up the steep and stony incline, so that I might be spared the breathless scramble of the last hundred yards.

Everything confirmed itself, like the quivering of a magnetic needle as it settles on the Pole Star, when I saw the house again in full sunlight. The great high hallway was cool and shadowy. The heifer and the barley alike had vanished. We climbed upon the balcony as if upon a cloud to watch a flock of white pigeons take off from the roof below and fan out in perfect formation on the blue, the flicker of their wings twinkling frostily like the early Pleiades.

We drank a glass of wine up there in the crisp air while Andreas Menas told the trees, with the sort of loving comprehension that comes to those who have planted them and watched them bear. 'A vine here and a vine there,' he said stroking his moustache with a brown hand, 'and in a year you could give this whole balcony shade. Why bother with concrete?' He pronounced the word after the village fashion, 'gon-gree'. Meanwhile Michaelis explored the two fine cellars and pronounced them large enough to house anything up to two camels. Andreas Kallergis sat drawing in the dust with his finger, waiting to see what ideas I had for the place.

Outside in the stony street a crowd of small children and several old men had gathered. Quite a conversation was going on— in such pure *patois* that I couldn't follow it, but Michaelis clicked his tongue disapprovingly and glared down upon them from the high balcony, asking whether he might be permitted to throw a little water on them. 'Why?' I asked. He looked very distressed. 'It's that fellow Morais, saying things again.'

Morais was carrying on a grumbling monologue in a harsh voice which went something like this: 'And now if we are going to have the swine actually living in our villages . . . It's bad enough to have them as masters. . . .' He was not receiving any moral support from his audience I noticed, even though they must all sympathize with his views. Indeed, I could see from their expressions that this outburst was regarded as in very poor taste—for it infringed the iron law of hospitality. 'You go down,' said Andreas to Michaelis, 'and tell him off.'

But I thought that here I saw an opening for my talent. Long residence in remote Greek islands had made me not unskilful in dealing with ruffled feelings—and, after all, Morais was only behaving like a Scotsman or a Welshman when faced with the foul invader. Indeed Cypriot manners at their worst never came near the stupidities and impertinences I endured from the Scots on my only visit to the Rump. Besides, being of a somewhat scientific turn of mind I wished to see whether Morais would prove an exception to the law I had formulated about Greek character, namely: 'To disarm a Greek you have only to embrace him.'

Accordingly I said: 'Let me go. After all, we are to be neighbours.'

They looked most anxious as I went down the staircase into the hall and out through the front door. Morais stood there in the street with a troubled aggressive expression on his face, holding a willow crook. Knife and water-bottle were at his waist. He was leaning against the wall of the old water-tank. I walked up to him and embraced him saying: 'Neighbour, I have come to live with you. I know what Greek hospitality is. I want you to know that I am always ready to be of service to my neighbor. I have heard praise of you everywhere in the village as a fine honest farmer.'

Inexorable chain of scientific reasoning! He looked absolutely amazed and put out of countenance. He began to stammer out something, but I ducked back into the door and left him to the mercy of his friends who had shown an evident delight and appreciation of this little performance. 'Well said,' cried an old man, who looked as if he wanted to snatch a kiss while they were flying about; and from the balcony above Andreas and Michaelis growled approvingly. Poor Morais! He made one or two ineffectual attempts to speak but was drowned by the voices chiding him. 'There!' they cried. 'Is that any way to behave to a neighbour? You see what you've done with your boorishness? Given us all a bad reputation.'

He stamped up the hill to his house looking extremely thoughtful. My friends on the balcony greeted me with chuckles and acclamations, as if I had pulled off a splendid diplomatic *coup*—which perhaps I had. At any rate it was a valuable test of the public temper for it showed that, despite the political tide, I could count on sympathies based in common neighbourliness. Indeed never once in the dark days to come did the affection of my village neighbours falter.

THE VANISHING LANDMARKS

(FROM *BITTER LEMONS*, 1957)

TERRORISM ITSELF BEGAN TO spread rather than to diminish—an ominous clue to the temper of things; and to the nauseating foulness of the street-murder of soldiers and policeman was added the disgusting, and typically Balkan, murder of civilians suspected of being traitors. Apart from this of course there was many an old score settled in the name of Enosis. The black mask was protection enough. 'When you give a chap a mask and a pistol,' said Wren thoughtfully, showing that by now he was fully abreast of the Mediterranean temperament, 'the first thing he does is bump someone he owes money to before getting on with more ethnic business.' He had become—we had all become—bitter.

But this disgraceful hunt for unarmed civilians who were shot down like rabbits in church, at the coffee-house, even in hospital, drove the last effective wedge between myself and my villagers whose obstinate and unwavering friendship had not faltered. It did not even now. With the old Cypriot obstinacy they still walked to Kyrenia to post me a wedding-invitation—I had on an average one a week—lest I should think that anything had changed. But now it was I who did not dare to go, for informers were everywhere and I could not bear to think of Andreas or Frangos or fat Anthemos having to answer for 'treachery'. Yet still the invitations came, there came flowers and mandarins and bulbs; and still Andreas the 'Seafarer' came to discuss the merits of concrete brick, though the balcony was finished. Wherever I met a villager I was welcomed with a cry and a handshake—even on a lonely road beyond Famagusta which was an eerie enough place for a Greek to be seen talking to a foreigner in a car. And then Panos was shot dead. He had walked out for a breath of air at dusk, through the winding narrow streets near the harbour. The walls around wore the familiar autograph of Dighenis though I doubt if Dighenis himself pressed the trigger of the pistol which killed him.

Two days before we had spent the day together out at Marie's headland at his own request; he was anxious to study the ambitious tree-planting programme she had begun, and I for my part was glad of advice as I did not quite trust her factotum Janis, and made a point, while she was away, of keeping an eye on the trees. It was a warm cloudless morning, and we set off in high good spirits for there had been a full two-day lull in bomb-incidents and killings and the warm lassitude of the island had begun, as always, to fill one with the illusion of a peace which now lay far back in memory, in a prehistoric era of the consciousness it seemed, yet was always ready to be revived by such a lull in operations. Clito had loaned us a wicker-covered demijohn full of white wine, while Panos' own salad-garden had provided lettuce and cucumber and slender shallots. A loaf of the rough brown peasant wholemeal and some slices of cold beef topped off the supply which we calculated would last us all day. With this provender loaded we tanked up the car and set off through the silvery olive-groves to Saint Epictetus, across the peaceful green flanks of the Gothic range, now drowsing in the warm sunlight of a spring morning, and crisply etching its delicate outlines upon a clear blue sky. The great cliffs which crowned the range gleamed brown-gold as loaves. 'Where to?' I said, for I had promised him a private visit or two before we made our way down to the headland. 'Klepini,' he said. 'My calendar tells me the cyclamen will be starting.' Panos had his own favourite nooks and corners of the range, familiar from years of walking about it—just as a lover will have favourite places in which to plant an expected kiss—the nape of the neck, or the curve of a pectoral muscle; moreover he carried in his head a veritable flower-calendar which told him, almost to the day, that the almond-blossom would be out in Carmi, or the dog-roses above Lapithos. In his memory he carried a living flower-map of the range, and knew where best to go for his anemones and cyclamens, his ranunculuses and marigolds. Nor was he ever wrong.

As a concession to the sunshine he wore an open-necked shirt; but nothing, not even an August heat-wave, could have persuaded him to wear anything but his rusty old black suit with its chalk marked sleeves. As we rolled along the coast-road he exclaimed delightedly at every glimpse of the sea through the carobs and olives, puffing at his cigarette, his spectacles gleaming. 'Today we shall forget everything—even the situation, eh?' he smiled, settling himself firmly in the front seat with the air of a man determined upon pleasure, whatever it may cost. I did not tell him that I had a small radio under the front seat, and that I would have to keep in touch with the news bulletins to see whether or not there might be a sudden call for my services which would send me racing back to the capital. The dreadful tug of my work was still there—yet in this benignly slumbering morning we seemed to be far from the bondage of politics or war. The little pistol itself seemed an anachronism in all this pastoral blue and yellow—the young barley struggling to its feet upon the tobacco-coloured winter fields. We ran on round the loops and curls of the road, the sea marching bravely with us, until we came to the little village dedicated by its name to a saint about whom nobody knew anything. Epictetus the philosopher might have been intended, but the ascription is doubtful; it is more likely that some rock hermit with the same temperamental predisposition as Saint Hilarion had lived and died there, bequeathing in the memory of his name something of the austerity and pain of a solitary life to which the villager could cling as a symbol for holiness.

The narrow streets of the little village were empty and most of the shops closed, save for the coffee-house in the main square where half a dozen farmers sat before their morning coffee idly scanning the newspapers of yesterday. This peaceful and traditional scene was only belied by the heavily sandbagged police station with its stalwart Commando guarding the front door, his keen blue eyes in a brown face turned towards us in hostile curiosity, one finger on the trigger of his Sten. His alertness was comforting; when I waved at him he smiled and waved his hand back at me, comforted perhaps by a familiarly English face among so many dark ones. 'How I wish,' said Panos, turning an admiring eye upon the young soldier, 'things were normal. But they won't be.' He shook his head and sighed deeply. 'For a long time yet, my friend, unless . . . unless . . .' But he shook his head. 'They won't take us seriously until the hotheads gain control. Look, oleanders. It is too early for snakes is it not? I thought I caught a glimpse of one.'

A few miles beyond the village, after a series of vertiginous loops and dips of the road, one finds great bunkers of sand shored up against the road—a quarter of a mile from the beach. The carobs and olives hereabout stand a couple of feet deep in the drifts which year by year move inland, smothering the light scrub and holm-oak in brown suffocating dunes. The whole great Pachyammos beach is marching inland, though precisely why I cannot tell. But these dunes athwart the road are a godsend for builders who send out lorries to collect the sand for use in Kyrenia; and here we came upon Sabri, sitting unmoved under a carob in a red shirt and grey trousers, while a grunting team of young Turks filled a lorry for him. We stopped and he came delightedly across to talk to us. Panos and he were old familiars, if not actually cronies, and it was warming to see the genuine friendliness between them. They were co-villagers first, and the link of the village was stronger here, on neutral ground, so to speak, than any differences of race or belief. 'Are you buying more houses?' he asked, and the smiling Panos answered for me. 'Never without your help. No, we are going to gather wild flowers.' Sabri said: 'I am gathering money,' nodding towards his little team of workers in their coloured head-cloths. 'We poor men,' he added wryly, 'cannot take the day off when we wish.' He was busy building a big house for an English lady, he added. 'It is not arty like yours, my dear, but rather *posh,* as you say.' I knew exactly what he meant. It would be called 'Auchinlech'.

We sat for a while in the warm sand under the ancient carob tree, trading a sip of our wine against a couple of rosy pomegranates which he had stolen from a wall in Kasaphani, while the sunny morning began to make the foothills glow and tremble in the humidity, and the old grey crocodile-skin of Buffavento turned to violet. The moon was still in the sky, pale and bloodless. Somewhere in the thin blue beyond the range of eyesight a plane cracked and re-cracked the sound-barrier and sent a wave of thunder flowing over the hills. 'Bombs?' said Sabri comfortably—in the warmth and contentment of that perfect morning it was impossible to make such a word sound any different from the word 'lizards' or 'wildflowers'. Panos turned and yawned. Our own silence surrounded us like a cocoon, softly woven by the briny air which climbed the hot dunes to stir the breathing shadows under the carobs. 'Summer is beginning,' said a Turkish youth, wiping the sweat from his dark brows with the end of a coloured headcloth. It was quite an effort to tear ourselves away from these warm dunes and follow the little signpost which said 'Klepini', but Panes' thirst for cyclamens was not to be denied, and so we reluctantly turned the little car off the main road and began the slow ascent upon the less kindly surface of the village road.

Though it was only a few hundred feet up we had moved into different air. The faint luminous tremble of damp had gone from the sky, and the sea which rolled below us among the silver-fretted screen of olives was green now, green as a Homeric adjective. The foothills began here, and the village itself lay higher up on a platform of reddish sandstone, remote and smiling. And here were the cyclamens and anemones we sought—sheets and sheets of them glittering like young snow, their shallow heads moving this way and that in the sea-wind so that the fields appeared at first sight to be populated by a million butterflies.

'What did I tell you?' said Panos, catching his breath with pleasure as we breasted the slope and rolled down the shady inclines among the trees to come to rest noiselessly on the thick felt of green. We sat with the engine switched off, listening to the wind among the trees, silent. Reality was so far in excess of expectation that we were suddenly deprived of all desire to pick the flowers which dusted these quiet terraces to a starscape—thick as the Milky Way. One could not walk among them without doing them damage. Panos sighed deeply and puffed his cigarette, indulging the relish of his eyes as they travelled across the enchanted slopes whose familiarity had never once staled for him in fifteen years of repetition. 'Embroidery,' he said under his breath in Greek, and with his hand followed the soft contour of the hills, as one might run one's hand affectionately over the flanks of a favourite horse. 'I knew that last thunderstorm would do the trick.'

We unpacked our hamper, placing it on a great smooth stone, and walked slowly to the edge of the cliff, to look down the coast towards Akanthou with its brilliant yellows and sere browns where the corn and barley grew wave upon wave. And as we walked across the carpet of flowers their slender stalks snapped and pulled around our boots as if they wished to pull us down into the Underworld from which they had sprung, nourished by the tears and wounds of the immortals. Here the trees perched upon the dear rock walls which their roots had penetrated, overhanging the valleys where the rooks turned and cawed in the wind, ruffled by the slightest air current. And beneath it all, drawn in long quivering strokes across the middle distance, swam the green sea, the opiate and legend of Europe, drawing itself like a bow back and forth upon the steely Taurus which flanked our horizon in and bound the earth to the sky in tempering the magnificence of both.

My companion was silent now, as he climbed into the branches of a tree to look down with delight upon the rolling relief map below with its bearded curves of lowland falling downwards at one corner to the sea-line, and then climbing and sweeping away towards the sky-blue edges of the world where the Karpass threw up its snouts of stone, and the boundaries of the peninsula were marked by the crash of water on stone and the plumes of spray turning in the air. 'I shall be sixty next year,' said Panos, 'what a pleasure it is to get old.'

The white wine tasted sharp and good and as he raised his glass Panos gave me the toast of the day: 'That we may pass beyond' (i.e. the present troubles) 'and that we might emerge once more in the forgotten Cyprus—as if through a looking-glass.' In a way, too, he was toasting a dying affection which might never be revived—one of those bright dreams of deathless friendship which schoolboys still believed in, of an England and Greece which were bondsmen in the spirit.

How stupid such figments sound to the politicians and how vital they are to young nations!

'You know,' said Panos quietly, 'I received a threatening letter from EOKA—a second-grade letter.'

'How do you mean—second-grade?'

'There are different types. First there is just a warning letter. Then there is a letter with a black dagger and a definite death-threat, which encloses a razor-blade. That is what I got. I expect one of my pupils decided to get his own back by trying to frighten me.'

'What would they have against you?'

Panos poured himself another glass of wine and watched his cigarette-smoke disperse in the still air. He was still absently smiling with his eyes, as if at the memory of our first glimpse of Klepini with its petal-starred glades. 'My dear fellow, how should I know? In these situations everyone informs on everyone else. There is no circumstance of my private life not open to view.'

'Perhaps because I stayed with you—though I haven't visited you more than once since the serious trouble started.'

'I know. I guessed why and I was grateful.'

'Then why did you come out today?'

He stood up and dusted the chalk-marks off his sleeve. He heaved a long sigh. 'Because I wanted to. Life is going to be intolerable enough with all these curfews and fines and strikes; it would be unendurable if one had to obey the dictates of the hot-heads. And besides, I am only one of dozens who have received such letters, and nothing has happened to them.'

'But I am a Government Official.'

'Yes, that is true.'

'They might suspect you of giving information.'

'What do I know? Nothing. It is true I am not as patriotic as most people, though I believe that Enosis is right and must one day come; I am a Greek, after all, and Cyprus is as Greek as . . . Vouni. But of course I shrink from violence though I see that it will certainly bring Enosis sooner than polite talk will.'

'How do you mean?' He stretched himself upon the rock now, face downward, and thrust out his hands until his fingers were buried in the dense clumps of anemones. 'O Lord!' he said, 'I promised myself not to talk politics. But sometimes you ask such silly questions. Can't you see? First there was no Cyprus problem. Then a few bangs followed and you agreed there was a problem, but that it couldn't be solved ever. More bangs followed. Then you agree to try and solve it, but in fact only to bedevil it further. Meanwhile however EOKA has seen that a few bombs could change your inflexible "Never" to "Sometime"; now they feel they have a right to provoke an answer to the question "When?" They are not politically as stupid as the authorities believe them to be. They have, in fact, very much shaken the British position and they realize it. The peasants of your village have two little proverbs which illustrate the present state of Cyprus perfectly. Of a stupid man they say "He thought he could beat his wife without the neighbours hearing." In this case the neighbours are your own Labour Party, UNO, and many others; we are provoking you to beat us so that our cries reach their ears. Then, from another point of view, your operations against the terrorists must be conducted across the body of the Cyprus people—like a man who has to hit an opponent through the body of the referee. As you say in Bella-paix, "He can't gather the honey without killing the bees." How, then, can you gather the honey of a peaceful Cyprus?'

We began to gather great bunches of the flowers now and stow them in the wicker basket; and while I carefully dug out the bulbs I needed for my garden Panos contented himself more easily, winding his cool wet stems about with the broad leaves of the arum lily. 'We could go on like this for weeks,' he said, 'and even today if we worked at it we couldn't make any impression on the field.' He was walking about from point to point as he picked his flowers, matching the various shades as he did so, composing each handful with a skill that showed practice. I could already see them glowing in the blue Lapithos vases which decorated a shelf in the kitchen, strategically placed beyond the reach of his children. After they had gone to bed he would take the flowers down and place them before him as he fell to work upon the great piles of grey copy-books with their school essays in spidery Greek straggling over the pages; and sighing, pause for a moment to refresh the 'eyes of his mind', as he said, with a glimpse, in them, of the Klepini groves.

We picked and picked until the back of the car was brimming with flowers—'like a village marriage' as Panos said—and then sank back upon our thrones of granite to unpack the bread and the meat.

The sun was approaching mid-heaven and the great lion pads of rock among the foothills were already throwing forward their reflections of shadow. Panos put away his spectacles and fell to cutting up the coarse brown loaf, saying as he did so: 'On days like this, in places like these, what does it all matter? Nationality, language, race? These are the invention of the big nations. Look below you and repeat the names of all the kings who have reigned over the kingdoms of Cyprus; of all the conquerors who have set foot here—even the few of whom written records exist! What does it matter that *we* are now alive, and *they* dead—we have been pushed forward to take our place in the limelight for a moment, to enjoy these flowers and this spring breeze which . . . am I imagining it? . . . tastes of lemons, of lemon-blossom.'

As he spoke there came the sound of a shot among the olive-groves, the echoes of which rolled about for a while on the range, sinking and diminishing as if they described the contours of the land in sound; then the silence closed in again, and everything was still save for the rustling foliage in the trees around us. We looked at each other for a long second. 'I thought the shot-guns were all in,' I said; he smiled and relaxed his pose as he lit a cigarette. 'It was a shot-gun all right,' he said, 'and quite near.' With a sudden soughing of wings three jackdaws passed over our heads, as if alarmed by something in the valley beneath. 'Last year one would not have turned one's head,' said Panos with a chuckle, 'and look at us. It's some poor fellow shooting at crows to keep them off his fields.'

A small foreshortened figure now appeared at the cliff-edge and stood looking down the slope towards us. He had a shot-gun under one arm, and he appeared to be listening as he watched us. I said nothing, and without his spectacles Panos 'had no horizons' as he always said in Greek. 'There is a man,' I said quietly, and as I spoke the figure started to stroll towards us at a leisurely pace, holding his uncocked gun in the crook of his arm. As he came nearer I saw that he was dressed in the conventional rig of a village farmer and wore a game-bag at his belt. His heavy brown snake-boots with their corded tops made no sound in the deep grass. Through the open neck of his shirt I caught a glimpse of the heavy flannel sweat-shirt that all peasants made a point of wearing, summer or winter. He walked slowly towards us across the glade at a deliberate and unhurried pace, only stopping for a few seconds every ten paces, the better to eye us. 'He is coming this way,' I said. Panos did not put on his spectacles, but propped his chin with his hands, and began to swear under his breath. I had never heard him use bad language before. 'I swear,' he explained, 'at the humiliation of having to feel afraid in the presence of an unknown man—a sensation so foreign to Cyprus as to be quite frightening in itself, the very idea of it. God! what have we come to?'

I did not answer, for the strange man was standing still, indulging in one of his regular little pauses. He had a large square head with a thatch of greying hair upon it. The wide wings of his black moustache were swept back and up from his mouth. He cocked a barrel of his shot-gun now with a clumsy sort of gesture, intended no doubt to be unobtrusive. The sound of the hammer clicking back was quite audible—like someone cracking his knuckle-bones. 'Measure for measure,' I said, and slipped the little pistol under the napkin on my knee, consoled by the cold butt under my fingers and at the same time disgusted—for Panos' sake. He observed the gesture and made a wry mouth. 'That won't be much use,' he said. I went on eating my sandwich and watching the newcomer lazily out of the corner of my eye. He had stopped now and stood undecidedly beside the trunk of a carob tree. 'Ho there,' he called in a deep hoarse voice, and I knew at once from his tone that we had nothing to fear. Sticking the pistol still wrapped in the napkin back into the basket I raised the demijohn of wine and gave him the traditional Cypriot greeting. 'Kopiaste—sit down and join us.' He relaxed at once, uncocked his gun, and stood it against the tree before walking over to us.

'Why Sir Teacher,' he said reproachfully as he took Panos' hand. 'Why did you not say it was you?' Then he turned his dark curious eye upon me and explained gruffly, 'The Sir Teacher stood godfather to my second son.' Panos was now sitting up and putting on his glasses the better to enter into the spirit of recognition. 'Why Dmitri Lambros,' he said. 'What are you doing here?'

'I've been shooting crows,' replied the newcomer, with a flash of white teeth in a face as dark as a plum cake. 'I know it's forbidden,' he added as if to forestall an inevitable question. 'But up here . . .' he waved a hand in the direction of the mountain, 'we are so far away. You can hear a car as it turns off the highroad at the bottom of the hill. Plenty of time to put it away.' He winked and with a brief word of thanks raised his glass with a friendly nod at me before drinking deeply and exhaling his breath in a rapturous 'Ah! that was good.' He wiped his rough brown hands with their ragged nails on his thighs before accepting the hunk of bread and meat which Panos offered him, asking as he did so, the dozen conventional questions which, like the opening moves of a game, must be made before any real conversation can begin in peasant Greek. His naturalness and the frank roughness of his glance were pleasing, and I could see from Panos' expression that he held the man in good esteem. In his game-bag reposed three bedraggled and crumpled corpses of the jackdaws against which he had been waging war, and these he showed us with some pride. 'I've got a good eye,' he explained.

'How are things up at the village?' asked Panos, and I was not surprised to hear him answer 'Quiet as the grave,' for the village was far more secluded among the foothills even than my own. 'Of course,' he added after a moment, 'we've got one or two of Them. They watch us. But so far there has been nothing. But of course if the English hang this boy Karaolis . . .' Panos interrupted him gravely to say: 'The Kurios is English,' and Lambros turned upon me a pair of dark sweet eyes, full of a sort of bravado. 'I guessed— in fact I have seen him down at the land where the Desposini Maria is building a house, have I not? And her man Janis is my cousin. So you see, nothing can be hidden in Cyprus!' He lit a cigarette swiftly and deftly and sat back on his haunches blowing out the smoke with a long exhalation of rare pleasure. 'Why is there so much feeling about Karaolis,' I said, 'since everyone knows he was guilty?' He looked thoughtfully at the ground and then raised his face to mine, gazing earnestly into my eyes. 'Guilty but not cul-pable,' he said. 'What he did was for Enosis not for gain. He is a good boy.' I sighed: 'This is wordplay. Suppose a Turk Hassan killed someone on behalf of Volkan and then said it was for Enosis.' He stroked his moustache with the backs of his fingers. 'The Turks are cowards,' he said. Panos sighed. 'Don't be a twisted stick, Dmitri, it is true what the Kurios says. Crime is crime what-ever the motive.' The man shook his head slowly from side to side like a bull and gazed up through lowered eyebrows. His mind refused the jump; Karaolis was a young hero. Once again I could not help remarking how absent was any conception of abstract guilt—abstract justice. Who could discern in the thought-processes of a modern Greek the exercise of a logic which was Socratic? They thought like Persian women, capriciously, way-wardly, moving from impulse to impulse, completely under the domination of mood. Had Karaolis been killed outright he would still have been canonized as a martyr but everyone would have accepted the fact and shrugged it off—to get shot is part of the penalty for shooting. A martyr no less, his death would have been accepted as part of the hazard of ordinary life. But the long-winded processes of the European juridical system were an intol-erable bore, an incomprehensible rigmarole to a people which valued action first and the pallid reflections thrown by its moral values afterwards. Here, they thought, comes the old hypocritical Anglo-Saxon mania for trying to justify injustice. The boy was a hero, and they were trying to slip a noose about his heroism. 'We know the truth,' he said, setting his jaw obstinately, and Panos glanced at me with a twinkle and an expression which said: 'Argu-ment on this topic is useless.' I knew it was.

We changed the subject now before it bred a taciturnity and ill-nature which would have been foreign to this chance meeting among the carob trees, and spoke about village affairs which were nearer to his heart. Helen and Maria, the daughters of the school-master, had married last week, and their wedding was the most sumptuous they had had in the village for years. The wine flowed like a canal. 'Even now after five days my head rings with the wine,' he said smiling, rubbing his chin with a tanned hand. It had been like old times. And in the afternoon some English people had come to look at the church; at first the children shouted 'EOKA' and were inclined to throw stones, but when they found the strangers spoke a little Greek and were 'gentle' everyone felt rather ashamed. So while they were in the church the children gathered flowers for the lady and they left with bundles of them in their arms, smiling. 'Such are the children of my village,' he said proudly, thrilling at the mere thought of hospitality upheld in the face of intense antagonism. Then he added, turning to me: 'Such are the Greeks.' I knew this too.

The sun was in mid-heaven now, and the wine low. It seemed a crime to leave the cool deep grass and the shady trees; but if Panos was to see Marie's land we should be on the move. 'Dmitri,' said Panos, whose mind was still busy with his flower-calendar, 'there is a favour I must ask of you.' The man smiled delightedly. 'Any-thing, Sir Teacher,' he said, pronouncing the most revered title in vernacular Greek with pride. 'You know the little ruined mill above the village? There is a glade there by the stream where the mushrooms grow. Set some of your famous children to pick me a basketful and bring them when next you come to Kyrenia, will you? And tell them I will send them sweets in exchange.' 'With the greatest pleasure,' said Lambros standing up and pitching away his cigarette.

I turned the car while Panos packed the food away in the hamper and gazed ruefully at the demijohn. 'It's amazing,' he said. 'We've drunk nearly half. Let us have one more glass for the parting.' We stood in a circle under the great carob and raised our glasses. 'Health,' cried Lambros, and we echoed him; and then, as if anxious to provide a phrase which would bridge the unhappy gap between himself and the hated-loved foreigner, he stuck out his hand to take mine and said, 'All will be well one day.' 'All will be well,' I echoed.

TROUBADOUR
(1960)

POVERTY AND POETRY HAVE BEEN REGARDED as bedfellows for so long now that I doubt whether I shall be believed in saying that I once knew a poet who made a living from his work. Nevertheless it is so. He was a wandering ballad-maker of Cyprus called Janis, and he travelled about on a moth-eaten motorbike with his saddle-bags stuffed with broadsheets. The Mediterranean has always been full of poets and every village in Cyprus has at least two. It is a communal gift rather than a personal one, and poetry has not yet been completely banished to the parlour as it has with us, though modernity (in terms of movements and periodicals) is fast catching up with feudal life. But village poetry is based upon spontaneity of rhyming, and every year there is a sort of Cypriot Eisteddfod on the Troodos mountains to which each village sends its best poets. They compete in an open contest of sixteen syllable rhymes, the challenger hooting out the first line which must then be capped without hesitation by his rival. Public applause decides the winner. Sometimes these wit contests continue interminably, all through the night, until the winner is declared. The arena is wired for sound and the contestants dress up in the full glory of their traditional attire, proud as peacocks. First one will advance to the microphone and hoot out his line, accompanying it with a vaunting gesture as befits a challenger—twirling his moustache or rubbing his boots on the ground like a bull when it is about to charge. Then his rival must take his place and cap the first phrase with something better. The best poets are full of dirty tricks and frequent linguistic fouls are committed, though there are no referees beyond the audience. Quite a high proportion of the verses are below the belt, which used to raise awful broadcasting problems: for what is regarded as joyful poetic licence in a community gathering was often deemed a trifle indecorous to put out on the radio in the course of a community programme.

But poetry is also still regarded as a solace and a fitting art with which to enshrine marriages, funerals and births. The professional keener still exists. Once I saw an elderly man standing outside Kyrenia post office plaintively singing a song of woe which had something to do with his son being unable to get a pension from the Army authorities. He had had it printed and was selling copies at a millieme each. It was a mournful little thing entitled 'The Sad Case of Aristides Koutsos and his plaint against the British Empire'. It was in the traditional village metre which goes something like this:

> Now listen all ye villagers and I will now rehearse
> The sorrows of a family which went from bad to worse
> Because the British Empire has denied my boy his pension
> And filled our hearts with agony and awful apprehension.

The old man, after finding that he had no redress in law for his grievance, had decided to solace himself in this artistic fashion. He was listened to with deep sympathy and his ballad sold well.

But Janis, compared to these, was a professional writer and the greater part of his ballads were news-ballads as were those of our own early ballad-makers like Nat Elderton (he of the 'ale-crammed nose'). Janis wrote them with the greatest facility and had them set up on credit by a printer in Nicosia. Stuffing the saddle-bags of his motorbike with them he set off on an island circuit made familiar by many years of ballad-selling. He was careful to base his circuit on such country fairs as were taking place at the time, since he knew that a fair tended to draw all the villagers of neighbouring localities into town for the day. In the main square he would set up shop. Putting his bundles of broadsheets around his feet he would start in his pleasant singsong voice to half sing, half declaim, his latest production. He was a small good-looking man in his early forties, always clad in a neat black suit and spotless white shirt open at the neck. Long practice had taught him the strength and staying power of his own voice, so that he was careful always to husband his energies, and never try and compete with raucous hucksters or café loudspeakers. He chose his position just out of the central mêlée where he could be best listened to. He nearly always began with a juicy murder.

> *Now listen men and maidens all, at what last week befell*
> *A virgin maid, Calliope, in a lone Paphos dell.*
> *The river ran with blood for weeks, and blood stained all the grass*
> *A virgin's blood for vengeance cries to heaven up above.*
> *In darkness was the dagger sheathed, in silence stole away*
> *The ravisher of Paphian youth, he did not stop to pray*
> *As if the fiends of hell were there to hiss him on his way,*
> *While the poor girl, her life blood spent, just gurgled where*
> *   she lay.*
> *Now who would cut that soft white throat so neat from ear to ear*
> *But Hadjilouk the barber with a shop right next the pier.*
> *For years he'd lusted for the lass, for years she had refused,*
> *Her brother once spat in his eye and he was not amused. . . .*

So the ballad would unroll in that pleasant unhurried voice, while the villagers gathered round in a tight circle, with many a pleasant shiver of horror, to listen to him. When he had finished he picked up a bundle from the ground, crying 'Who will buy?' in a pleasant chirping voice. His sales were usually good, and his wares not expensive; two milliemes was a price of a ballad. They could be either recited aloud in the chimney corner or sung to traditional airs. He had several types of poem to offer and they were graded according to subject matter; there were folktales set in verse, or local news-events (usually murders of the Arden of Feversham type), and there were also a number of what he called 'Erotika'—rather ferocious songs of naked passion and hopeless love. These were done up in rather a special way—for on each cover there was the reproduction of a Rank starlet which the printer had cunningly overprinted; sometimes she had a dripping heart with a dagger in it, and gouts of blood dripping down over her vital statistics. At other times there was a masked man peering over her shoulder with another dagger, preparing to let her have it from behind. Sometimes, too, she had a noose around her neck. I often wondered whether Janis had ever heard of copyright but my native tact prevented me from asking him. After all, what is such a small matter between poets?

When he had sold all he could, he would usually retire to the tavern for a glass of wine before resuming his journey. Once I was able to sit for an hour with him and question him on his work. He answered my questions with good nature, and with a touch of the resigned weariness which comes over poet's faces under questioning. He told me that his poetic skill was a gift which his father had handed down to him. His father, too, had sold ballads but had never been successful at it. He could never make ends meet while he, Janis, the son, was making a small but decent living. It was hard in winter, however. 'What makes it possible,' he said 'for the poet today is the motorbike. You see, in my father's day he had to be content with a camel which is very slow. It took ages to get from fair to fair; whereas now I can often cover three or four fairs in a day and motor from one end of the island to the other in a couple of hours. This morning, for example, I began at Paphos and when I leave you I'll run over to Larnaca this evening for the fair there. It makes a difference.'

I had several meetings with Janis and we became quite good friends; and later that year I got him to agree to let me take some photographs of him to illustrate an article which I had in mind to write. But the wretched crisis intervened before I could do so, and his friendship, like that of so many Cypriots, was temporarily submerged in the hate and despair of the times. We nodded when we met, but I was careful not to force my company upon him lest his acquaintance with a British official might earn him the unwelcome attentions of the nationalists. Once I was in his printer's offices when I saw him come in to pay for his broadsheets. He looked tired and ill. He had a saddle-bag full of millieme pieces which he poured out in a stream over the counter. They took an age to count. He did not see me as I was seated in shadow at the back of the shop.

Later again I had news of him from a villager. He had been forced to give up poetry as all movement was hampered by troop movements and curfews. He had decided to retire to the home of an aunt at Paphos until he could once more resume his trade.

The day before I left the island I bumped into him coming out of a church in Larnaca. 'Janis,' I cried, 'well met,' and for a moment he smiled. But then he checked the involuntary gesture of pleasure and his face clouded over. 'I am leaving tomorrow,' I said. I made as if to shake hands with him but he placed his hands behind his back. He said quietly, 'You did not write the article, did you? I am glad, for it would have made trouble for me.'

'One day I will,' I said. 'In happier times.'

'In happier times,' he said gravely, and inclining his head turned and moved slowly off in to the twilight.

SICILY

Durrell traveled to Sicily with a tour group in 1975, and his 1977 book about the two-week trip reflects his nostalgia for the days when he lived on islands. The book also echoes with Durrell's regret for a young English girl—Martine—whom he met during his time on Cyprus. Martine had died in Sicily (in the Greek colony of Naxos). Durrell's interest in Sicily reflects his interest in ghosts—both Martine's spirit and the island's ancient history as a former part of Greater Greece. But by contemporary humanity, in the shape of his fellow tourists, also captures his attention.

ARRIVAL

(FROM SICILIAN CAROUSEL, 1977)

As I EXPLAINED TO DEEDS more than once during the course of our breakneck journey round Sicily in the little red coach, nobody has ever had better reasons than I for not visiting the island. I had let my visit go by default for many a year, and now with increasing age and laziness and the overriding fact—no, Fact in upper case—of Martine's death, what on earth was the point? I could surely spare myself the kind of sentimental journey which would be quite out of place and out of context? Yes or no? Deeds only shook his head and tapped out his pipe against a wall. "If you say so," he said politely, "but you seem to be enjoying it very much." I was.

The bare fact of my arrival in Martine's own private island had in some way exorcised the dismal fact of her disappearance from the scene—so much had it impoverished life in general, and not for me alone. Moreover the luck was that I was able to talk a little about her, for though Deeds had not known her he had actually seen her quite often driving about Cairo and Alexandria, and lastly about Cyprus where I had helped her to build the ambitiously beautiful house which Piers had designed for her around a cruciform central room which both vowed was based on a Templar motif. But now they were both dead! In some of those long telephone conversations which somehow never succeeded in fully repairing our long-relinquished attachment to the Cyprus past, I could hear, or thought I could hear, the chatter of waves upon the beach of Naxos, the Sicilian Naxos where she had at last come to roost like a seabird, secure at last from politics and civil strife alike.

Happy, too, in the possession of the Man That Never Was and her "blithe and beautiful" children.

Unexpected and fateful is the trajectory which life traces out for our individual destinies to follow. I could not have predicted her Sicilian life and death in Cyprus, years ago. In fact, the Sicilian invitation was one of long standing, and the project of a visit to Naxos was one which had hung fire for many years. But it had always been there. I must, I simply must, she insisted, visit her on her home ground, see her children, meet her husband. And once or twice we almost did meet, the very last time in Rome. Yet never here, for each time something suddenly came up to prevent it. I think neither of us had seriously reflected on the intervention of something as unusual as death—though my wife, Claude, among her warmest friends, had suddenly surprised and saddened everyone by falling ill of a cancer and disappearing. Lesson enough, you would think; but no, I delayed and procrastinated on the Sicilian issue until suddenly one day Martine herself had floated out of reach. That last long incoherent letter—no, absolutely indecipherable—had not alarmed me unduly. An impulsive girl, she was accustomed to write in letters a foot high on airmail paper, and so terribly fast that the ink ran, the pages stuck together, and the total result even under a magnifying glass was pure cuneiform; say, an abstract drawing done in wet clay by the feet of a pigeon. But now the plane hovered and tilted and the green evening, darkening over the planes of coloured fields girdling Catania, swam up at us. The island was there, below us.

Thrown down almost in mid-channel like a concert grand, it had a sort of minatory, defensive air. From so high one could see the lateral tug of the maindeep furling and unfurling its waters along those indomitable flanks of the island. And all below lay bathed in a calm green afterglow of dusk. It looked huge and sad and slightly frustrated, like a Minoan bull—and at once the thought clicked home. Crete! Cyprus! It was, like them, an island of the mid-channel—the front line of defence against the huge seas combing up from Africa. Perhaps even the vegetation echoed this, as it does in Crete? I felt at once reassured; as if I had managed to situate the island more clearly in my mind. Magna Graecia!

But it wasn't only Martine I had come to see. I had other pressures and temptations—inevitable when half my living came from travel-journalism. Yet it was she who placed her darts most cunningly in spots where they cost me most pangs of guilt. For example: "You are supposed to be somewhat of an authority on Mediterranean islands—yet you neglect the biggest and most beautiful! Why? Is it because I am here?" A question which must remain forever unanswered. "After all," the letter continued, "fifteen years is a long time. . . ." It wasn't that either. It was just my old slavish habit of procrastination. The invitation had always been accepted in the depths of my own mind. But circumstances were against it—though I made several false beginnings. And of course we missed each other elsewhere—Paris, New York, Athens; it was extremely vexatious yet it could not be helped. And of course there would always be time to repair this omission and repair the fifteen-year-old breach in our friendship. . . .

In Cyprus, during those two magnetic summers we had discussed at great length the meaning of the word I had invented for people stricken by the same disease as ourselves: islomanes. I had even written a trilogy of books about Greek islands in a vain attempt to isolate the virus of islomania—with the result that later, in an age of proliferating tourism, the Club Méditerranée had even adopted the phrase as a *cri de guerre*—blessed by the French glossies. I had the impression that it had all but made the *Medical Encyclopaedia.* And now?

Well, I had brought with me a few of those long amusing and tender letters to look over as we voyaged; almost all that I knew of Sicily today came from them. In Cyprus she had been a fledgling writer and I had tried to help her tidy an overgrown manuscript about Indonesia called *The Bamboo Flute.* Somewhere it must still be knocking about. It had moments of good insight and some metaphors vivid enough to incite cupidity for I borrowed one for *Bitter Lemons,* but *con permesso* so to speak, that is to say, honestly.

There were of course other strands woven into the skein, like the repeated invitations from an editor in New York to consider some long travel articles on the island. I visited my travel agent in the nearby town of Nîmes where, like an old stork, he nested in a mass of travel-brochures and train-tickets. He was rather a cultivated old man, an ex-schoolmaster who had a tendency to think of himself as a cross between a psychiatrist and the Grand Inquisitor himself. "The thing for you," he said pointing a long tobacco-stained finger at me, "is the Sicilian Carousel—every advantage from your point of view. You will have Roberto as guide and a fine bus." My soul contracted. But truth to tell, the invitation from New York had in some queer way settled the matter. It was also as if Martine had given me a nudge from beyond the grave: had summoned me. But the thought of facing up to the chance adventures of the road made me uneasy. I had become a bit spoiled with too much seclusion in my old bat-haunted house in Provence. My friend must have divined my train of thought for he at once said, "You need a change—I feel it. And the Sicilian Carousel will give you what you need." He handed me a clutch of tomato-coloured brochures which did nothing to allay my misgivings at all. The beauties of Taormina—I knew of them. Who does not? I did not need French commercial prose to excite me. Yet as I drove homeward across the dry garrigues of the Languedoc I was in some obscure way rather happy—as if I had taken a decision which was, at that particular stage, appropriate and necessary. So be it, I thought. So be it.

On arriving home I switched on the lights and took a perfunctory look at Sicily in the encyclopaedia. They made it sound like the Isle of Wight. Then the evening papers arrived with their talk of strikes and lock-outs and so on, and my resolve faltered at the thought of spending days and nights asleep on my suitcase at Nice or Rome or Catania. But somehow I could not draw back now. I lit a log fire and put on a touch of Mozart to console me against these dark doubts. Tomorrow my friend would ring me with the reservations. I cannot pretend that my sleep was untroubled that night. I regressed in my dreams and found myself in the middle of the war in Cairo or Rhodes, missing planes or waiting for planes which never came. Martine was inexplicably there, behaving with perfect decorum, dressed in long white gloves, and subtly smiling. It was the airport but in the dream it was also Lord's and we were waiting for the emergence of the cricketers. I slept late and indeed it was my friend's call which shook me awake. "I have the whole *dossier* lined up," he said. He liked to make everything sound official and legal. "When do I leave?" I quavered. He told me the dates. Technically the Carousel started from Catania; my fellow-travellers were converging on that town from many different points in Europe.

So it was that I began to land-hop sideways across France on a strikeless fifth of July with the pleasant feel of thunder in the air and perhaps the promise of a night storm to come and refresh the Midi. And there was no sign of that old devil the mistral, which was a good omen indeed. It is always sad leaving home, however, and in the early dawn, after a spot of yoga, I took a dip in the pool followed by a hot shower and wandered aimlessly about for a bit in the garden. Everything was silent, the morning was windless. The tall pines and chestnuts in the park did not stir. In the old water-tower the brood of white barn-owls snoozed away the daylight after their night's hunting. The old car eased itself lingeringly away across the dry garrigues with their scent of thyme and rosemary and sage. The Sicilian Carousel was on. All my journeys start with a kind of anxious pang of doubt—you feel suddenly an orphan. You hang over the rail watching the land dip out of sight on the circumference of the earth—then you shake yourself like a dog and address yourself to reality once more. You point your mind towards an invisible landfall. Sicily!

Agrigento

(FROM SICILIAN CAROUSEL, 1977)

MARTINE: "BUT AGRIGENTO FOR ME IS THE ACID TEST and I am sure you will feel it as I have; it reminded me of all our passionate arguments about the Greekness of a Cyprus which had never been either geographically or demographically part of Greece. What constituted its special claim to be so? Language of course—the eternal perennity of the obdurate Greek tongue which has changed so little for thousands of years. Language is the key, the passport, and unless we look at the Greek phenomenon from this point of view we will never understand the sort of colonisers they were. It was not blood but language which gave one membership of the Greek intellectual commonwealth—barbarians were not simply people who lived otherwhere but people who did not speak Greek. It is hard for us to understand for we, like the Romans, have a juristic view of citizenship—in the case of the British our innate puritanism makes it a question of blood, of keeping the blood untainted by foreign admixtures. The horror for us is the half-caste, the touch of the tar-brush. It is a complete contrast to the French attitude which resembles in a way the ancient Greek notion in its idea of Francophone nations and races. The possession of the French tongue with its automatic entry into the riches of French culture constitutes the only sort of passport necessary for a non-French person whatever the colour of his or her skin. It is easier to find a place in a French world than in a British—language determines the fact; yes, if you are black or blue and even with a British passport it is harder to integrate with us.

"This little homily is written in the belief that one day you will visit the temples in that extraordinary valley below the horrid tumble of modern Agrigento's featureless and grubby slums—and suddenly feel quite bewildered by finding yourself in Greece, one hundred per cent in Greece. And you will immediately ask yourself why (given the strong anti-northern and secessionist sentiments of the Sicilians) there has never been a Greek claim to the island. You will smile. But in fact if we judge only by the monuments and the recorded history of the place we are dealing with something as Greek in sinew and marrow as the Argolid or as Attica. How has it escaped? *Because the language is no longer a vital force.* There are a few pockets where a vestigial Greek is still spoken, but pathetically few (luckily for the Italians). There is an odd little Byzantine monastery or two as there is in Calabria. But the gleam of its Greekness has died out, its language has been swamped by Italian. Only the ancient place-names remain to jolt one awake to the realisation that Sicily is just as Greek as Greece is—or never was! The question of Greekness—and the diaspora—is an intriguing one to think about. If we take Athens (that very first olive tree) as the centre from which all Greekness radiates outward . . . Sicily is about like Smyrna is—if we take its pulse today. O please come and see!"

Not very well expressed perhaps, but the sentiments harked back to our long Cyprus arguments in the shade of the old Abbey of Bellapais. The dust raised around the question of Enosis with Greece, which constituted such a genuine puzzle to so many of our compatriots. Their arguments always centred around the relative amenities offered the Cypriots under our unequal, lazy but relatively honest regime. No military service, standards of living etc. . . . all this weighed nothing against a claim which was purely poetic, a longing as ancient as Aphrodite and the crash of the waves on the deserted beaches of Paphos. How to bring this home to London whose sense of values ("common sense") was always based upon the vulgar contingencies of life and not on its inner meaning? You would hear nice-minded civil servants say: "It's astonishing their claim—they have never been Greek, after all." Yet the Doric they spoke had roots as deep as Homer, the whole cultus of their ethnographic state was absolutely contemporary, absolutely living. Was it, then, the language which kept it so? The more we disinterred the past the Greeker the contemporary Cypriot seemed to become.

Through all these considerations, as well as many others—for I had been living in the Mediterranean nearly all my adult life—I had started very tentatively to evolve a theory of human beings living in vital function to their habitats. It was hard to shed the tough little carapace of the national ego and to begin to see them as the bare products of the soil, just like the wild flowers or the wines, just like the crops. Physical and mental types which flowered in beauty or intelligence according to what the ground desired of them and not what they desired of themselves or others. One accepts easily enough the fact that whisky is a product of one region and Côtes du Rhône the product of another; so do language and nationality conspire to evolve ways of expressing Greekness or Italian-ness. Though of course it takes several generations for the physical and mental body to receive the secret imprint of a place. And after all, when all is said and done, countries as frequently overrun and ravaged as Greece cannot have a single "true" Greek, in the blood sense, left.

If indeed the phrase means anything at all. What is left is the most hard wearing, even indestructible part, language whose beauty and suppleness has nourished and still nourishes the poet, philosopher and mathematician. And when I was a poor teacher in Athens striving to learn demotic Greek. I found with surprise that my teacher could start me off with the old Attic grammar without batting an eyelash. Much detail had obviously changed, but the basic structure was recognisably the same. I could not repay this debt by starting my own students off with Chaucer, the language had worn itself away too quickly. Even Shakespeare (in whose time no dictionary existed) needed a glossary today. What, then, makes a "Greek"? The whole mystery of human nationality reverberates behind the question. The notion of frontiers, the notion of abstract riches, of thought, of possessions, of customs. . . . It all comes out of the ground, the hallowed ground of Greece—wherever that was!

This train of thought was a fitting one for a baking morning with a slight fresh wind off the sea. The little red bus had doubled back on its tracks and was heading north briefly before turning away into the mountains. Today we would climb up from sea-level into the blue dozing escarpments which stretched away in profile on our left. Mario plied his sweet klaxon to alert the traffic ahead of us—mostly lorries bringing building materials to Syracuse. Roberto hummed a tune over the intercom and told us that it would be nice and cool in the mountains, while tonight we would find ourselves once more at sea-level in a good hotel just outside Agrigento. Deeds felt like reading so I pursued my long argument with Martine's ghost, upon themes some of which had invaded my dreams. I saw her irritating the Governor at dinner by being a trifle trenchant in support of the Greek claim—it made him plaintive for he felt it was rather rude of her, which perhaps it was. What could he do about a situation fabricated by his masters in London?

But in fact these old arguments had a burning topicality for me, for they raised precisely the questions I had come to Sicily to try and answer. What was Sicily, what was a Sicilian? I had already noticed the strongly separatist temper of the inhabitants which had won them (but only recently) a measure of autonomy. The island was too big and too full of vigorously original character to be treated as if it was a backward department of a run-down post-war Italy. In every domain the resemblance to Greece was fairly striking—and Sicily was politically as much a new nation as the Turk-free modern Greece was. Indeed metropolitan Greece was itself still growing—acquiring back places like Rhodes from Italy itself. All this despite the predictable tragedy of the Cyprus issue, envenomed by neglect and the insensitivity and self-seeking of the great powers with their creeping intrigues and fears of influence.

What was the Mediterranean tapestry all about anyway; particularly when it came to extending the frame of reference in the direction of art, architecture, literature? Italy, Spain, Greece, the Midi of France—they all had the same light and the same garden produce. They were all garlic countries, underprivileged in everything but the bounteous sense of spareness and beauty. They were all naïfs, and self-destroyers through every predatory Anglo-Saxon toy or tool from the transistor to the cinema screen. Yet something remained of a basic cultural attitude, however subject to modification. But why wasn't Spain Italy, why wasn't Italy Greece, or Greece Turkey? Different attitudes to religion, to love, to the family, to death, to life. . . . Yes, deep differences, yet such striking likenesses as to allow us to think of such a thing as a Mediterranean character. After all, there are many varieties of the olive tree, which for me will always mark the spiritual and physical boundaries of that magical and non-existent land—the Mediterranean. Martine was right. How I regretted not having come here before.

We passed Augusta again—how dismal it looked by daylight with all its rusty refineries and sad clumps of rotting equipment. But oil had come to Sicily, and with it prosperity and of course the death of everything that makes life valuable. They were doomed to become soft, pulpy and dazed people like the Americans so long as it lasted. But in a generation or two, after the land had had its fill of rape and disaster the magnetic fields would reassert their quiet grip once more to reform the place and the people into its own mysterious likeness—the golden mask of the inland sea which is unlike any other. How lucky France was to have one foot in the Mediterranean; it modified the *acerbe* French northern character and made the Midi a sort of filter which admitted the precious influences which stretched back into prehistory. It would not be the first time or the last that a whole culture had plunged to its doom in this land. The long suppurating wars of the past— Etruscan against Italian, Carthaginian against Greek against Roman. After every outburst of hysteria and bloodshed came an era of peace during which the people tried to reform their scattered wits and build for peace. It never lasted. It never would. A spell of years with the promise of human perfection—then collapse. And each succeeding invader if given time brought his own sort of order and beauty.

Such a brief flowering fell to the lot of Sicily when the Arabs came, during their great period of ascendancy, at the invitation of the Byzantine admiral Euphemius. It was a fatal invitation, for the island slipped from the nerveless fingers of Byzance into the nervous and high-spirited fingers of the Arabs who immediately entered the struggle and at last succeeded in mastering the masterless island. Then there was another period of productive peacefulness—just as there had been when Syracuse had enjoyed its first flowering of peace and prosperity. They were astonishingly inventive and sensitive these newcomers from over the water, people with the austere desert as an inheritance. For the Arab knows what water is; it is more precious to him almost than oxygen.

So were rural areas resettled, inheritance laws revised, ancient waterways brought back into use for irrigation. They were planters of skill and choice, they brought in citrus, sugar-cane, flax, the date palm, cotton, the mulberry with its silkworms, melon, papyrus and pistachio. Nor was it only above ground for they were skilful miners and here they found silver, lead, mercury, sulphur, naphtha and vitriol—not to mention alum and antimony. The extensive salt-pans of today date from their inspired creative rule. But they also vanished within the space of a few decades—like water pouring away down a drain; the land took over once more, trying to form again its own obstinate image.

We were entering the throat of a plain which led directly into the mountains, and here I got a premonitory smell of what the valley of Agrigento must be like—it was purely Attic in the dryness, in the dust, and the pale violet haze which swam in the middle distance foxing the outlines of things. To such good effect that we found ourselves negotiating a series of valleys diminishing all the time in width as they mounted, and brimming with harvest wheat not all of which had yet been garnered. It is impossible to describe the degrees of yellow from the most candent cadmium to ochre, from discoloured ivory to lemon bronze. The air was full of wisps of straw and the heat beat upon us as if from some huge oven where the Gods had been baking bread. I expected Argos to come in sight at any moment. What is particularly delicious to me about Attic heat is its perfect dryness—like a very dry champagne. You are hot, yes, you can pant like a dog for water; but you don't sweat, or else sweat so very lightly that it dries at once on your skin. In such heat to plunge into an icy sea is marvellous—you get a sharp pain in the back of the throat as if from an iced wine. But here we were far from the sea, and starting to climb amidst all this glaze of peacock-blue sky and yellow squares of wheat. Underneath that hot heaven the sun rang as if on an anvil and we were glad of Mario's cooling apparatus which sent us little draughts of cool air. Dust devils danced along the plain, and the few lorries we passed were powdered white—they had left the main roads for the country paths. Half-way up Roberto announced a "physiological halt" as he called it, and we pulled into a petrol station in order to fill up and, by the same token, to empty out.

There was a canteen where we had a few moments of quiet conviviality over wine and a strange white aperitif made from almond juice and milk. Like everything in Sicily it was loaded with sugar though a delicious drink when sufficiently iced. The Petremands stood treat and Mrs. Microscope was back in sufficient form to engulf a couple of glasses before Mario honked and we all trooped back to the bus to resume our ascent which was now to become a good deal more steep as we left the plain behind. It was pleasant to look down on it as it receded, for the sinuous roads curved snakewise in and out among the hills and the fine views varied with angle and altitude. We were heading for a Roman villa where quite recently the archaeologists had discovered a magnificent tessellated floor of considerable importance to them—and in consequence to us, the curious sightseers of the Carousel. We would base ourselves at Piazza Armerina in order to see the Villa Imperiale and have lunch before crossing the scarps and descending with the descending sun upon Gela and Agrigento. This gave us our first taste of the mountains and it was most refreshing. In one of the rock-cuttings there were little tortoises clicking about and Mario stopped to allow Deeds to field one smartly and hand it to Miss Lobb who did not know what to do with it. It was an astonishingly active animal and ran all over the bus into all the corners, upsetting all of us and causing a full-scale hunt before it was caught. Finally she freed it. Its little claws were extremely sharp and it fought for dear life, for its freedom. I had always thought of tortoises as such peaceable things which simply turned into stones at the approach of danger. This little brute attacked all along the line and we were glad when at last it clicked off into the bushes.

Piazza Armerina is a pretty and lively little hill town, boasting of more than one baroque church, a cathedral and a castle, and several other sites of note in the immediate environs. But it is quite impossible to convey that elusive quality, charm, in writing—or even in photography which so often deludes one with its faked images and selected angles. The little town had charm, though of course its monuments could not compare in importance to many another Sicilian town. Yes . . . I found myself thinking that it would be pleasant to spend a month there finishing a book. The walking seemed wonderful among these green and flourishing foothills. But the glimpse we had of it was regrettably brief; having signalled our presence to the hotel where we were to have lunch we set off at once to cover the six or so kilometres which separated us from the Imperial Villa—a kind of summer hideout built for some half-forgotten Roman Emperor. What is intriguing is that almost no ascription ever made about a Sicilian site or monument is ever more than tentative: you would have thought that this important version of Government House everywhere would offer one a little firm history. No. "It has been surmised that this hunting lodge could have belonged to the Emperor Maximianus Heraclius who shared his Emperorship with Diocletian." The site they chose for the Imperial Villa is almost oppressively hidden away; it makes one conjecture why in such a landscape one should plank down a large and spacious building in the middle of a network of shallow ravines heavily wooded, and obviously awash in winter with mountain streams. Instead of planting it on a commanding hillock which (always a problem in hill architecture) drained well during the rains. There was something rather unhealthy and secretive in the choice of a site, and it must be infernally hot in August as a place to live in. It buzzed with insects and butterflies. We arrived in a cleared space where, together with a dozen or so other buses, we dropped anchor and traipsed off down the winding walks to the villa, marvelling at the sultriness and the oppressive heat—so different from the Attic valleys we had traversed with all their brilliant cornfields.

We came at last to a clearing where an absolute monstrosity greeted our eyes—a straggling building in dirty white plastic which suggested the demesne of a mad market gardener who was specialising in asparagus. I could not believe my eyes. None of us could. We stood there mumchance and swallowing, wondering what the devil this construction was. Roberto, blushing and apologetic, told us.

So precious were the recently uncovered mosaics and so great the risk that they would be eaten into by the climate that someone had had the brilliant idea of covering them in this grotesque plastic housing through which a series of carefully arranged plankwalks and duckboards allowed the curious to walk around the villa. It was a groan-making thing to do and only an archaeologist could have thought of it. Moreover the mosaics, so interesting historically that one is glad to have made the effort to see them, are of a dullness extraordinary. But then the sort of people who build villas for Governors are for the most part interior decorators with a sense of grandiose banality, a sense of the expensively commonplace. Of such provenance is the Imperial Villa, though of course the number and clarity of the decorations merit interest despite their poor sense of plastic power. Historians must be interested in these elaborate hunting scenes, the warfare of Gods, and the faintly lecherous love scene which ends in a rather ordinary aesthetic experience. And all this in a white plastic housing which turned us all the colour of wax. Was this the pleasure dome of an Emperor, or was it perhaps (an intelligent suggestion by Christopher Kininmonth) more the millionaire's hideaway, constructed for the rich man who purveyed animals for the Roman arenas? The frescoes of animals are so numerous and their variety so great that it makes one pause and wonder. But as usual there is no proof of anything.

Dutifully we prowled the duckboards while Beddoes, who had culled a whole lot of Latin words from the Blue Guide, made up a sort of prose poem from fragments of it which he murmured aloud to himself in a vibrant tone of voice. Thus:

> And so we enter the Atrium
> By its purely polygonal court
> To the left lies the Great Latrine
> Ladies and Gents, the Great Latrine
> For those who are taken short
> But the marble seats are lost
> Yet ahead of us is the Aediculum
> Giving access to the Thermae
> The vestibule can be viewed from the Peristyle
> Do not smile.
> Next comes the frigidarium
> With its apodyteria
> Leading onwards with increasing hysteria
> To the Alepterion
> Between tepidarium and calidarium
> Whence into a court where the Lesser Latrine
> Waits for those who have not yet been

> *In construction sumptuous*
> *As befitted the Imperial Purple*

But here the Muse punished him and he wobbled off a duck-board and all but plunged down upon one of the more precious tessellations, to the intense annoyance of Roberto and the collective disapproval of the Carousel. The dentist's lady seemed particularly shocked and enraged and flounced about to register her disapproval. "That guy is sacrilegious," she told her companion with a venomous look at Beddoes who seemed only a very little repentant. Frescoed bathers massaged by slaves, animal heads bountifully crowned with laurel—yes, but it was a pity that so extensive and such energetic cartoons had not come from more practised or feeling hands. The commonplaceness of the whole thing hung about in the air; I was reminded suddenly of the interior decorations of the Castle of the Knights at Rhodes—which had been hatched by a Fascist Governor of the Dodecanese Islands who tried to echo the pretensions of Mussolini in this seat of government. The same empty banality—and here it was again—an echo from the last throes of the expiring Empire. "In richness and extent the villa can fairly be compared to Hadrian's villa at Tivoli or Diocletian's Palace at Split." I don't agree, but then who am I to say? The site alone militates against this opinion. These idle thoughts passed through my brain as we slowly negotiated the lesser latrine; "whose brick drain, marble hand-basin and pictorial decoration attest to the standards of imperial Roman comfort". Yes, but if it were just the home of the local Onassis of the day all would be clear.

The visit was long, it was thorough, and it explained why when Martine listed the places she wished that I might visit in order to write the "pocket" Sicily for her children, she had quite omitted to mention it. Perhaps she had just forgotten—such is the vast pro-lixity of memorable monuments in this island that one could be forgiven for simply forgetting one which made no particular mark on one's nervous system. I write these words, of course, subject to caution and with a certain diffidence, for the finds at the Imperial Villa, the most extensive in Europe, have become justly famous and it may well be that I am putting myself down as a hopeless Philistine. But I think not. And I am somewhat comforted by the fact that Deeds gave the place a very tentative marking in his little guide. But this he rather tended to explain away over the lunch table by saying that he was so deeply in love with the little red town of Aedoni which was a few kilometres off—and with the marvel-lous ancient Greek site of Morgantina—that all this heavy dun Roman stuff did not impress him. Indeed opinions were rather divided generally, and there were one or two of us who rather shared my view of the Villa. The dentist's lady was most unsparing in her open dislike for Beddoes who glimmered about everywhere like a dragonfly peering over people's shoulders and whispering things they didn't want to hear. "That man," she told her dentist at the lunch table, "is a pure desecrator." It was as good a way of viewing Beddoes as any we had invented, and her accent had an envenomed Mid-Western sting in it.

The lunch was toneless but the mountain air was fresh and we drank a good deal of wine with it; one had begun to feel rather fatigued, almost sleepy. We had been on the move for what seemed an age now, though in reality it was only a few days; but we had begun to feel the stress of travelling about, even over perfect roads, and being exposed the whole time to new sights and sounds. We took off languidly in the cool air, replete with wine, and for the most part with the intention of having a short doze as Mario nego-tiated the hairpins and forest roads on the way down to Agrigento.

The very old Italian couple who never spoke but tenderly held hands like newlyweds seemed in the seventh heaven of smiling joy. They sat back, quiet as apples, and smiled peacefully upon the world as it wheeled by. The little red bus chuckled and rippled its partridge-like way among the forests and pretty soon we once more came in view of the distant sea and the black smudges which marked the site of Gela. There was a good deal of fairly purposeful reafforestation among these cliffs and scarps but I was sorry to see to what extent the eucalyptus had been used, not because it isn't very beautiful as a tree—its shimmering spires of poplar-like green are handsome; but the shallow spread of its roots makes its demands for soil immoderate and nothing very interesting can be set beside it. I suppose that it was chosen precisely because the roots hold up the friable and easily washed-away soil. And Sicily has the same problems of reafforestation as Greece has.

And so from Caltanissetta the long downswing began into the plain where Gela lay; the sea-line today as misty and incoherent as only the heats of July can make it. Somewhere away to the left sweet Vittoria (another dream-town of Deeds which we were going to miss) whose smiling baroque remained to this day a suitable monument to the lady who founded the city, Vittoria della Colonna—was she not once Queen of Cyprus? The slopes lead enticingly downwards towards the Bay of Gela, one of the American landing places in 1943. The dust is rich in this long valley intersected by a number of lively rivers which seemed very high for the time of the year. For a long while, half dozing, we descended along the swaying roads through vineyards and clumps of cane, olive groves and extensive plantations of oranges. And at last of course we struck oil—as we neared the town which Aeschylus had chosen to spend his last years in, indeed to die in. There was probably a hotel named after him—there always is such a fitting memorial of the mercantile age we live in! The last whiff of the open country is soon extinguished at the approaches to this famous town whose great complex of petro-chemical installations seems to girdle it. There is little to see save what the museum has put on view—an extensive and fine historical collection of objects both votive and utilitarian. The bald skull of the Greek dramatist should perhaps have been among the relics? The legend says that an eagle mistook his skull for a stone and dropped a tortoise shell upon it in order to break it.

Now I took this story to be simply one of those literary fables with which we are so familiar until . . . one day in Corfu, long ago, I actually saw a big bird, perhaps a buzzard, doing exactly this, dropping shells from a great height, on to a seagirt rock and then coming down to inspect and peck. I watched it for over an hour and in all it tried out three or four different shells—they seemed to be clams of a sort, and not tortoises. Though a tortoise would be quite a logical animal for an eagle to sweep in its claws and try to crack apart in this fashion. One Doric column is all that is left unless you like a chunk of defensive ancient wall half silted into the sand. Oil rigs off the shore with their ominous message. But the sweep of the bay is in the grand style and even in the mess of modern Gela one sees how sweet a place it must have been, how rich in fruit and vine, and how splendid as horse-country because so well watered and green. Also it lay just back from the coast so that Syracuse and Akragas were in the front line as far as commerce and warfare were concerned; Gela must have been a little démodé, a little second-hand and old-fashioned, a fitting place for Pythagorean thinkers and poets who wanted a quiet life. At any rate that is what one feels even today. How ugly, though, they have allowed this important site to become (ah Demeter, where is your shrine!) with its haphazard modern development.

There was no time to go down to the sea for we were due in Agrigento that evening, so that after Gela we tumbled back into the bus and set off along the coastal road—the section leading us to Agrigento struck me as desolate and full of dirty sand-dunes; even melancholy, if you like, but not melancholy and depressing as some of the later stretches after Marsala. Perhaps it was the anticipation of the Vale of the Temples which lay ahead, or simply the sun made one drowsy and content to feel the ancient pulse-beat of the vanished Gela where now, off the coast, strange steel animals with long legs probed about like herons in a shallow lake. An idea came to me, and I jotted it down in order to chew it over later at leisure. (Before Christianity the sources of power were in magic, after it in money.) What is to be done? Nothing, it is too late.

On a remote country road, in the deep dust, we unexpectedly drew to a halt under a great carob-tree full of fruit, which is known as the locust-bean. There was an enclosure with trees and a wicket-gate behind which one could see a trimly laid-out little cemetery. This little halt had been organised specifically for Deeds by Roberto. It was a war-cemetery which came into his purlieu for inspection. Accordingly he somewhat apologetically took himself off in the direction of the British and Canadian graves, lighting a cigarette and promising us not to be long. Roberto turned us loose in the road and we straggled about for a while like lost sheep. I walked a little way and entered a vineyard where I found a patch of grass, almost burned brown by the summer heat. Here I lay down in its warm crackling cradle, dislodging swarms of crickets which hardly ceased their whirring as they retreated. The earth smelt delicious, baked to a cinder. Ants crawled over my face. In my heat-hazed mind dim thoughts and dreams and half-remembered conversations jumbled themselves together as a background to this throbbing summer afternoon with the cicadas fiddling away like mad in the trees. Every time a light patch of high cloud covered the sun the whole of nature fell silent—or at least the crickets did. Did they think that winter had suddenly returned? And when the heat was turned on again was I wrong to detect in their fervour a tremendous relief that such was not the case? I hovered on the edge of sleep and then called myself to attention, for the others did not know where I was and it would not do to miss the bus or keep poor Mario fretting and scowling by being late.

I hoisted myself sleepily to my feet and crossed the field back to the road where Roberto, who had been trying to explain something about the carob-tree to the rest of the party, had run into vocabulary trouble. Here I could help a little, for these great strong carob-trees were a handsome feature of Cyprus with their long curving bean. When wind or lightning broke a branch of the tree one was always surprised to see that the wood revealed was the colour of human flesh. The locust-bean, Roberto was trying to explain, was highly nutritious. He was picking a few—they were dry and snapped between his teeth— and handing them round for the party to try. We had often done this on picnics in the past and I was pleased once more to make the acquaintance of this noble tree whose produce is "kibbled" (an absurd word) very extensively in Cyprus for animal fodder. By now Deeds had sauntered back to us in time to take the long seed in his fingers and try it with his teeth. "Can I bore you with a story?" he asked diffidently. "Some of the boys in that cemetery came from a commando I trained in Cyprus. Now among our training tips was to keep an eye wide open for carobs if short of food. You can live almost indefinitely on carob-seed and water, and for a commando in this theatre it was most essential gen. In fact several of those men were lost between the lines during the first assault for about ten days, without rations of any sort. But they found fresh springs and they found locust-beans and lived to tell the tale. Alas, they were killed later in a counter-attack. But if we had been training a commando in the U.K. we would have forgotten about the nutritive qualities of the carob. I always think of Cyprus in those days when I inspect this little cemetery." He had been quite a time and seemed a trifle sad, and somewhat glad to pile back into the bus with us and start off again down the long roads which led onwards to Agrigento and the Temples which for Martine (and not ruling out Taormina) had been the great Sicilian experience. So on we sped now, eating carobs.

The land had gone yellower and more ochreous, the valleys had become longer and more spacious. It had a feel of wildness. But there were strings of lorries loaded with dust-producing chemicals which floated off into the air and powdered the bus until Mario swore and shook his fist at them. Somewhere some Herculean constructions were being mounted—I hoped it was not Agrigento which had come under the scourge of urbanisation. On one of these long declines we slowed down for an accident involving a lorry and a large sports car. A very definitive accident for the sports car with its occupant still in it had been pushed right into the ditch on one side, while the lorry responsible for the push had itself subsided like an old camel into the ditch on the opposite side. As in all scenes of terror and dismay everything seemed to have settled into a sort of timeless tableau. The police had not yet arrived. Someone had covered the form of the lorry driver with a strip of sacking— just a bare foot sticking out.

But the occupant of the sports car was a handsome blond youth, and he was lying back in his seat as if replete with content, with sunlight, with wine. The expression on his face was one of benign calm, of beatitude. He wore a blue shirt open at the throat.

There was no disorder in his dress, nor was he marked by the collision; he seemed as if asleep. The light wind ruffled a strand of blond hair on his forehead to complete the illusion of life, but the little man whose stethoscope was planted inside his blue shirt over the heart, was shaking his head and making the traditional grimace of doctors the world over. The front of the sports car, the whole engine, was crumpled up like a paper bag. Yet there was no blood, no disorder; the young man had simply ceded to the demands of fate. It was a death by pure concussion. He lay, as if in his coffin, while around him stood a group of half a dozen peasants who might have been chosen by a dramatist to give point and resonance to this classical accident in which so unexpectedly death had asserted itself. No one cried or beat his breast; the women had drawn the corner of their headshawls into their mouths and held them between white firm teeth—as if by this gesture to allay the possibility of tears. Two peasants, with mattocks held lightly in hands wrinkled as ancient tortoises, stared at the young man and his sumptuous car as one might stare (the operative phrase is perhaps "drink in") at a holy painting above an altar. Their black eyes brimmed with incomprehension. They did not try to understand this phenomenon—a dead boy in a brilliantly coloured car with yellow suede upholstery. But there was no sorrow, no breast beating, no frantic curiosity such as there would have been in the north or in Greece. Nobody crossed themselves. They simply stared, without curiosity, indeed with a kind of stern bravado. You felt that they and death were equals. It was simply that the island had struck home once more. This was Sicily! And one realised that even death had a different, a particularly Sicilian resonance. The groups of black eyes remained fixed and unwinking whereas the Greek or Italian eye is forever darting about, restless as a fly. In the background there was an older man with a mane of white hair, who stared as hard as the others—indeed with such concentration that his little pink tongue-tip stuck out and gave him an absurdly childish expression. But no fear.

It was we in the bus who felt the fear—you could see gloom and dismay on every visage as Mario drew up in a swirl of whiteness and leaned out to inform himself of the circumstances. Was there anything we could do? Nothing. An ambulance was on the way from Agrigento, also the police. The doctor with his open shirt looked more like a youthful vet. He had managed to edge his tiny Fiat right off the road into a nook while he examined the young man in the car. Nobody used the word for death either: the fact was conveyed with gestures of the fingers or the head. The whole thing was amazingly studied; it was as if all of us, even us in the bus, had been chosen by a dramatist to fill a part in this tableau.

The Bishop had put on an expression which read as: I told you so. He seemed rather like the chief cashier of a great Bank (Death Inc.) who had a good deal of inside knowledge. The old Italian apple-people stayed quietly smiling; perhaps they did not understand or remained locked in their dream of Eden. Renata, the German girl, closed her eyes and turned her head away. Miss Lobb looked severe, as if it reflected discredit on the tourist company to let people who had paid good money suddenly come up against this kind of thing. Beddoes straightened an imaginary tie furtively; you could see that death was for him a headmaster in Dungeness. How did I look? I caught sight of my reflection in the dusty glass and thought I looked a trifle sick—I certainly felt it; it was so unexpected on that brilliant afternoon with the sun sliding down into the mist-blue waters of the Underworld. Would we arrive before dark? We had gathered speed now, and had at last cleared the long file of lorries which were causing all the dust. The air was dry and hot; the limestone configuration of the land spoke of water and green, of spring and rivers and friendly nightingales. Deeds seemed rather remote and preoccupied by his own thoughts and I did not subject him to mine which as usual were rather incoherent and muddled—across the screens of memory old recollections of Athens and the islands came up like friendly animals to be recognised and stroked. Yes, we were in Attica, there was no doubt about it; just north of the capital, say in Psychico or perhaps east near Porto Rafti. . . . I must not hurt Roberto's patriotic feelings by all my Greek chatter. Sicily after all belonged to neither Greece nor to Italy now (geographical frontiers mean nothing) but strictly to itself, to its most ancient and indestructible self. On we sped, skimming the hills like a swallow.

It came in sight slowly, the famous city; at first as a series of suggestive shapes against the evening sky, then as half dissolved forms which wobbled in the heat haze to settle at last firmly into the cubist boxes of a modern city—and with at least two small skyscrapers to mark the ancient (I supposed) Acropolis. But as we approached, a black cloud of a particularly heavy and menacing weight began to obscure the sun. It was very strange—the whole of heaven was, apart from this cloud, serene, void and blue. It was as if the thing had got left over from some old thunderstorm and lay there undissolved, drifting about the sky. It was not to be regretted as it was obviously going to cause a dramatic sunset, threshing out the sun's rays, making it seem like the lidless dark eye of a whale from which stray beams escaped. If I make a point of this little departure from the norm of things it is because as we journeyed along we saw to our left a small cottage perched on a headland with two wind-bent pines outside it—the whole hanging there over the sea, as if outside the whole of the rest of nature. There was no other sign of human habitation save this desolate and memorable little cottage. With the black sunlight it looked deeply tragically significant, as if it were the backdrop for a play. Hardly anybody paid attention to the little scene, but Roberto with an air of sadness, announced over the speaker: "The birthplace of Pirandello. A little hamlet called Chaos!" He looked at his watch. The museum would be shut he thought. Perhaps one might just stop for a moment? If the idea was tentative it was because he knew that hardly anyone in the bus knew or cared much about this great man, this great original poet of Agrigento. We risked, by a detour, to arrive a trifle late and perhaps prejudice a trip to the valley of the Temples which were floodlit at night. Would anybody care to . . . but only three or four hands were raised so it was decided to press on.

Meanwhile, staring across the dusty *bled* on my left I saw the sunbeams lengthen and sink, like stage-lights being lowered for a play, while suddenly from the beaches behind the silhouette came a stream of grinding labouring lorries, like a string of ants upon a leaf. I suppose they were doing nothing more sinister than bringing up sea sand from the beaches, but the clouds of whiteness they sent swirling heavenwards contained so many tones of pearl, yellow, amber that the whole display, with the sunlight shining through it, was worthy of a nervous breakdown by Turner. It made my heart beat faster, it was memorable and at the same time a little ominous—as if by it we were warned not to take the famous city we were about to visit too lightly. To bring to it our real selves. Yet it was all over in a matter of half a minute, but it had a sort of finalising effect on our decision, for we turned our backs upon this vision and set about climbing into the sky, towards the town whose shabby outlines and haphazard building became slowly more and more evident as we advanced. Roberto uttered its name with a small sigh of fatigue.

I had not conveyed my impressions to Deeds believing him to be otherwise occupied, but the all-seeing eye had taken in the headland and he said now: "Pity about Pirandello. The little museum is very touching. But what a strange light. And the small scale is striking—like the humbleness of Anne Hathaway's cottage." It was an apt comment on the origins of greatness.

But by now the cloud had mysteriously vanished backstage and all was serene, a transparent, cloudless dusk with no trace of wind; and as we followed the curves and slants of the road up to the town it became slowly obvious that what was being unfolded before us and below us was a most remarkable site. Successive roundels led in a slow spiral up to the top of the steep hillock upon which once an Acropolis had perched, and where now two parvenu skyscrapers stood and an ignoble huddle of unwarranted housing did duty for the old city's centre. We had reached by now the commercial nexus of the new town which lies a bit below the city, makeshift and ugly. But the light was of pure opalescent honey, and the setting (I am sorry to labour the point) was Hymettus at evening with the violet city of Athens sinking into the cocoon of night. I tremble also to insist on the fact that from the point of view of natural beauty and elegance of site Agrigento is easily a match for Athens on its hills. Just as the ocean throws up roundels of sand to form pools, so the successive ages of geological time had thrown up successive rounds of limestone, rising in tiers like a wedding-cake to the Acropolis. From the top one looks down as if into a pie-dish with two levels, inner and outer ridges. It is down there, at the entrance to the city, that all the Temples are situated, like a protective screen, tricked out with fruit orchards, with sweeps of silver olives, and with ubiquitous almond trees whose spring flowering has become as famous as the legendary town itself.

We climbed down into the twilight with a strange feeling of indecision, not knowing exactly what was in store for us. It was only after a brief walk across a square, when we found ourselves looking down into the tenebrous mauve bowl where the Temples awaited us that we realised that our arrival at that precise time was an act of thoughtful good sense on the part of Roberto. "Before the city lights go on you may see more or less how the classical city looked at sunset." The air was so still up here that one could catch the distant sounds of someone singing and the noise perhaps of a mattock on the dry clay a mile below us. At our back the streets were beginning to fill up for the evening Corso, the tiny coffee-shops to brim over with lights which seemed, by contagion, to set fire at last to the street-lamps behind our backs and set off the snarling radios and juke-boxes and traffic noise. Ahead of us the darkness rose slowly to engulf us, like ink being poured into a well; but it was a light darkness, slightly rosy, as if from a hidden harvest moon. But we belonged to the scattered disoriented city now with its stridulations of juke.

We were about to turn away from this slowly overwhelming darkness and back into the raucous streets when Roberto, who still peered keenly down the valley, implored a moment's patience of us, for what reason I could not tell. He seemed as keyed up as if we were to expect something like a firework display. But it was better than that; presently there came the swift wingbeats of a church-bell which sounded like a signal and soundlessly the temples sprang to floodlit life all together, as if by a miracle. This was aerial geography with a vengeance, for they were to be our after-dinner treat tonight! But there were signs of raggedness and fatigue in the party and I could see that some of us might prefer to stay in the hotel and sleep. The Count's wife looked really ill with weariness and I wondered why they had embarked her on such a journey.

Mrs. Microscope too looked crusty though we had had no more news of her spleen. But there was to be a bit of delay as yet for our schedule called for half an hour's shopping halt in the town, to enable us to buy curios and generally take a look round. Not all set off for this treat; many stayed in the bus. While, rather cowardly, I took myself off with Deeds to a *bistro* where I anticipated dinner and the fatigues of temple-haunting by a couple of touches of *grappa* which was like drinking fumed oak in liquid form. Heartening stuff. Deeds fell into conversation with a eunuchoid youth who brought us coffee with a kindly but disenchanted air.

In the far corner, however, there was a small group of middle-aged to elderly men who attracted my instant attention by their hunched-up look and their black clothes and battered boots. They were gnarled and leathered by their avocation—could they have been coal-miners, I wondered? Dressed awkwardly in their Sunday best with heavy dark suits and improbable felt hats which looked as if very seldom worn. Or perhaps they were mourners attending the funeral of some local dignitary? They spoke in low gruff tones and in a dialect Italian. The sister of the eunuch served them exclusively and with such obvious nervousness that I finally concluded that they must be a group of Mafia leaders on a Sunday outing. Their little circle exuded a kind of horrid Protestant gloom, and most of their faces were baneful, ugly. They were drinking Strega as far as I could make out, but the massive sugar content was not making them any sweeter. It was a strange little group and all the other customers of the place beside ourselves shot curious glances at them, wondering I suppose like ourselves, what and from where. . . . The mystery was only cleared up when Roberto appeared in search of a quick coffee and caught sight of us. He seemed not unprepared for the question and it was clear from his way of looking at them when Deeds pointed them out that they did seem singular, almost like another race. But no, that was not the case. They were simply sulphur-miners on a night out in town.

"They are Zolfataioi," said Roberto with a smile. "We have been shielding you from the uglier side of Sicily, but we have our own black country here like you have; only it's not black, it's yellow. The sulphur-workers live a sort of grim separate life except for their occasional excursions like this—though it's usually to Caltanissetta that they go. It's the headquarters of the trade." The men looked as if they were waiting anxiously for transport and those at the two tables playing cards were doing so abstractedly, as if marking time. They were as impressively different from the other Italians as would have been, say, a little group of Bushmen, or Japanese. But they drank with precision. One of the elder ones with a leather face and expressionless eyes had the knack of tilting and emptying his glass in a single gesture, without swallowing. He looked like Father Time himself, drinking a whole hourglass of time at each quaff. I watched them curiously.

At that moment there came a diversion in the form of a large grey sports car which drew up outside the café. From it descended a couple of extremely well-dressed and sophisticated youths of a vaguely Roman allure—I put them down as big-city pederasts having a holiday here. But their manner was offensively superior and they acted as if they owned the place. They were fashionably clad in smart coloured summer wear and open collars, while their hair was handsomely styled and curled. They wanted to leave a message for some local boy and they engaged the flustered eunuch in conversation. Meanwhile, and the touch had a somewhat special insolence, they had left the car's engine running so that the exhaust was belching noisome fumes on to the terrace and into the café itself. One felt resentful; it was as if they were deliberately flaunting not only their classical proclivities but their superiority as well. Their tones were shrill and their Italian of the cultivated sort.

Their arrival produced a little ripple of interest in the circle of sulphur-miners, though the general tone was apathetic and not resentful. They eyed these two butterflies in their expressionless way and then looked at one another with a kindly irony. It was not malicious at all. Then the old man set down his tiny Strega glass and, wiping his moustache, said in a firm audible tone, *"Ah! pederastici!"* It was not offensive, simply an observation which classified the two, who must have overheard for they shrugged their shoulders and turned back to the eunuch with more questions about their friend Giovanni. Moreover the word fell upon the silence with a fine classical limpidity—five lapidary syllables. It was perfectly summed up and forgotten—the whole incident. The one eloquent word was enough. No further comment was needed, and the miners turned back to their inner preoccupations and sank ever deeper into their corporate reserve while the two turkeys gobbled on.

> *A Greek root with*
> *A Latin suffix*
> *A Grecian vice*
> *A Latin name*

But at last it was time to take ourselves off to the gaunt restaurant where a single long dinner-table had been prepared for us. There were to be some casualties among us, and about six of the wearier, as predicted, decided on an early night. We were anyway to have another look at the Temples by daylight on the morrow so that they were not to lose very much. It was only annoying for Mario, for the hotel was in the valley, some way off, and he would have to ferry them and then come back and ferry us to the Temples, going without dinner in the process. But he took it all with grave good humour and that undemonstrative courtesy that I was beginning to recognise as a thoroughly Sicilian trait. The weary therefore moved off, content to eat a sandwich in bed, while we doubled up our ranks and did our best to look joyfully surprised by yet another choice between spaghetti and rice. But the wine was good in its modest way. And we did full justice to it telling ourselves that we owed it to our fatigue, though Roberto warned us that we were only going to have a sniff at the Temples and not attempt to "do" them thoroughly until tomorrow. It was to see them floodlit, that was all. But how grateful one finally was for the glimpse, however brief, and how sorry one felt for the absentees.

We had hardly finished dinner when impassive Mario appeared with the bus and we were on the way down the hill, curving away upon the so-called *passegiata archeologica,* a beautiful modern road which winds in and out of the temple circles; one by one these great landmarks came out of the night to meet us, while a thousand night insects danced in the hot light of the floods. The bare ground—yes, it smelt of Attica again. The whiffs of thyme and sage, and the very soil with its light marls and fawn-coloured tones made the island itself seem like some huge abstract terracotta which by some freak of time might give birth to vases, amphorae, plates, craters. An ancient Athenian must have walked here with the sympathetic feeling of being back in Athens. And it was extraordinary to realise that this huge expanse of temples represented only a tiny fraction of what exists here in reality, and which remains to be unearthed. The archaeologists have only scratched the surface of Agrigento; stretching away on every side, hidden in the soft deciduous chalk through which the twin rivers have carved their beds, there lie hidden necropolises, aqueducts, houses and temples and statues as yet quite unknown to us; and all the wealth inside them of ceramics and jewellery and weapons. It seems so complete as it is, this long sparkling ridge with its tremendous exhibits. Yet Agrigento has hardly begun to yield up all its treasures, and in coming generations what is unearthed might well modify all our present ideas about it. Long shadows criss-crossed the night. Leaving the glare of the floods one was at once plunged into dense patches of fragrant darkness. There was another busload of dark figures round the Temple of Concord, all down on their knees. Were they praying? It seemed so.

In the circumstances, with the massive and blinding whiteness of the floodlights, the magical temple looking down upon us from some unimaginable height of centuries, the activity of the group of persons clustering about the stylobate, kneeling, bending, crawling, seemed to suggest that they were engaged in some strange archaic rite. Was it a propitiatory dance of some sort, an invocation to the God of the site? But no, the explanation was more prosaic. Yet before it was given to us the strangeness of the scene was increased by the fact that, as we approached upon the winding paths, punctuated by lanterns, we saw that they were Asiatics— Chinese I thought. Their faces were white in the white light, and their eyes had disappeared with the intensity of their concentration upon the ground. Our groups mingled for a moment to wander about on this extraordinary headland over the brimming darkness of the valley. Their guide was an acquaintance of Roberto's and provided a clue as to the mysterious behaviour of his group. Two of the more ardent photographers had lost their lens caps and everyone was trying to help them recover these valuable items. It was extremely hard. The floods were pouring up into the sky with such power that unless one was directly in their ray one could see nothing, one became a one-dimensional figure, a silhouette. They cast an absolutely definitive black shadow.

Even if you held out your hand in the light the underneath, the shadowy side, was plunged into total blackness. Thus to pick up something small from the ground just outside the arc of white light presented extraordinary difficulties. Which explained all the crouching stooping peering people. Standing off a little from them, feeling the velvety warmth of the night upon my cheek, I felt grateful to have outgrown the desire to photograph things; I had once been a keen photographer and had even sold my work. Now I preferred to try and use my eyes, at first hand, so to speak, and to make my memory do some work. In a little schoolchild's exercise book I occasionally made a note or two for the pleasure of trying to draw; and then later I might embark on a water-colour which, by intention, would try to capture the mood or emotion of a particular place or incident. It was a more satisfactory way of going about things, more suitable to my present age and preoccupations. The photograph was always a slightly distorted version of the subject; whereas the painting made no pretensions to being anything more than a slightly distorted version of one's feelings at a given moment in time.

Our Japanese couple seemed disposed to exchange a word with the Chinese, but the attempt made no headway and they retired into their shell once more, having pronounced the other group to be North Koreans. Some of us, with simulated good will, tried to join in the search for a moment, but it did not last long for we were now a little tired. Indeed we were glad to regain the bus, and after one more brilliant glimpse to coast quietly down the sloping roads towards the hotel where doubtless the others were already fast asleep. Fatigue lengthens distance mentally—we felt now as if we had been to the moon and back. And yet, despite it, a queer sense of elation and of freshness co-existed with the fatigue. The darkness was sort of translucent, the air absolutely warm and still; the hotel was rather a grand affair pitched at a main cross roads and obviously laid out for tourism. There was a huge swimming pool, and its lights were still on. A few people still lounged by it in deck-chairs or swam; and so warm was it that several of our party, notably the German girl and her boy friend, elected to have a dip before going to bed. I hesitated but finally decided upon a whisky on the balcony before turning in; Deeds had retired sleepily, and I did not fancy the company of Beddoes who had doubtless been peering through keyholes already.

In the little file there were no letters actually written from Agrigento though she had had plenty to say about the place which she had visited on numerous occasions with her little car. "In early February it is pure wedding-cake with the almond blossom of three tones and the fabulous later flowering of an occasional Judas. That is the real time to come, though of course it will be still too cold to swim." I had missed it, but I already had the configurations of the Temple hills clearly in mind and could visualise easily how they must look—like a series of flowered panels, Chinese water-colours, with the mist-mauve sea behind. From my balcony I could sit in the warmth of the scented night and see the distant moth-soft dazzle of the temples crowning the lower slopes of Agrigento; immediately underneath me in loops of artificial light swam the fish-white bodies of northern bathers who as yet had not become nut-brown with Sicilian sunlight. A slight splashing and the murmur of voices was rather agreeable from the second storey of this comfortable if nondescript building. I read for a little while, dipping here and there among the letters to recover references to the temples, and listening with half an ear to the voices in the pool. "Whole conversations at Bellapais in Cyprus came back to me when

I visited the Temples at night—they have only just started to flood-light them, and the result is marvellous—the whole of nature takes part; every insect in creation, every moth and butterfly comes rushing to this great kermess of light, like people impelled to go to war, only to perish in the arcs. In the morning they are swabbed off with cloths. I picked up a most beautifully marked moth which looked as if it came from India specially to see Pythagoras or the other one—who is it? The one you find so great with his two-stroke universe, operating like a motor-bike on the Love and Hate principle? O and yes, when I saw the ring of the temples, the so obviously defensive ring of them here on the outer slopes of the town I thought of your notions of ancient banking."

It was not simply banking, though we had canvassed pretty thoroughly the notion of the temple as a safe-deposit of values, both sacred and profane. I had been trying to sort out some muddy notions about the idea of Beauty, and its origins in history and myth. You could not well take on a more intractable field to hoe—for we cannot even establish a working notion which defines excellence ("purity of function?" "congruence?") let alone something as absolute as an aesthetic ideal of Beauty. Greece was an appropriate place to chew such an idea to death, since it was in Greece that all these unanswerable questions had first been ventilated. But riffling a large book of ancient Greek sites drawn and described for architects I had been struck by the frequency with which the temple or the sacred fane had found its place, not in the interior of the city or fortress, but along its defensive walls. The temples with their magical properties were a more efficacious defence against piracy in a world of superstition than bolts and bars and moats even. And thinking over the theory of value as another mystery of our time (unless you accept the Freudian or Marxian notions which oppose each other) it seemed to me that in ancient times the whole notion of sacred and profane had not been separated; the riches of the temple were protective; and a site protected by the magic of its temples and its Gods would encourage investment in the form of artisanship—workers in metal and precious stones and furs. The numen would protect them and let them work in peace, while in their turn they would render the city rich and notable with their products. There was an underground connection between the Bank and the Temple and it has cropped up over and over again. In the Middle Ages the Order of Templars, themselves vowed to frugality and poverty, became the bankers of kings, and their temples the actual banks where treasure was deposited for safety.

The Greek temple implicated the whole of nature in its magical scheme—the world of animals as well as Gods. The notion of value was twofold, namely, material gain and also a degree of beauty which enslaved and ennobled, which enchanted and enriched on the spiritual plane. But how inadequate words were when it came to trying to point up the difference between these two degrees of excellence. There was, however, a continuity between the Greek temple with its ex-votoes and the modern Christian or Orthodox Church with its same pathetic objects of gratitude or propitiation. And the notion of beauty worshipped in icons, in paintings, in holy relics. One thinks of the golden statue that Cicero found "beslubbered by the kisses of the faithful who loved its unique beauty"; today the icon is still kissed, but not for its beauty. For its power.

Martine took the idea and played with it for a while, making fun of my woolliness and vagueness—it is impossible to be too precise, for so many fragments of the jigsaw are missing. Everything is supposition.

But we have had enough experience now of the thought-schemes of savages to be thoroughly on our guard when it comes to trying to imagine how primitive peoples think, how they associate. Were the ancient Greeks, with their highly organised and, to them, very logical superstitious systems, any different? I don't think so. Why, the notion of gold being valuable may well have come from the first golden Aryan head which the Greeks saw, with its marvellous buttercup sheen. The men went mad over this hypothetical girl—Circassian or Scythian or British perhaps? Gentlemen preferred blondes even then, so it became necessary to manufacture golden wigs, or tresses of beaten filigree gold as a head ornament. We know that prostitutes in ancient Athens were forbidden by law to imitate the blandishments of respectable married women by wearing rich gold ornaments, fillets or clips, in their hair. That is probably why they set about finding cheap dyes in order to effect a transformation that was legitimate. They tried saffron and, like the modern Egyptian of the poorer classes, common soap with its strong bleaching agent. The story of Goldilocks. A theory of how beauty came to be evaluated. But where, then, did the metal come into this scheme of things? These matters we used to argue to the point of sheer irritation with each other. In one of her letters she records our violent disagreements.

"I couldn't help thinking of you and your wretched relativity notions the other evening when I went to see Loftus Adam who now lives here, just down the coast from me. He too said how irritated you made him by trying to subject everything to the merely provisional: and all truth as subject to scale. Yet he himself at last admitted that if you selected your co-ordinates you could prove anything from any evidence; he wants to write a modern history of Europe based on three co-ordinates, namely the moustaches of Hitler, Marinetti and Chaplin, which have formed our unhappy age. They were all the same little smudge moustache which must prove something. And between them the new European sensibility was forged and founded. It sounds highly fanciful but why not? He is going to call the book *THE MOUSTACHE; and why*".

I went to sleep quite late that night and had a dream in which I recovered the name of the philosopher which had escaped her— the great Empedocles who was a native of the town and around whose name and memory gathered so many tales of necromancy and witchcraft as to almost obscure his real fame as a philosopher as eminent and as fruitful as any of the great men of his time. Is it nothing to have won the respect of Aristotle, or to have influenced Lucretius? Moreover enough of his system remains extant today for our scholars to evaluate and describe. Why has he been written off as a mythomane? In the case of Bertrand Russell the reason is plain; great as Russell is, he was, in the affective and intuitional sense, colour-blind. He is no poet but a geometer. And it was inevitable, given the type of temperament that was his, that he should be as unfair to Plato as he was to Empedocles. Then one recalls the gibes and sneers of Epicurus when he referred to Plato's attempts to systematise reality and to comprehend nature. To him everything that Plato beheld was the purest illusion, the purest self-deceit. He believed in a world which held no mysteries and in consequence no great dangers. Temperamentally Empedocles lies on a tangent between the absolute behaviourism of one and the pure subjective vision of the other. To each his truth, and *qui verra vivra* to adapt the phrase to suit philosophers who are also visionaries (charlatans to the Russells of this world and the last). The two functions, however, the two arts of deduction and of intuitive vision must be complementary at some remove. Plato to Aristotle, Freud to Jung. . . . In this sharp diversity is born the marriage of true minds.

For Empedocles also the world was arranged in not too mysterious a fashion, though it was far from an impulse-inhibition machine run by invisible and soulless engineers. One could best comprehend it as a sphere ceaselessly agitated by two primordial impulses or dispositions which in turn acted upon four primary roots of all being—fire, air, water, earth. This joining and separating motor (the Love and Strife machine) in its quite involuntary convulsions manipulated matter and shook it out in a million differentiated patterns and mixtures like a kaleidoscope shakes out pictures at the slightest jog. The arch-movers of all process were Love and Hate—the joining and separating impulses. The domination of one or the other produced quite recognisable effects in nature, alloys of the four basic elements. It seems fair enough.

The original condition of matter was to be envisaged as a sphere in which Love played the dominant role and where the four basic elements were perfectly accorded and mixed. Into this primordial harmony entered the principle of Strife which set off the whole dance of process and foxed up the original harmony of things. First air became separated, then fire, then earth—the motion acted like a milk-separator, forging unexpected unities and dissonances; and the effects of these changes were reflected in every department of man's life and thoughts. Quantity was all-important—a hint perhaps of a Pythagorean influence? The present world—the world he knew and which has not noticeably changed since his time—is a theatre where Love is being everywhere assailed by Strife; and where Strife becomes dominant species and sexes become separated, lose their coherence and identity—it is matter in a state of hysteria. But at the other end of the cosmic seesaw—for the gain of one element turns to loss by overplus and gives ground to its opposite—the overwhelming force of undiluted love could bring about bizarre physiological changes in nature. Empedocles, in his vision of the disorder brought about by the mixture of unequal quantities of the four elements, speaks about separate limbs being begotten, arising and walking around, as in the canvases of Dali; hands without shoulders and necks, bodies without hands. And all sorts of singular combinations, like oxen with human heads, fishes with breasts, lions with hands, birds with ears. . . . A chaos of undifferentiated forms ruled.

But nature aspired to the functioning rule of the sphere, and only the sphere mixed the elements rightly, in the proper proportion and harmony. Yet the slightest push from one side or the other and one got an imbalance in nature which only hazard could redress. This then was the reality of things as we were living it, for we were part and parcel of the whole convulsion, our thoughts and feelings were all influenced by it. As for thought, Empedocles was convinced that we think with our blood, and more especially with the blood around the heart, because in the blood here all the elements are more correctly fused than in other sectors of the body. What is endearing, and indeed peculiarly modern, is his interest in embryology and in the growth-systems of plants; whenever possible he drew his analogies from this department of knowledge. For him thought and perception were materially functions of our bodily constitution. All this was down to earth, was perfectly functional, was the fruit of sweet reason and not of fantasy; somewhere at heart he was temperamentally akin to Epicurus.

Yet in spite of this rational disposition the visions kept intervening—Nature kept unfolding itself before his eyes, delivering its secrets to his curious and poetic mind. By some strange alchemy, too, he somehow managed to include a purely Orphic notion about the transmigration of souls into his system, where it sits somehow awkwardly. But so much of his work is missing that it is really a miracle that the extant remnants present as coherent a view of things as they do. It is rather like trying to reassemble a beautiful vase from a few recovered bits and pieces of it—the task which faces the archaeologist. Inevitably there will be here and there a shard which does not fit. In the case of this great man I was always struck by the fact that he felt that he himself had forfeited the final happiness; he describes himself as an "exile from a possible Bliss", because he had put his trust in "senseless strife". Was there any way to escape from such spiritual contamination? Apparently there was—by fasting, abstention from animal flesh, and the performance of certain mystical rites. . . .

For him also the first completely realised forms to grow on earth were trees in whom male and female sexuality were so perfectly conjoined. And so on. Apparently the intoxication of these high thoughts was matched by a brilliant fuliginous style which made Aristotle christen him the first of rhetoricians or the father of rhetoric.

Yes, it is not hard to see why the notions of magic, of necromancy, clung to the name of old Empedocles—one thinks of his final leap into the maw of Etna. A suitable way for a great magician to take his leave of his fellow Sicilians. But the truth appears to be that he actually died far away, in the Peloponnesus. He must have been a very dramatic figure, this great rhetor, poet, visionary. In my mind's eye I see always someone of the aspect of the modern Greek poet Sikelianos, who so charmed and bewildered us all with his strange mixture of greatness and histrionic absurdity. He became as much beloved for his aberrations and exaggerations as for his truly great verse which he insisted on declaiming at gale force and with gestures—which so often all but disguised its real merits. He too chose "big" subjects like his contemporary Kazantzakis—St. Paul, Buddha, Socrates. . . . They were grist to his poetic mill. I remember how Martine used to adore anecdotes about the Greek poets of our time—she was fully aware of their European stature in a period when Greece had yet to find its immortal echo outside Athens and Alexandria. Sikelianos at that time was already a walking reincarnation of an ancient God. He had founded the Delphic festival not as a piece of tourist folklore but, in true Empedoclean fashion, because he believed that the spirit of place was ever present, and that Delphi despite its silenced shrine of the Pythea was still pregnant with life. The meeting of great European minds at this sacred spot could have an incalculable effect on the poetic destiny of Europe—so he thought. He did not lack detractors, as may be imagined; but the incontestable greatness of his poetry silenced them. But sometimes he got so carried away by his vatic role that people thought of him as a mountebank. Yet the peasants at Delphi saw him as a sort of magician of today.

He was a strange mixture of vagueness and gentleness; and his great unassuming physical beauty made one sit up, as if in the presence of the Marashi. Nor was he foreign to the most endearing absurdities. One hopes that there will soon be a biography to enshrine the many anecdotes born of his flamboyant life and thought. One that Martine particularly enjoyed was concerned with death, for old Sikelianos believed so firmly in the absoluteness of poetic power that he went so far as to declare that a great poet could do anything, even bring a dead man to life by the power of his mind and vision. He was rather belabouring this theme while sitting in a little taverna, having dinner with Kazantzakis and, I think, Seferis, when the waiter, who had been listening to him with sardonic disgust stepped forward and informed him that someone had just died on the second floor, and if he wished to prove his point he had a subject right under his hand. Everyone smiled at this but Sikelianos appeared enchanted with the chance to show, not his own greatness, for he was a modest man, but the greatness which resides in poetry. Moreover he believed in what he said, he could bring the dead man back to life as he had promised. They did not ask how he proposed to do such a thing. But anyway, the poet rose and asked to be taken to the room where the corpse lay. In a resigned mood the others continued their dinner; they were not entirely unconvinced that the old poet might, by some feat of magic, actually be as good as his word and make the dead man breathe again. But he was a long time gone. They listened but there was no sound of poetic declamation. He must have chosen some other method of raising the dead. Well, after quite a time a crestfallen Sikelianos made his appearance once more, deeply disappointed. Pouring himself a glass of wine he said: "Never have I seen such sheer obstinacy!" He was very sad about the failure of the Muse to come to his aid.

This was the delightful man whom once Seferis brought to meet me—indeed it was to chide me for a bad translation of one of his great poems. I was terrified, but he rapidly put me at my ease by his gentleness. He had just come from the doctor where he had been informed that he was in danger of a thrombosis. A vein in the brain. . . . But far from being despondent he was wild with elation. "Think of it," he said to Seferis, "a little gleaming swelling in there, shining like a *ruby*!" And he placed his long index finger upon the supposed place in his skull where the swollen vein was situated. He should have disappeared into Etna like Empedocles, or have been found half-eaten by the Minotaur in Crete, or suffocated by the Pythean fumes at Delphi. But his death was the more tragic for being so banal. He suffered from a chronic sore throat and to soothe it drank quantities of a glycerine mixture the name of which differed by one letter from that of Lysol. He sent a boy out to the pharmacy for a bottle of his medicine and by a tragic mishearing the boy bought instead a bottle of the poisonous detergent.

Without thinking the poet raised the bottle as he had always done with his throat mixture and half drained it before he realised the full horror of what he had done. By then it was too late.

I could not sleep, with all these thoughts fluttering about in my mind. I lay for a while on the balcony quietly breathing in the warm unmoving night air; it was strangely light, too, as if from somewhere offstage there was a bronze moon filtering its light through the vapours of the night. But before I realised it the dawn had suddenly started to come up, the distant sea-lines to separate from the earth like yolk from white of the cosmic egg. The hills with their soft chalk tones rose slowly, tier upon tier, to where the city stood once more revealed with its two baleful skyscrapers. But an infinity of pink and fawn light softened every outline, even the huge boxlike structures looked well. I slipped down and coaxed the night porter to open the changing-room door; the pool was delicious, not a tremor of coolness. I was swimming in something the temperature of mammals' blood.

Yes, Sikelianos belonged to that old assured classical world where only great men wrote great poetry—there was an assumed connection between the power to write and orate great verse and the power to be morally and psychically superior to one's fellow men. Greatness, though thrust upon one by the Muse, did not absolve one from being a great example to one's fellows. An epic grandeur of style was believed to match an epic grandeur of insight and thought. They were another race these men—they were bards, whose sensibilities worked in every register, from uplift to outrage. The poet was not cursed, but blessed in his insight; and his themes must be equal to his mighty line. It is probably a fallacy to imagine that with the Symbolistes, with Baudelaire, there comes a break and the poet becomes a passive object of suffering, a sick man, a morally defective man like Rimbaud, like Leopardi. His work comes out of sickness rather than an overplus of health. Swinburne, Verlaine. . . . No, this is donnish thinking, for Sikelianos existed side by side with Cavafy, just as Mistral lived in the epoch of Apollinaire. But we should avoid these neat ruled lines between men and periods. The distances are much vaster than that and the poetic constellations move much more slowly across the sky. I betook myself to the coffee-room where the majority of my fellow-travellers were hard at work on breakfast, and where Deeds had emerged in some magical fashion with a brand new *Times*. This always made him vague, and over his coffee he was repeating "Sixty-three for five—I can't believe it." It seemed that a disaster had overtaken Yorkshire, and that Hampshire . . .

It was by far the hottest day yet, and brilliantly invigorating; there was no wind, the sea had settled into long calms like a succession of soft veils. Agrigento glimmered up there on the sky and Mario in some mysterious fashion had succeeded in giving the bus a wash and brush-up for the floors were still moist from his mop.

The temples were bathed in an early morning calm and light, and there were no other tourists at the site, which gave us the pleasant sense of propriety, the consciousness that we could take them at our ease. Drink them in is the operative tourist phrase—and it wasn't inapposite, for the atmosphere on this limestone escarpment with its sweeps of olive and almond, and its occasional flash of Judas was quite eminently drinkable. The air was so still one was conscious that one was breathing, as if in yoga. The stolid little temples—how to convey the sense of intimacy they conveyed except by little-ising them? They were in fact large and grand, but they felt intimate and lifesize. Maybe the more ancient style of column, stubby and stolid, conveys this sense of childishness. It was not they but the site as a whole which conveyed a sense of awe; the ancients must have walked in a veritable forest of temples up here, over the sea. But one slight reservation was concerned with the type of light tufa used in the Sicilian temples; it was the only suitable material available to the architect, and of course all these columns were originally faced with a kind of marble dust composition to give the illusion of real marble. In consequence now when they are seen from close to the impression is rather of teeth which have lost their glittering dentine. They are fawnish in tone, and matt of surface; while embedded in the stone lie thousands of infinitesimally small shells, tiny worm-casts left by animalcules in the quarries from which the stone was taken. This is not apparent at night during the floodlighting unless one looks really closely. But by day they strike a somewhat second-hand note which forces one to recall that originally all these temples were glossy—fluted as to their columns while their friezes and cornices were painted in crude primary colours. It is something too easy to forget—the riot of crude and clumsy colour in which the temple was embedded. Statues painted. . . . It is my private opinion that the Greeks had, for this reason, little of what we would call plastic sense in our present-day terms. I speak of our lust for volume and our respect for the parent matter out of which our sculptures are shaped. Obviously for them wholly different criteria obtained; it is intriguing to try and imagine whether we would not have been shocked rather than moved by these sites if they had been today in their ancient state of repair, bright with colour-washes. It might have seemed to our contemporary eyes as garish but as refreshingly childish as the painted sideboards of the little Sicilian carts which from time to time we passed in the streets of the towns. I thought back to the Pausanian description of the Holy of Holies on the Acropolis; perhaps one should make the mental effort to compare our impressions of, say, Lourdes (horrible!) or St. Peter's or the Cathedral of Tinos. . . .

So we slowly passed down at a walking pace in that pleasant sunshine following the sweet enfilade of the temples as they curved down towards the one to the Dioscuri—like a descending chromatic scale. One by one these huge mythological beasts came up to us, as if they were grazing, and allowed us to pat them. The image had got muddled up in my mind with another thought about temples as magical defensive banks; and by the same token with the thought that all religious architecture carries the same sort of feeling. In America the most deeply religious architecture (in the anthropological sense) is the banks, and some are watched over by precisely the same mythical animals as watched over the temples here, animals staring down from a frieze—lions or boars, bulls or bears. Just as in the Midi, added Deeds jokingly, the deeply religious architecture of the wine co-operatives betrays the inmost religious preoccupations of the inhabitants. He thinks this a *boutade* but has in fact made an observation of great perspicacity and truth. They are indeed very much alike, and quite religious in their style, like stout laic churches.

The Bishop now elected to fall into a shaft, gracefully and without damage, and for a moment a terrible beauty was born. One touch of music-hall makes the whole world kin. All we heard at first was a kind of buzzing and booming. It was his voice from the depths giving his rescuers instructions as to how to help him clamber back into the daylight. Beddoes at once suggested that Hades had mistaken him for Persephone and had made an unsuccessful snatch at his coat-tails, almost dragging him into the Underworld. He would have been disappointed one supposes. At any rate a pretty scene was enacted not unworthy of its ancient Greek echoes, for his saviour turned out to be none other than Miss Lobb who (like Venus on a similar occasion) undid her plaited goat-skin belt and extended the end of it to the upraised hands of the holy man. The idea was simple and efficacious. We all formed up, myself with my arms round Miss Lobb and the rest linked on as in a childish game and with a tug or two we raised the Bishop into the daylight, where he seemed none the worse for this brief adventure. The one who was really pale with anxiety was of course Roberto who at once realised that his charge could have broken an ankle. The shaft was not profound, however; the sides had subsided, that was all; and as for the Bishop he was only wounded in his *amour propre.*

The theory of Hades snatching at him was all the more plausible as down here there had once been a shrine to the chthonic deities—another bewilderment of contradictory ascriptions—and it was just the place where a Protestant Bishop might expect to run foul of a pagan God. Anyway, this accident put us all in a very good humour and we felt a little touch of pride in the classical aspect of the whole affair. Though we were mere tourists we had a touch of the right instinct. As for poor Persephone, that is another story. But I could feel no trace of her sad spirit calling from its earthen tomb—the sunlight made such fictions too improbably cruel to contemplate. The chthonic deities had little reality for us on that sunny morning. It was hard to admit that one so beautiful had, as one of her attributes, the title of "bringer of destruction".

But what was a real knockout on this extensive and rather chaotic site was the enormous figure of the recumbent telamon— that gigantic figure whose severed fragments have been approximately assembled on the ground to give an indication of his enormous height and posture. This temple of Zeus is the most extraordinary in conception and has a strangeness which makes one wonder if it was not really constructed by some strange Asiatic race and left here. It feels somehow unlike anything else one may think of in the Greek world of temples, and particularly here in Sicily. I found the thing as barbaric and perplexing (despite its finish) as an Easter Island statue, or a corner of Baalbek. Who the devil executed this extraordinary Bank—which could have been the City National Bank in Swan Lake City, Idaho, or that of Bonga Bonga in Brazil? My elated puzzlement communicated itself to Deeds who raided his battered hold-all and finally found a copy of Margaret Guido's admirable book on the archaeological sites of the island. He used no other, it seemed. From it he read me a bit, sitting on a fragment of pediment to do so. The great temple had, like so much else, been toppled by an earthquake; but the fragments had fallen more or less in order and some notion of its construction could be deciphered. With this lucky factor, and with the description of Diodorus Siculus who had seen it standing, it was possible to work out its shape. But the real mystery begins at this point for the wretched thing is unlike anything else in the island—it is overgrown and vainglorious and, if one must be absolutely truthful, overbearing and grim. It makes you uneasy when you look at the architectural reconstruction.

The whole thing, to begin with, stands on a huge platform about 350 feet long, reposing on foundations nearly 20 feet deep. Around this chunk had been strung a series of Doric half columns of staggering size. Their diameter is 13 feet. The top of this wall was surmounted by a sort of frieze of enormous stone men—the telamones. They supported the architrave with the help of an invisible steel beam linking column to column. Each of these giant men was over 25 feet tall, male figures, alternately bearded and beardless. Feet together and arms raised to support the architrave they must have been really awe-inspiring. Some of this feeling actually leaks into the dry-as-dust description of Diodorus who notes with wonder that the simple flutings of the columns were broad enough to contain a man standing upright in them. "The porticos," he writes, "were of tremendous size and height and on the eastern pediment they portrayed the battle between the Gods and the Giants in sculptures which excelled in size and beauty, while in the west they portrayed the Capture of Troy in which each one of the heroes may be seen depicted in a manner appropriate to his role."

Nothing but ruins and conjectures remain of all this. Mutilated fragments of statues and coins and walls marked by fires. But here to my astonishment the Japanese couple suddenly began to behave strangely, overwhelmed I suppose by the giant stone figure on the ground. They screamed with laughter and pointed at it. They started to talk one hundred to the dozen and to nod and giggle. They climbed on it and photographed each other sitting on it. They clucked and beamed. They behaved like children with a new toy. And climbing about its defenceless body they reminded me of illustrations of *Gulliver's Travels*. It was an intriguing reaction and I would have given a good deal to ask them what had provoked such an expression of feeling, but the limitations of language made it impossible. We walked thoughtfully around the recumbent warrior, wondering at the coarseness of the workmanship yet aware that in terms of imaginative pictorial originality the temple marked an important point in the architectural history of Sicily. There was only one other construction which in style resembled it—and that we had not seen as yet; but I made a mental note to watch out for the Temple labelled F at Selinunte, and was struck by the suggestion that perhaps this heavy treatment of the building may have come here via Egypt—where of course they worked in heavy and recalcitrant stones for their religious buildings.

But what earthquakes and weather began was more often than not finished off by the marauders—not necessarily foreign invaders, but simply lazy local builders who picked these choice bones of history and culture simply because they lay to hand and saved transport costs. Every architect will tell you what a godsend it is to find your building materials on the site, instead of being forced to transport them.

The party had spread out to visit the further corners of the site but Deeds, who knew from old not to waste time, headed me away across the meadows towards a pleasant little bar where we celebrated the Bishop's narrow escape from Hades with a glass of beer and a roundel of salami. "It was a very singular sound he made," said Deeds. "Like a bumble bee in a bottle. I heard it from quite a distance. It sounded like the bees in Agamemnon's tomb." It was another reference which carried a small built-in pang—for a whole generation had heard and remembered those bees at Mycenae; but an unlucky spraying with insecticide had silenced them and the great tomb has sunk back into its original sinister anonymity.

But the mystery of the Japanese behaviour was absolute; we could not evolve a theory to account for this little wave of hysteria. Unless, as Beddoes suggested, they were suddenly filled with the conviction that this gorgon-like figure was a sort of carnival joke, placed there to evoke innocent merriment.

Miss Lobb walked about with a pleasant air of having done her duty. The two old apple-people sat down in a clump of bushes and began to eat fruit which the old man peeled with a small pocket knife. They were radiant, obviously without fear of the Underworld. The Bishop had recovered his composure and was once more pacing out the temples and behaving as if he were suspicious about being overcharged for them. If they were not of the stipulated size he would report them to the agency. Roberto, still shaken, drank Coca Cola. Mario blew his sudden horn at last and we awoke to action once more.

ERICE

(FROM SICILIAN CAROUSEL, 1977)

AT ERICE ONE FEELS that all the options of ordinary life are reversed. I do not know how else to put it. We steer our lives by certain beliefs which are perhaps fables but which give us the courage to continue living. But what happens even before you reach the "sickle" of Trapani is that you lose your inner bearings, become insecure. It's as if the giant of the mountain up there, riding its mists, had kicked away your crutches. History begins to stammer; the most famous and most privileged temple to Aphrodite in the whole of the Mediterranean has vanished without leaving a trace. The one late head of Aphrodite is nothing to write home about. The holy shrine of Eryx has been blown out like a light, yet as at Delphi, one can still smell the sulphur in the air. You feel it in the burning sun like a cold touch on the back of the neck. But I am going too fast for we are still approaching Trapani, that deceptively happy and unremarkable town so beautifully perched upon its seagirt headland. The old part of the town, rather as in the case of Syracuse, occupies a firm promontory thrust out into the sea like a pier; the town has developed on the landward side. Salt-pans and windmills, yes, and the view from the so-called Ligny Tower is a fine one; but what is really fine is the fresh sea-wind, frisky as a fox-terrier, which patters the awnings and bends the trees and sends old sailors' caps scuttering along the cobbles of the port. Westward a fine expanse of the Tyrrhenian Sea, smouldering in the sinking sun; two of the Egadi Isles with the choice names of Levanzo and Favignana glow with a kind of mysterious malevolence.

We were tired, we were really in no mood for further sightseeing, and Roberto let us off easily with a short visit to an indifferent church and a glimpse of the stern battlements constructed by Charles V. But the main thing was the frolicking wind whose playfulness allayed somewhat the curious feeling of tension and misgiving which I felt when I gazed upwards towards the ramps of Monte Giuliano and saw the sharp butt of Erice buried in the mountain like a flint axehead which had broken off with the impact. There was a short administrative pause while Mario made some growling remarks to the world at large and some adjustments to his brakes. Somewhere in the town a small municipal band had slunk into a square and started to play fragments of old waltzes and tangos. The sudden gusts of wind offered the musicians a fortuitous nautical syncopation—the music fading and reviving, full of an old-world charm. The Petremands ate a vividly coloured ice-cream and bought one for Mario. The Bishop had broken a shoelace. The old pre-Adamic couple were fast asleep in their seats, arm in arm, smile in smile, so to speak. It is pleasant when sleeping people smile and obviously enjoy their dreaming; they looked like representations of the smiling Buddha—though he is very far from asleep, sunk rather in smiling meditation. At last we began the ascent.

The sun was over the border now, rapidly westering, apparently increasing speed in its long slide into the ocean. Our little red bus swung itself clear of the crooked streets of Trapani and then started its tough climb up the dark prow of Eryx. Adieu Via Fardella, Via Pepoli! The road now began to mount in short spans on a steepening gradient, swinging about first to the right, then to the left; and there came a gradually increasing sobriety of spirit, a premonition perhaps of the Erycinean Aphrodite whose territory we were approaching. I am not romancing, for several of my fellow-travellers expressed a sharpened sense of excitement in their several ways. Mario varied his engine speeds with great skill and the little motor had us valiantly swarming up the steep cliffs in good order.

The vegetation gradually thinned away, or made room for hardier and perhaps more ancient plants to cling to the crevices and caves in the rock. The precipices hereabouts were bathed in the condensations of cloud, as if a rich dew had settled on them; or as if the whole of nature had burst into a cold sweat. Yes, there were clouds above us, hanging lower and lower as we climbed, but they seemed to part as we reached them to offer us passage. At each turn—for we were still tacking up the cliffs like a sailboat—the view increased in grandeur and scope until the whole province of Trapani lay below us bathed in golden light and bounded by the motionless sea. Far off twinkled the Egadi, with Marettimo printed in black-letter—the island which Samuel Butler so surprisingly decided must be the historical Ithaca in his weird book about the supposed female author of the *Odyssey*. I love wrong-headed books. But a short residence in modern Greece would have made Butler somewhat uncertain about the main theme of his book. Only a man, only a Greek could have written the poem—at least so think I.

We worked our way with elephantine determination round the north-eastern flank of our two-thousand-metre odd mountain. There was only one little village to traverse, Parparella, perched up in solitude like a nest and empty of inhabitants at that hour. Bare rock now, with sudden ferns, cistus, caper and an occasional asphodel to surprise one. And the views below us went on steadily unwinding like a scroll. The air had become purer, colder, as if filtered by the passing clouds. Once or twice our engine sneezed and Mario cocked an alert ear; but there was no trouble and on one of the penultimate loops we called a halt designed to let the amateur photographers in the party record the scene below. But while they clicked happily away at Trapani I found myself craning upwards to gaze at the crest of Eryx, printed on the unfaltering blue of the evening sky, still touched by the sun's rays. You could see a dabble of ancient wall and some higgledy-piggledy towers and minarets just below the summit. They must mark the site of the now vanished temple of Aphrodite. From the rugged Cyclopean bases the walls mounted in a faltering and somewhat ramshackle fashion— improvised in layers, in tiers, in afterthoughts and false starts— Phoenician, Greek, Roman and Norman.

Once we had broken the back of the ascent the road spanned pleasant but lonely pinewoods which scented the still air and led us in mysterious hesitant fashion to the gates of the little town, the Porte Trapani, where Roberto got down for a long confabulation with a clerk from the Mairie while the rest of us set about digging into our luggage for pullovers. The dusk was about us now though the higher heavens were still lit by the sun, and up there the swifts darted and rolled, feasting on insects. A chill struck suddenly and the Bishop shivered.

There had been a hitch, said Roberto, and we had been switched to an older hotel; this was irritating. Like all guides he decried the old-fashioned and only respected modernity. But in this case there was no need for apologies; the hotel was a fine old-fashioned tumbledown sort of place but with all the right amenities. Mario turned the bus round and conducted us steeply downhill upon a forest road; but it was not far, for we emerged upon a sort of ledge like an amphitheatre above the sea. It was a spacious site and belonged to spacious times when they built hotels with comfortable billiard-rooms and lounges and terra-cotta swimming pools. It was fine to be thus perched over the sea in the middle of a pine forest. The wooden floors creaked under our feet in comfortable fashion. There were several dusty bars full of dusty half-full liqueur bottles. But at the back underneath the dining-room there came a short stretch of forest followed by an astonishing vertical drop—a sheer drop to the bottom of the world as represented now in diagrammatic fashion by a Trapani with its salt-pans and harbour picked out in lights. We were a bit below the castle here and the little town was not visible. A heavy mist from the precipice rose and dispersed, rose and dispersed. "It's all very well, but I have got cold feet and I want my money back," said Beddoes to the distress of Roberto who took everything he said seriously. Despite the season the mountain chill and the fatigue had chastened us and we were glad to settle for a drink and dinner and early bed.

The Count walked about in the dark for a while before turning in—I saw the glow of his cigar. Deeds found a crossword in an ancient paper while Miss Lobb replaced her book and appropriated another. I retired to my narrow wooden chamber which reminded me a bit of a ship's cabin, or a room in a ski-chalet. The wood smelt lovely and it was not too cold to step out upon the balcony with its great view. All along the horizon line there was a tremulous flickering of an electrical storm, soundless from this great distance. It reminded me of the only naval engagement I have ever witnessed—if that is the correct word; the ships were all out of sight and only this steady flicker (followed centuries later by the thunder of guns) was to be seen. It went back and forth regular as a scythe-stroke.

I watched, straining to hear the following thunder, but none came for ages. It was up here, perhaps in this very room that Martine had spent a night of "intense nervous expectation". It was so intense that she could not sleep, and it was at last with weary elation that she had watched the dawn break over the exhausted sea. She felt as if she had escaped whatever it was that had been haunting her subconscious in the form of vague premonitions of something doom-laden which she would encounter here at Erice. Nor was she completely wrong. Nor had she escaped, for months afterwards she realised that it was here, and more especially on that sleepless night, that she had felt the first twinges in the joints, the first stiffness of the neck and backbone which were only to declare their meaning long months afterwards. "I recognise now in retrospect just what I went to Erice to find. It was a rendezvous which would finally lead me towards death—one must not fuss too much since it is everyone's lot. Only now I know what I did not at Erice—I know roughly when. Yes, I am going into a decline in a year or two. Or so they say, the professors in Rome. I like the Victorian phrase, don't you? It has pride and reserve—though I was never a woman of ice, was I?"

But all this was at another season, and the hotel had been deserted, and the rock-levels of Venus' temple had been smothered in tiny spring flowers she could not identify. Now I had followed her, not with quite such an acute apprehension of momentous happenings, but with something nevertheless which troubled and disturbed me and made me expectant. During that first night (I could hear the desultory click of billiard balls, where Beddoes was still up. Floors creaked.), during the long vigil she had spent some time "scratching about among the bewildering debris of legend and conjecture which makes everything Greek in Sicily such a puzzle. It is as if everything has been smashed into dust by a giant trip-hammer; one can reach nothing coherent among these shattered shards; just the tantalising hints and glints of vanished people and their myths. So finally one says, to hell with Daedalus the engineer, and first labyrinth-maker—what did he find to do here in Sicily? Head of public works for old King Cocalos? Why did he assent to the murder of Minos his old patron? One becomes so weary of the oft-repeated tales which make up the historic pattern. It is hopeless! And then what about the ultra-famous temple of Venus—Astarte-Aphrodite-Venus—the goddess had diverse roots and multiple attributes? Everything, woman, wife, nurse, mother, Muse, as well as ritual prostitute. . . . There was no aspect she did not rule over. In this grim temple there was ritual prostitution, as well as fertility rites—while for the sailor the place was a notable navigational seamark to guide him to Trapani; and just as today the sailor asks for weather reports, so his ancestor took the omens for the voyage from the temple and acted according to whether they were fair or foul.

"But how could it have disappeared so completely from sight, this world-famous place? Nothing but a tiny bit of stone ramp remains to mark the site of the temple. Nothing? Well, only this intangible feeling of dread, of something momentous preparing itself. And the empty sockets mock one in the one late banal head of Aphrodite."

Youth, beauty, death—the three co-ordinates of the ancient world. Martine wrote: "I told myself that in Sufism and Taoism (it would take too long to convince you that the original Astarte of Erice was much older than Greek) they do not have any truck with the notion of disease as we see it. They do not talk of getting cured but simply of modifying conduct. It is presumed that your wrong action has procured a disharmony with the universe which manifests itself in disease. I believe this with all my heart, but I also believe in destiny, as well as in just wearing out like a pot. Then there is another aspect of things—I hate the Christian notion of prayer as an act of propitiation. But I like the old Byzantine notion of turning it into a sort of heart-beat—each man his own prayer-wheel so to speak. Everything you feel in Erice goes way back beyond any notion which the monkey mind or tongue can formulate. Into the darkness where those great vegetable forms, tuberose creatures, wait in order to munch your flesh when you are once in the ground. The chthonic gods and goddesses as they are so strangely called. . . ."

The light went out—the hotel generator packed up at midnight. It was still very light—a white milky light as if of moonlight diffused through a silk screen. I was weary now and I set down my papers and slept—but it was a light, nervous sort of sleep without great density.

At about three I woke with a start and sat up to look at the forest. I thought at first what I had heard was muffled sobbing somewhere in the building. I am still not sure. But what had happened was that a powerful surge of wind had sailed upon the promontory and bent the pines. It made a sudden rich hum, like a sweep of strings long drawn out but slowly dying away. Then the quivering silence returned. But one felt excited, on the *qui vive*. It was exactly as if one woke in the middle of the night on the African veldt slowly to realise that the noise which had wakened one was the breathing of a lion. The forest stirred and shook and resettled itself. A kind of breath of music had passed over it—like breath passing over embers. No, there was nothing particularly disquieting or singular about it, but waking, I felt the need to get up and drink some water. It was icy. I went to the balcony and looked down at the necklace of lights etching in their diagram of Trapani. It was some time off dawn yet but I felt completely rested and wondered if I would get to sleep again. Hesitating there I suddenly caught sight of a figure advancing towards the hotel through the pines. It was the German girl and she was naked.

The light, though diffused, was extremely bright and I saw quite clearly that she had no clothes on. I wondered if she could be sleep-walking but it did not seem so for she looked about her, turning her head now this way and now that. She carried her hands before her, palms turned up, but lightly and without emphasis. And her walk was slow and calm.

Perhaps the sweep of wind in the pines had woken her also, or else the forest had evoked in her her native Bavarian landscapes? Or more simply still, she felt the incoherent stirrings of a primeval inheritance—suppose she were, without realising it, some Nordic goddess who had come on an accidental visit to a remote cousin called Aphrodite of Eryx? She walked slowly and calmly under my balcony and disappeared round the corner of the house. And that was all. I dwelt a little while on the spectacle, wondering about it. Then I turned in again and at once fell into the profound sleep which up to now had been lacking. The sun was up when I awoke. And the disquiet had been replaced by a calm elation. Yet in a sort of way I felt that it was a relief to have traversed the night without incident.

Breakfast was very welcome on that fine sunny day; and we had been promised a look at the castle before being spirited away to Segesta and thence Palermo. Our trip was soon going to be at an end, and the consciousness of it provoked a new sense of friendliness. Conversations became warmer and more animated. A Microscope helped the Japanese girl change a film. I looked curiously at Renata the German girl when she came down but she seemed perfectly normal and assured, and of course one could not question her about her nudist escapade. I wondered if her boy friend knew of it. They were both very obviously much in love and went to no pains to hide it—which crucified poor Roberto as he watched, biting his nails.

It was necessary to set the red bus to rights this morning, for the little town of Erice was only going to be a brief stop on the road to Segesta whence we would face a long haul into Palermo.

I rather feared the ardours of this journey but in fact the cal-
culations of Roberto were fairly exact and we arrived at night not
too late and not too fatigued. But Erice in that bright blue
morning was something for a glider-pilot's eye or an eagle's. The
drops, the views, the melting sea. Light clouds frolicked way below
us. The little town had tucked itself into the nape of the mountain
while the successive fortresses had been squarely planked down
on the site of the ancient temple, thus obliterating it. But the rock
promontory, sticking out like a stone thumb, was a perfect
emplacement for a place of worship. "It makes me wonder," said
Deeds, "since all the ancient shrines have served as Christian foundations for our churches, whether there isn't always a little bit of
the pagan devil leaking into the stonework of our Christian edi-
fices. I would like to think there was; we seem such a rigid and
unfunny lot. But I don't think I dare ask the parson."

The little town stumbled up and down its net of cobbled streets
below the fortress garden. The architecture was all that one finds
in the Aegean—houses built round a courtyard tessellated with
coloured pebbles and decorated with old corned-beef tins full of
sprouting basil and other sweet-smelling plants. It was Samos, it
was Tinos all over again. We were warmly bidden to enter several
courtyards to admire the arrangements of the house; these dark-
eyed smiling people might have been Corfiots. The snug little
courtyards bounded-in their lives, and one felt that here, when
once night fell and the mists began to climb up from the valley
below, people did not hesitate to lock their courtyard-gates. After
midnight one could knock a long time on a door without getting
an answer, for their world was both ancient and also one of contemporary goblins and fays. And with the temple site brooding up
there. . . . But the domestic organisation of their houses was that
of birds' nests, and they had all the human force which comes

from living on top of one another in a small place; making room for children, for livestock, for everything important to life—and not less for the sacred icons which ensure that the dark spirits shall be kept at bay.

Roberto had a small chore to do and it was quite a compliment that he should ask Deeds and myself if we would like to accompany him. He had to visit the ancient grandmother of a friend and give her some messages of congratulation for her eighty-sixth birthday plus various assorted messages. We found the house without much difficulty and when the portals opened to us we saw that quite a number of people were there on the same errand. It was rather a spacious house on its own courtyard, and a short flight of steps led up to the upper room and gallery where the old lady lay in state to receive her visitors, in a great bed like a galleon with carved headboards. It looked, as Deeds said afterwards, as if one could have hitched a horse to it and just ridden off into the sky, there were so many cherubs and saints carved upon it, all *con furioso.* She wore an old-fashioned shawl of fine black lace with a white fichu and her long witch-like white hands with their filbert nails were spread on the sheet before her, while her clever old eyes accepted the compliments of her visitors with grace and no weariness. Her fine room was furnished with graceful Sicilian earthenware plates beautifully painted, and flowers in bloom. Two small children played with a sailboat upon a handsome carved trunk under the window. She must have been a person of great consequence, for several of her visitors were local dignitaries, as Roberto explained later—the barber, the chemist, the *podesta* and *medico condotto.* It all went off with great style and ease, but the appearance of Roberto was a thrilling surprise and his presence evoked questions and answers which took a good twenty minutes. She had questions to ask involving several generations and several families and

I had the impression that nobody was passed over—she checked up on the whole lot of them, for who knows when she might have another chance? The peasant memory and the peasant sense of life is a tenacious and determined thing—it draws its strength from this sense of a corporate life, shared by all, and to which all contribute a share of their sap. Moreover I think the old lady felt that she was not long for this world and that she must make the most of things, such as this surprise visit which had brought her all the gossip of a far corner of the island.

Duty thus done, Roberto kissed the long patrician fingers of the old lady and we made our way back into the sunshine to negotiate the little curling streets back to the main square where by now the rest of the party must be sitting under awnings and writing postcards or drinking lemonade. The day was bright and hot, and it was quite a contrast to think back to the evening before with its mists and murmurs of another world, another order of life. Nothing could be more ordinary in its beauty than Erice by day, with all the little shops functioning—post office, bank, gendarmerie. The minute main square was built upon a slope—indeed such an acute tilt that everything tended to slide about and run down to the bottom. Tables at this angle were in danger of falling over, as were chairs; as one wrote one's postcards or drank one's beer, one found one was insensibly sliding downhill. People who came out of the café had to brake sharply in order not to find themselves rolling about like dice.

A very fat policeman made something of an act of this natural attribute of Erice's Piazza Nationale by allowing himself to slide helplessly downhill until he ended up on the lap of a friend who was trying to eat ice-cream at an angle of fifty degrees. Just how the poor café owner managed to dispose his tables and chairs was something of a mystery—it would have seemed necessary to wedge them in place. Over the lintel of the butcher's hung a peeled and dry little kid which bore a label reading *"Castrato"* and giving a price per pound. This intrigued Beddoes who said: "It's a rum word, I thought it meant something frightful that Monteverdi did to his choirboys to enable them to hit high C." The kid was so neatly cut in half that it looked rather like a violin hanging up there; the rest of the meat on display was pretty indifferent-looking stuff; of course, like all Mediterranean islands Sicily is a lamb country.

Our little visit had cost us a bit of time and by now the others had already done the cathedral and the Church of St. John as well as the public gardens, so full of yellow broom; but the real heart of the place was the restored towers and the old castle standing grimly on its sacred site, sweating with every gush of mists from the lowlands. What a farewell sweep the eye takes in up there—the whole sweep of western Sicily exposed in a single slice, as if from an aeroplane! Roberto was disposed to be knowledgeable about the *Aeneid* with its famous cruise along this coast which is described in poetic detail—but to my shame I have never read it, and I rather doubted whether anyone else had either. But the few lines he quoted from memory sounded sinewy and musical on that fine silent air and I made a mental note to repair this grave omission as soon as I could happen upon a version of the poem in parallel text. We were leaving and suddenly as we entered the bus I had a sudden reversion to the mood of the night before—a sudden atmosphere of unreality in which some momentous happening lay embedded, encysted, waiting to flower. But the faces of my fellow-travellers did not seem to express any untoward emotion and it was perhaps my own imagination. But whatever they were, these small preoccupations, they were swept away like cobwebs by the fine speed of our descent, for Mario was in a particularly expansive humour and swung the little bus about with a professional dexterity that was marvellous—in the sense that it caused us no alarm, so confident were we in his ability. And the land swept about with him on this turntable of a road, swinging like a cradle this way and that. At one corner he slowed for the Japanese girl and her camera and I caught a glimpse of a couple of appropriate eagles sitting motionless in the mid-heaven, staring down at the vanished altars of Erice.

TAORMINA

(FROM *SICILIAN CAROUSEL*, 1977)

"TAORMINA, THE OLD BULL MOUNTAIN—I'm so glad I followed my instinct and saved it up for the last. It was like a kind of summation of all that went before, all the journeys and flavours this extraordinary island had to offer. Like a fool, I loped up it with Loftus in an old racing-car at full moon; but something made me aware of the sacrilege and next day I walked humbly down to the bottom where I left a propitiatory candle in the little Christian shrine of St. Barnabus (isn't it?) and retraced my way up again. Of course it must have once been a sort of sacred way, laid out against the breast of this steep little mountain so that one could approach it step by step, loop by loop. The long steep zigzags of the road must have been punctuated significantly with statues and flowering shrubs and little fanes to take an offering of the first fruits. One arrived, slowly and breathlessly, watching the scene widen out around one, and deepen into a screen of mountain and sea and volcano."

Thus Martine. In the garden of the Villa Rosalie to which I had been assigned, two white-haired men played chess amidst dense flowering shrubbery which suggested rather the cultivation of a spa like Nice than the wild precincts of Sicily; I had come back to Europe really. I left my bags and walked the length of the main street with its astonishing views. It was so good that it aroused indignation: one almost suspected it to be spurious; but no, it simply outstripped language, that was all. And a wonderful sense of intimacy and well-being suffused the whole place. Yes, it was sophisticated as well—and as if to match the idea I found a small visiting card from Loftus waiting in my box inscribed in that fine old-fashioned lace hand which he had cultivated in order to write ancient Greek. A message of greeting, giving me his phone number. But tonight I was in a mood to be alone, to enjoy and to regret being alone. It was a strange new feeling, not unconnected with fatigue. But the sinking sunset which one drank out of one's glass of Campari, so to speak, was as extraordinary as any that Greece or Italy has to offer. And Etna did her stuff on the skyline. "However blasé one is, however much one has been prepared for the aerial splendours of the little town, its freshness is perennial, it rises in one like sap, it beguiles and charms as the eye turns in its astonishment to take in crags and clouds and mountains and the blue coastline. Here one could sit in a deck-chair gazing out into the night and thinking about Greek flair and Roman prescience—they married here in this place; but why was it a failure at last, why did it fall apart?"

Because everything does I suppose. And now after so long, here come I with my valedictory admiration, inhabitant of yet another culture which is falling apart, which is doomed to the same decline and fall, perhaps even more suddenly. . . . How marvellous to read a book at dinner. I had chosen that fussy but touching civil servant Pliny; his pages tell one all one wants to know and admire about Rome.

And how pleasant, too, to dawdle the length of that main street—like walking the bridge of a Zeppelin. And how astonishingly still the air is at this great height. It is what constitutes the original feature of Taormina, I think; one's thoughts naturally turn to places like Villefranche or Cassis (as they must have been a hundred years ago); and then, quite naturally, to Capri and Paleocastrizza. The difference is not only in variety and prolixity of classical views—the whole thing has been anchored in mid-heaven, at a thousand feet, and up here the air is still and calm. The white curtains in my hotel-room breathed softly in and out, like the lungs of the universe itself. There were cafés of Roman and Venetian excellence, and there were the traditional hordes of tourists perambulating up and down the long main street. Its narrowness grew on one after the sixth or seventh turn upon it.

And in the little side streets there were unforgotten corners of the real Italy—by which I mean the peasant Italy with its firmly anchored values and purity of heart. At dusk next day I walked up to have a look at the villa Lawrence occupied for three years. It was modest and quite fitting to the poems he wrote here in this pure high tower of silence which is Taormina at night. But at the first corner of the road there stood a tattered trattoria with a dirty cloth across the door to keep the flies at bay. In the street, under a faded-looking tree, stood a rickety table and two chairs. Just that and nothing more. A tin table which had been racked with smallpox and perhaps some hunter's smallshot. A slip of broom was suspended from the lintel. And here I was served a harsh black wine by a matron with a wall-eye and hairy brown arms. She was like Demeter herself and she talked to me quietly and simply about the wines of the island. Hers was Etna, volcanic wine, and it tasted of iron; but it was not sugary and I bought a demijohn as a present for Loftus when I should decide to take up his invitation. If I hesitated, it was for a rather obscure reason; I wanted, so to speak, to let the Carousel experience evaporate before I changed the whole key. For I knew that encountering Loftus and his life here meant that I would find myself back in the Capri of the twenties; in the world of Norman Douglas—a world very dear to me precisely because it was a trifle precious. Martine had had one foot in this world, to be sure, but what I had personally shared with her had not belonged to this aspect of our islomania. Capri had long since sunk below the horizon when Cyprus became a reality. Yet she had loved Douglas as much as I, and Compton Mackenzie as well, while the silent empty villa of Lawrence up the hill also carried the echoes of that Nepenthean period where *Twilight in Italy* matched *South Wind*.

But Taormina is so small that it was inevitable that from time to time I would bump into other members of the Carousel. I saw the Microscopes in the distance once or twice, and the American dentist waved from the April café as I passed. I also saw the Bishop—he had taken up a stance in order to "appreciate" a piece of architecture, while his wife sat on a stone and fanned herself with her straw hat. But that was all. There was no sign of Deeds. After two days of this delicious privacy in my little pension where I knew nobody, I visited the bookshop and bought a guide to the island, intending to spend my last few days filling in the lacunae in my knowledge. I could not leave without bracing Etna for example, or standing on the great "belvedere of all Sicily", Enna; then Tyndarus . . . and so on. I thought I would rent a small car to finish off the visit in a style more reminiscent of the past than by having any truck with trains and buses. It would be interesting to see what Loftus thought.

I rang him, and was amused and pleased to recognise his characteristic drawl, and the slight slurring of the r's which had always characterised his speech. He had a little car he could lend me, which was promising, and so I agreed to dine at his villa the following evening. In a way it was reassuring that nothing much had changed for Loftus; he had ruined a promising diplomatic career by openly living with his chauffeur, an ex-jailbird, and then, as if that were not enough, winning notoriety by writing a novel called *Le Baiser* in French which had a *succès de scandale*. Someone in the Foreign Office must have known that the word "baiser" didn't only mean "kiss" (though it is difficult to think who) and Loftus was invited to abstract himself from decent society. This he did with good grace—he had a large private income—and retired to Taormina where he grew roses and translated the classics. He had been one of the most brilliant scholars of his time, though an incurable dilettante. About Sicily he knew all that there was to be known. But of course now he was getting on, like the rest of us, and hardly ever moved from the Villa Ariadne—a delightful old house built on a little headland over the sea, and buried in roses. He too was a relic of the Capri epoch, a silver-age man.

I hardly recognised the chauffeur-lover after such a long lapse of time—he had grown fat and hairy, and spindle-shanked. But he panted with pleasure like a bull-terrier at meeting me again and ushered me into the car with a good deal of friendly cere-mony. I was glad that I had been fetched when he started to nego-tiate the steep descent from the mountain to the coast where the villa was. It was a labyrinth of criss-crossing roads, with snatches of motor road to be crossed. But at last we arrived in that cool garden full of olives and oleanders and the smell of rushing water in dusty fountains—the house had been designed by water-loving Romans. And there was Loftus frail and smart as always, though a little greyer, waiting for me.

Terraces led down to the sea; there were candles already burning on a white tablecloth; wide divans with stained cretonne covers were laid out under the olives. The parrot Victor had gone to bed, his cage was covered in a green baize cloth. Smell of Turkish tobacco. "Dear boy," said Loftus, "I can't rise to greet you as is fitting. I had a small ski-mishap." His crutches lay beside him. The tone and temper of his conversation was reassuringly the same as ever, and I was glad to feel that now it would never change. It belonged to an epoch, it marched with the language of the eighteenth century whose artists (like Stendhal?) discovered how to raise social gossip to the level of an art. The trivia of Loftus had the same fine merit—even though he had not much at present to recount. Various film nabobs from Beverly Hills had come and gone. Then Cramp the publisher from London. There were two amusing local scandals which might lead to a knife-fight. "All this is simply to situate you, dear boy. You are in Taormina now which has its own ethos and manners. It is very degenerate in comparison to the rest of Sicily which is rather strait-laced."

In this easy and languid style the conversation led him closer and closer to the last days of Martine. She had spent a lot of time with him; she would bring over her two children and a picnic and spend the day on his little beach, reading or writing. She had never been happier, she said, than during that last summer. She had spoken of me with affection, and indeed had rung me up once or twice for advice about a book she was planning to write about Sicily. I surmised it must have been the "pocket Sicily" for her children—Loftus agreed that it was. "Finally she gave up and said she would make you do it. She found that in Sicily there is no sense of time; her children inhabited a history in which Caesar, Pompey, and Timoleon were replaced, without any lapse of time, by Field-Marshal Kesserling and the Hermann Goering division—the one the Irish knocked about." He smiled. "It's difficult to know how you would have dealt with that sort of Mediterranean amnesia. Everything seems simultaneous." By the same token Martine seemed as ever-present as Loftus himself—the mere intervention of death seemed somehow unreal, untruthful. "She took everything calmly, gaily, lightly. Her husband was marvel-lous, too, and made it easy. Also she wasn't encumbered by any heavy intellectual equipment like a theological attitude. She wasn't Christian, was she?" As far as I knew she wasn't anything, though she observed the outward forms for fear of wounding people—but that was just part of a social code. What Loftus really meant was that she was a Mediterranean, by which he meant a pagan; she belonged to the Astarte-Aphrodite of Erice rather than to Holy Mary of Rome. I did not elaborate on all this, it was not our business.

At any rate she had satisfactorily managed to answer the question I had put to her in the Latomie at Syracuse; the word "yes" had been exactly where I had asked her to arrange for it to be. But about the question, it went something like this: "Do you remember all our studies and arguments over the Pali texts and all the advice you got from your Indian princeling? Well, before you finally died did you manage to experience that state, however briefly, which the texts promised us and which was rendered no doubt very inadequately in English as 'form without identity'?" Rather long-winded, but it is hard to express these abstract notions. Yet I was delighted to think that perhaps she might have experienced the precious moment of pure apprehension which had so far eluded me—which I could intuit but not provoke: poems are inadequate substitutes for it.

Loftus said: "After dinner I must put you on a tape-recording of a dinner party we had once here; she wanted to ask me some questions about Theocritos and Pindar, and then she forgot to take the tape. I found it long afterwards. It's pleasant to hear her voice again."

So it was, and the setting was not the less pleasant, this warm olive grove steepening towards the sea. The chink of plates and the little rushes of laughter or the clash of people all talking together. Marline's swift Italian. Somewhere she said that she had given instructions to her lawyers to let her lie in state one whole night on the beach at Naxos, close to the sea, so that like a sea-shell she could absorb the sighing of the sea and take it with her wherever she was going. "I don't know if she did," said Loftus, "but the idea struck me as typical of her and I dreamed about it for several nights. Martine, all dressed in white, lying in her beautiful coffin which was like a Rolls, lying on the beach almost within reach of the waves, under the stars."

It was late when the chauffeur finally dropped me back in Taormina, but despite the lateness of the hour there were cafés open and I felt sufficiently elated by my evening to want to prolong it for a while; to have a quiet drink and think before turning in with my Pliny. I had, in a manner of speaking, recovered contact with Martine. It was reassuring to feel that she was, in a sense, still there, still bright in the memory of her friends. On the morrow I had promised to return and lunch with Loftus, bathe, and work out an itinerary for my last few days in Sicily. He on his part would have the little Morris serviced and fixed up for my journey on which he would have accompanied me had it not been for his ankle. I must say I was glad, for though he was good company, I still felt a little bit as if I was on a pilgrimage and wanted to spend the time alone before I took off once more for France.

I sat long over my drink, tasting the cool balm of the midnight air and listening to the occasional chaffering voices in the dark street. Taormina had fallen asleep like a rooks' nest; occasionally there was a little movement, a few voices—as if a dream had troubled the communal sleep. Then everything subsided once more into a hush. My waiter was almost asleep on his feet. I must really finish up, I thought, and have pity on him. Yet I lingered, and if I reflected upon Martine the thoughts were relatively down to earth and free from all the nostalgias which tend to lie in wait for one when the mysterious matter of death comes to the front of the stage. I was still very conscious of that tiny chuckle with which my friend had always demolished anything slack or sentimental, anything sloppy in style or insipid. Truth to tell, I hardly dared to mourn the girl so much did I dread the memory of that chuckle. For her even death had its own rationale, its strictness and inevitability. It was thus. It was so. And it must be accepted with good nature, good grace, good humour.

Even Loftus, *homo beatus* as he used to call himself (sitting in the garden in a deck-chair looking out to sea through an old brass telescope)—even he could not speak of her without a smile, as if of recognition. "You know," he said, during our dinner, and apropos of the tape-recording of her voice, "the English can be disappointing in so many ways, but in friendship they have no peers." Due, I think, to this quality of smiling good sense which made it easy to confront life and death without a false Roman stoicism.

I spared the waiter at last and walked slowly back to my lodgings, savouring the soft airs of the invisible dawn with delectation. I did not feel a bit sleepy, and indeed it was almost too late to go to bed. I was sorry not to be on the beach at Naxos, for I should have bathed and waited for the light to break before making myself some breakfast. I compromised with a tepid shower and a lie-down of an hour which was interrupted by the breakfast-gong.

That morning I had some shopping to do, and a suit to get cleaned. At the post office I ran into the two French ladies. They had had a great shock, and they gobbled like turkeys as they told me about it. As usual they had been sending off clutches of postcards to their friends and relations in France—they seemed to have no other occupation or thought in mind. But peering through the grille after posting a batch they distinctly saw the clerk sweep the contents of the box into the lap of his overall and walk into the yard in order to throw all the mail on to a bonfire which was burning merrily on the concrete, apparently fed by all the correspondence of Taormina. They were aghast and shouted out to him—as a matter of fact they could hardly believe their eyes at first. They thought they had to do with a madman—but no, it was only a striker. He was burning mail as fast as it was posted. When they protested he said "*Niente Niente* . . . questo e tourismo . . ."

I transcribe phonetically, and consequently inaccurately—but that is what they said he said; and I took him to be telling them something like "It's nothing at all, my little ladies, just a clutch of tourist junk."

But the links of our friendship had, I observed, begun to weaken already for I had forgotten their names. I racked my brains to recall them. Anyway they were leaving in the morning and were half nostalgic and half irritated by the high price of things and the general slipshodness and insolence of the small shopkeepers. But it is ever thus in tourist centres.

Soon I was to begin my solitary journeys in the little borrowed car, trying, in the days which were left me, to fill in the jigsaw of names and strike up a nodding acquaintance with so many of the places mentioned in the letters of Martine and in the guide. It was rather a breathless performance. I realised then that Sicily is not just an island, it is a sub-continent whose variegated history and variety of landscapes simply overwhelms the traveller who has not set aside at least three months to deal with it and its overlapping cultures and civilisations. But such a certainty rendered me in the event rather irresponsible and light-hearted. I took what I could get so to speak, bit deeply into places like Tyndarus, revisited Segesta, crossed the hairy spine of the island for another look at Syracuse; but this time on different roads, deserted ones. In some obscure quarry I came upon half-carved temple drums which had not yet been extracted from the rock. I had a look at the baby volcanoes in their charred and stenchy lands. Islands whose names I did not know came up out of the mist like dogs to watch me having a solitary bathe among the sea-lavender and squill of deserted estuaries near Agrigento. But everywhere there came the striking experience of the island—not just the impact of the folklorique or the sensational. Impossible to describe the moth-soft little town of Besaquino with its deserted presbytery where once there had been live hermits in residence. Centuripe with its jutting jaw and bronzed limestone—an immense calm necropolis where the rock for hundreds of yards was pitted like a lung with excavated tombs. Pantalica I think it was called.

But time was running out. I had decided, after a chance meeting with Roberto in the tavern of the Three Springs, to keep Etna for my last night—the appropriate send-off. He had promised to escort me to the top to watch the sun come up, and thence down to the airport to catch the plane.

I burnt Martine's letters on a deserted beach near Messina— she had asked me to do so; and I scattered the ashes. I regretted it rather, but people have a right to dispose of their own productions as they wish.

It was the end of a whole epoch; and appropriately enough I spent a dawn in the most beautiful theatre in the world—an act of which Etna itself appeared to approve because once, just to show me that the world was rightside up, she spat out a mouthful of hot coals, and then dribbled a small string of blazing diamonds down her chin. Roberto had been a little wistfully drunk in the tavern; he was recovering from his heart attack over the girl Renata, but he was rather bitter about tourism in general and tourists in particular—there was a new Carousel expected in a few days. I wondered about Deeds, what he was doing with himself;

and then I had the queer dissolving feeling that perhaps he had never existed or that I had imagined him. Roberto was saying: "Travelling isn't honest. Everyone is trying to get away from something or else they would stay at home. The old get panicky because they can't make love any more, and they feel death in the air. The others, well, I bet you have your own reasons too. In the case of the officer Deeds you know his young brother is buried in that little cemetery where he told us about the locust-beans—one of the commandos he mentioned. Much younger than him I gather." He went on a while in a desultory fashion, while we drank off a bit of blue-black iron-tasting wine—I wondered if our insides would rust. I had done my packing, I had bought my postcards and guides. I wondered vaguely what Pausanias had been trying to get away from as he trudged round Athens taking notes. A Roman villa on the Black Sea, a nagging wife, the solitary consular life to which he had, as an untalented man, doomed himself?

We walked slowly back to my hotel in the fine afternoon light; and there another surprise awaited me. In my bedroom sat an extraordinary figure which I had, to the best of my knowledge, never seen before. A bald man with a blazing, glazed-looking cranium which was so white that it must have been newly cropped. It was when he removed his dark glasses and grinned that I recognised, with sinking heart, my old travelling companion Beddoes. "Old boy," he said, with a kind of fine elation, "they are on my trail, the carabinieri. Interpol must have lit a beacon. So I had to leave my hotel for a while." I did not know what to say. "But I am sneaking off tonight on the Messina ferry and Roberto has arranged to have me cremated, so to speak."

"Cremated?"

"Tonight, old boy, I jump into Etna like old Empedocles, with a piercing eldrich shriek. And you and Roberto at dawn scatter some of my belongings round the brink, and the Carousel announces my death to the press."

"You take my breath away. Roberto said nothing to me. And I have just left him."

"You can't be too discreet in these matters. Anyway it is just Sicilian courtesy. They often let people disappear like that."

"Beddoes, are you serious?"

It sounded like the sudden intrusion of an *opera bouffe* upon the humdrum existence of innocent tourists. And then that amazing glazed dome, glittering and resplendent. It looked sufficiently new to attract curiosity and I was relieved to see that he covered it up with a dirty ski-cap. Clad thus he looked like a madly determined Swiss concierge. "Roberto asked me to leave my belongings here with you. When he calls for you at midnight just carry them along; he will know what to do. And it's quite a neat parcel."

"Very well," I said reluctantly, and he beamed and shook my hand as he said goodbye. Then, turning at the door, he said: "By the way, old scout, I forgot to ask you if you could loan me a few quid. I am awfully pushed for lolly. I had to buy a spare pair of boots and an overcoat to complete my disguise. Cost the earth." I obliged with pardonable reluctance and he took himself off, whistling "Giovanezza" under his breath.

His belongings consisted of a sleeping-bag and a mackintosh, plus a pair of shapeless navvy's boots. The suitcase was empty save of a copy of a novel entitled *The Naked Truth.*

Roberto was punctual and accepted full responsibility for the plot concerning Beddoes' disappearance. Apparently the authorities often turned a blind eye to the disappearance of people into Etna. He said: "There's only one other volcano where one can arrange that sort of thing for hopeless lovers or bankrupts or schoolmasters on the run like Beddoes. It's in Japan."

The car drummed and whined its way into the mountains and I began to feel the long sleep of this hectic fortnight creep upon me. I had a drink and pulled myself together for we had to envisage a good walk at the other end, from the last point before the crater, the observatory. It became cooler and cooler. Then lights and mountain air with spaces of warmth, and the smell of acid and sulphur as we walked up the slopes of the crater. Somewhere near the top we lit a bonfire and carefully singed Beddoes' affairs before consigning them to the care of a carabinieri friend who would declare that he had found them on the morrow. The boots burned like an effigy of wax—he must have greased them with something. Poor old Beddoes!

Then the long wait by a strange watery moonlight until an oven lid started to open in the east and the "old shield-bearer" stuck its nose over the silent sea. "There it is," said Roberto, as if he had personally arranged the matter for me. I thanked him. I reflected how lucky I was to have spent so much of my life in the Mediterranean—to have so frequently seen these incomparable dawns, to have so often had sun and moon both in the sky together.

PROVENCE

Durrell moved to France in 1957, soon after leaving the civil strife of Cyprus. Durrell lived in Southern Provence for the next thirty-three years. He published his last book Caesar's Vast Ghost: Aspects of Provence in 1990, the year of his death.

In Praise of Fanatics

(1962)

THE JOB OF A PROVINCIAL EDITOR may not be a particularly enviable one in any country, but my friend Lejoie who guides the destinies of the largest of the country newspapers in Provence
manages to make it sound full of variety and interest. He weaves
his way with skill and tact among the diplomatic and political
quicksands of the post—always gay, always tireless, always good-
humoured. Also, being a Frenchman, he has a keen eye for the
downright ridiculous, and provincial life is full of it—to the brim.

Nevertheless it is not easy to mediate effectively between all the
different factions which assail the provincial daily and its chief—to
poultice (for example) the wounds of a village mayor whose name
has been spelt wrong twice running, to represent a strongly felt
case for an augmentation of salaries without falling foul of government policy, to criticize an art show as honestly as possible within
the limits of fair comment . . . ('Sir: I feel I must protest strongly on
behalf of the village of Plages (200 souls) against the gross calumnies
levelled against our artist-mayor in your columns.')

Perhaps it is the very intricacy of the job which has made Lejoie
into a 'spare-time student of fanaticism'—as he says; I did not
exactly know how he qualified the word until one day he cited,
among the great number of French eccentrics who have left works
of art behind them, the name of the Postman Horse—Le Facteur
Cheval. He was delighted to find that I had never heard of this
estimable man, or of the Ideal Palace which he built in response to
a vision. 'As a spare-time work it is certainly unique,' said Lejoie
wistfully. 'The man was a village postman in the Drôme whose

duties involved him in a thirty kilometre tramp every day. On his return at night he would surrender himself to the intoxication of his vision and set about building this extraordinary monument which, if it had not been built in such an out-of-the-way place as his native village, Hauterives, might well have earned him a reputation similar to that other naïf Douanier Rousseau.'

'You think so?'

'I certainly do; and you will agree. I'll tell you more of him and unearth some pictures which will give you an idea. He's a sort of Gaudi—only touched with French fanaticism.'

'You mean a monomaniac?'

'No. Just a Frenchman. I'll find the pictures.'

He was as good as his word and on a subsequent visit he tumbled out onto the table between us a number of postcard views of this strange monument.

'Why, it's a sort of private Albert Hall,' I said.

'Except that it's got every style mixed into it. It isn't consistent to a single style or influence. It's got the whole blasted world of assorted architectures all rolled into one cake mix.'

The Ideal Palace of the Facteur Cheval was begun in 1879 and only finished in 1912, single-handed. The pictures which Lejoie showed me depicted one of the weirdest monuments which it has ever been my good fortune to gaze upon—a sort of giant wedding-cake of styles and moods all welded together into a building which was twenty-six metres long by fourteen broad; it was about twelve metres high—the height of a modern two-storied villa.

Only an inspired lunatic would have hoped to juxtapose and marry up all these different styles in one work—or at least that is what one feels as one looks at the pictures. To this proposition Lejoie replied: 'Yes, but there is something else which these pictures don't quite capture; they emphasize only its apparent eccentricity. There's more than that in it. It really deserves to be seen. As a matter of fact the thing is in my own village in the Drôme, and as a child I spent my holidays playing in the ideal Palace of the old Postman—his private Xanadu, you might say. It left the strangest impression on me. As a matter of fact I am distantly connected to the postman's family—hence the fine streak of fanaticism in my own make-up. Would you care to come north for a week-end and have a look at it? I could promise you other things of interest. My mother lives there and she is married to Chabert, the great chef. They run a tiny hotel to which they admit only friends who care about . . .'

'Don't tell me; let me guess. Food!'

'Sometimes for an Anglo-Saxon you are quite discerning. Yes, in a word, food. Such food!'

'I am your man,' I said solemnly.

When he left that evening he allowed me to keep the strange pictures, and also a small autobiographical fragment written by the Postman in his old age—a document almost as strange as the pictures.

It was written in simple schoolboy French which gave it an oracular ring, both touching and authoritative. It was a sort of artistic credo—but it smelt strangely of the direct vision of somebody like Blake. I read it over slowly and with growing admiration.

'The son of peasant folk [it began], and myself therefore a peasant, I would like to live and die in such a manner as to prove that even in my own order of life men of genius and energy can be born, can exist. I've been a village postman for twenty-nine years now. Work has been my only glory, honour my only well-being. Up to today, then, here is my strange history. Once in a dream I conceived and built a place, a château in which there were grottoes. . . . I don't know how to explain it . . . but so ravishing, so picturesque, that for ten years the whole thing stayed engraved in my memory. I could not get rid of it. Of course I took myself for a fool, a maniac. I was no mason, to start with; I had never touched a trowel. As for sculpture I'd never touched a chisel. As for architecture—leave it right out of the picture—I know nothing of it. I did not dare to breathe a word about my dream to a soul for fear of being laughed at in the village. To be truthful, I laughed at myself a bit. Fifteen years later, when I had almost forgotten this remote dream, a chance slip of the foot jogged my memory. I tripped and fell over an object. It was a stone of a form so bizarre that I slipped it into my pocket, in order to study it at leisure. The next day I went back to the same spot and found others, even more beautiful. The stone was of a softish kind, deeply worked by river-water and finally hardened by time into something as tough as possible; but the shapes—they represented a sort of sculpture so bizarre that I doubted if any man could imitate it. It was full of different species of animal, human caricatures. I said to myself then: "Well, if nature can sculp so easily I am sure I can master masonry and architecture." Here then was my dream at last. "To work," I said to myself!'

From that moment the Facteur Cheval was fully awakened to his real mission in life. A dream was trying to get born, to get transformed into a reality. He began to keep a sharp lookout on his thirty kilometre tramp for rare and curious stones—the raw material for the Ideal Palace. His vision was sharpened, his appetite whetted. Soon these lovely objects of *virtu* began to invade his heavy post-bag as he tramped along. It should be remembered that the Facteur in France does not only deliver letters. He has several other onerous duties as well—to pay pensions, for example, and to collect receipts. It is not an easy job, particularly when in addition to your mail-bag you load yourself up with stones. He also began to extend his range in his search for new beauties. Dry river-beds yielded him beautifully polished gems, the lush flanks of the rolling Drôme hillsides other treasures. A Japanese artist would have understood immediately what had happened to the Facteur Cheval, but in his own village they began to whisper that he was showing signs of incipient insanity. No matter. He was in the grip of the curious insatiable fever which only the artist knows and recognizes. Sometimes the stones grew so many that he was forced to leave them in piles by the roadside, strategically, stacked for loading. At night when he got home he would take his old wheelbarrow and walk back to get them by moonlight, tireless, grim— absorbed in the first aesthetic pleasure he had ever known. Sometimes he was up until two or three in the morning ferrying stones for the Ideal Palace. One begins to see what the good Lejoie means when he uses the word 'fanaticism'. . . .

But you cannot please everybody—not even by trying to build a Xanadu. The Facteur's wife began to complain bitterly that his clothes were getting worn to rags by his exertions, and by the stones he carried. His pockets were all shot to hell and his trousers covered in mud. Sometimes just the *corner* of a beautiful stone caught his eye and he simply had to dig it out. Grimly he persevered, turning a deaf ear to family scolding and village gossip alike. But it wasn't only the stones; his poor wife, who watched the Ideal Palace growing in the rambling garden by the river, began to complain of the expense. Every spare sou was spent on bags of cement and lime. How could all this be done on a postman's pay? One can understand that from her point of view the whole thing was a grotesque folly, a monomania. In the final analysis the Dream Palace was to cost them 3,500 sacks of cement, and to represent 1,000 cubic metres of masonry; and on the Eastern Facade the old Postman was to engrave the legend:

'1879–1912

10,000 days

93,000 hours

33 years of hardship

If there is anyone more obstinate than I, let him fall to work.'

It was a splendid credo, and in the course of time the Postman's dream justified all these heroic efforts. But phew! It made my back ache just to think of the plain man-hauling involved for the project, let alone the task of building.

'It is not really a building,' said Lejoie patiently; 'nor is it quite a sculpture. It's a work which creates its own crazy idiom. Now in our age it is easy to recognize the force and charm of the naive, we are trained to it. But this strange lump, chunk, object was completed in the year of Picasso's first cubist experiments. That is what is so odd about it. Anyway, wait till you see. By the way, all the arrangements are made. We set off tomorrow.'

We did. It was a Saturday. He was carefree. The great Chef Chabert had deigned to allow us to stay at his hotel, after many careful questions as to whether I merited the sort of cuisine in which he specialized. We could take an easy trip north, visit the Ideal Palace, and return to Tain which was only half an hour's drive from Hauterives. The first stop was to be somewhere near Perols where a meal had been planned which would serve, I gathered, as a sort of spiritual launching pad towards our objective.

So we followed the left bank of the Rhone which was relatively unencumbered by northbound holiday traffic, and once we crossed the border into Ardèche my friend, as if to signify a formal throwing off of responsibility towards his station in life, removed his coat and tie and donned a comfortable wind-breaker and scarf. He was no longer the grave and responsible editor of an important southern daily, but a holidaymaker like everyone else. It was only in his home department of the Gard that he risked being stoned to death by outraged painters, or torn to ribbons by ministers without portfolio, quizzed by communes, or caught with his pants down (metaphorically) by regional officials. That little sign by the roadside 'Vous êtes dans l'Ardèche' allowed him to feel, all at once, quite unbuttoned, uncorked, and set by the chimneypiece to breathe, like a good bottle of wine.

We sang a few songs, but not loudly enough to disturb the nightingales which had responded to a few light showers the day before and decided upon a snap daylight appearance. No, our music, which perhaps was not good of its kind, was at least without prejudice to man or beast. Here and there, too, we made a pretence of needing petrol and turned into inviting routiers' inns where, in a sunny garden, we took the measure of the country by addressing a local wine with gravity and aplomb.

If Lejoie had, so to speak, cast off the editor, I for my part was quite ready to cast off the writer and thinker. A touch of the scholar-gipsy was what the situation seemed to warrant, and I felt I had just that. This week-end, I told myself, I should be free to devote myself to higher living and lower thinking. Why not?

But once or twice I did seem to catch the reproachful voice of the Postman Horse whispering in my ear that laziness was all very well, but that nothing really gets done without brutish labour. I had brought his little autobiography along in my pocket, and we had been discussing it. 'I can't go into all the details,' writes the old Postman, 'nor describe the troubles and miseries that I had to endure; it would be wearying. Nor indeed does my limited education permit me to express it all. But quite simply I carried everything on my back, working night and day for twenty-six years, without a halt, without mercy. The visitors who come now from other countries—and in increasing numbers—have difficulty in believing the evidence of their own eyes; they have to be reassured by the testimony of the local inhabitants before believing that a single man, all alone, could possibly muster the courage and will-power to build such a masterpiece. They marvel, and keep saying: "No, it's not possible." "No, it's unbelievable." '

It sounds a little immoral I know, but the thought of all that back-breaking labour added a certain vicarious luxury to these moments of sunny ease and relaxation—the two of us sitting before a wineglass in a sunny arbour by the ancient Rhone. 'But then,' said Lejoie, spreading his hands in a self-excusing gesture, 'any gourmet will tell you that to eat and drink creatively is also a labour.'

'Yes, but rather a pleasant one.'

'Besides,' he added, 'one carries the raw material for that sort of work inside one, and not on one's back.'

'Thank God.'

But he had something there and I told him so. We faced up to the invisible spectre of the Postman's reproaches and ordered another glass before rolling on northward in the direction of Tournon, towards that beckoning table which stood under a lime-tree in an orchard, dappled with sunlight. For my part I was some-what suspicious of the lunch, fearing first of all that if I overdid it my sensibility would be too blunted to take in the Ideal Palace; and secondly that I might find myself unable to do justice to Chabert's creations that evening. It would be horrible to be expelled from the hotel as a godless and unworthy guest, thus bringing discredit on my friend and sponsor. But Lejoie clicked his tongue reproach-fully at me when I voiced these sentiments. 'Fear nothing,' he said, 'I have ordered a light meal which is calculated to sharpen the sensibility without wearing out your lining or overtaxing the liver. We will proceed according to a carefully graduated scale I have worked out.'

'In calories?'

'No. In tastes and smells.'

He was as good as his word and when finally we settled down at that sunny table, neatly spread with its check cloth, my doubts began to fade; after all it had been a long drive, full of intellectual conversation which takes it out of a man. Moreover the faint whiffs of cooking which curled out of the kitchen on to the tideless air of that vernal afternoon were curiously stimulating. A splendid bosomy matron had been charged to attend to us; rosy-cheeked and blue-eyed, she gave off waves of motherly confidence. A mother-figure, a repository for confidences—that is how one felt as one watched her roll across the lawn with a basket of bread. No. No harm could come to us here; we were among people who could be trusted not to send us reeling out into the main road with purple faces, with gorged, starting eyeballs. Well, we lunched according to the severely graduated scale of my friend, on a *tarte aux morilles,* a splendid sort of mushroom tart, and a *truite aux amandes.* At least these were the two main features of an excellent lunch. If there was any fear that the trout, dappled in the browned almonds, might prove a somewhat cumbersome dish for aesthetes, it was easily dispelled; we managed a couple each with the greatest ease, the most effortless sang-froid. The wine which my friend unearthed for the occasion was a delightful little Chante-Alouette (a 'Sing-Lark') calculated to put even the tone-deaf into a good mood. So we lingered, gossiping our way through cheese and fruit, and finally sat replete to watch the blue smoke of a good cigar hang above us in the sunlight, mixing its exotic flavour with that of the limes and the wet flowerbeds.

We had broken the back of our journey; it was only about half an hour's drive to the Xanadu of the Facteur Cheval. The sun was well past meridian when we crossed the river and rolled eastward, cutting directly across the two great northbound arteries with their rushing traffic, and nosing out towards the greener country in which the village of Hauterives nestled in its green seclusion.

The landscape changed softly as we headed towards Hauterives, becoming gradually greener and more densely wooded. The clear limestone formations talked of subterranean rivers, of chalk, and of rich soil; the little hills wore dense green topknots out of which peeped the eaves of old châteaux; the roads began to turn and twist, to rise and fall like a conductor's baton. It was another of those empty corners of France, rich with farms but sparsely populated, where the jerry-builder and the money-mad industrialist have as yet seen nothing they could exploit, nothing they could rape. We ran down an inclined plane into the village and drew up in the market-place, surprised to find that the noise of the engine was replaced only by the cooing of doves and the drone of bees. There was not a soul about. 'From here,' said Lejoie, 'we walk a few hundred yards to Xanadu.'

It was late afternoon. There were few people stirring in the village of the Postman Horse. Once or twice we heard the clank of pots or the sound of someone stoking a furnace, but the only people we actually met were a few children eating sweets and talking in low voices.

Here and there some of the plaster had fallen from the wall of a house and I was interested to notice that it had been built entirely of rounded river-stones cemented by mortar; stones the size of ostrich eggs. There was a man trimming fruit trees in a desultory fashion. The sound of the sécateurs fractured the silence. Finally we skirted a long high wall and knocked at an iron gate. It was opened by a dark pleasant-looking girl to whom Lejoie said a word; she was at once all smiles, drying her hands in her apron. But I had already caught sight of the Ideal Palace, of which she was the custodian. It stood there, imposing yet modest in an ineffaceable sort of way, neither inviting nor repelling scrutiny. The gardens surrounding it were full of tall trees. It smelt of peace and repose and verdure.

We entered the little office to buy our tickets and I saw, with something bordering on irritation, that this girl—an ordinary peasant girl, talking with a marked provincial accent—was reading a book about abstract painting. It was lying face down, where she had left it in order to answer our knock. Really the French drive you mad with anxiety and frustration! Wherever you go, whoever you meet, you find them engaged in some intellectual pursuit, reading recondite books, painting, cooking, playing the harp or writing sonnets. Damn them, it is unfair that the whole country is creative, or trying to be; the whole blasted population, regardless of education or breeding, is obsessed by the maniacal desire to manufacture a work of art. Finally it gets you absolutely mad with envy when you think of your own damn nation, loafing about in a brutish daze, a sort of Philistine dementia. What ails these big-arsed cart horses at home that they cannot enjoy drinking from the source of all the fun in the world?

In a sort of way the Facteur Cheval, whose monument stood outside waiting to be examined, increased my feeling of self-reproach. We approached Xanadu in silence and Lejoie, with the typical tact of his kind, turned aside into one of the corners in order to let me take the thing in slowly, in the round. Well, it is not really large, of course. It is not the size of the Parthenon; indeed I should say that it is about the size of the Theseum. But there is a mystery about it, which has nothing to do with the strangeness of the subject matter. It is—and here I am weighing my words—one of the most *unexpected* of works. It is very much more than a folly: and I realized with shame that, despite Lejoie's warning, I had come prepared to be touched and amused by a folly. How British! I had really come to Hauterives to Betjemanize! And all of a sudden I was face to face with the fiery Blakeian vision of an uneducated postman, but something brimming with a queer kind of authenticity of its own. Where did it lie?

Before I answer this question I must, so to speak, subtract the fantasy—this extraordinary monument, crawling like a Hindu temple, with a thousand different things: heads of martyrs, soldiers, monkeys, palm-trees, peacocks, apes, palm-trees, Crusaders, Romans, Greeks, Druids, Persians . . . but this is not all; almost every type of known architecture was represented here from Stonehenge to Altamira, from Rome and Greece to Babylon, from the White House to a Swiss chalet! There was a cascade, a labyrinth, a Saracen tomb, a menhir, a mosque, a Norman belfry, a labyrinth, a . . . but the thing was a sort of dictionary of every known style. I understood now why the Surrealists had claimed the Facteur Cheval as one of them (at least Breton did on their behalf): the juxtaposition of styles and modes was fantastic and gave one the requisite Surrealist shock.

But this was not all; there was something else, something troubling and exciting about the whole work, which was not due to this eccentric mix-up of dissimilar styles and objects. I caught Lejoie as he was climbing the twisted turret staircase to the first floor, so to speak, and expressed my excitement by saying, as I pressed his arm: 'But the whole bloody thing has congruence.' He sighed as if with relief, but said nothing. Smiling we mounted the spiral staircase, bringing a whole new set of frescoes into sunny relief. The gargoyles of Notre Dame stuck out their tongues at Apes from Barbary; two Crusaders confronted an effigy from a sarcophagus of the age of Semiramis.

Then, all of a sudden, I understood why this whole piece of

work enjoyed a kind of completeness of its own, the kind of completeness which only true works of art enjoy. The Facteur had been neither a madman nor somebody trying to show off. He had responded to the sacred vision honestly, that was all; he had actually copied his dream accurately, trusting it implicitly to carry him where it would, faithful only to it. There was, so to speak, not a dishonest thought, a *factice* element in the whole of this grotesque monument. In fact one might characterize it as a 'naturalistic' work—for where your naturalistic painter reproduces nature as fairly as he sees it, so did the Facteur Cheval. . . . If he had been a Surrealist, a gimmick-artist, a Dali, something would have smelt wrong about the whole work.

As it was, it had an extraordinary perfection, a repose. The Ideal Palace is indeed ideal—it is the palace of the world's childhood, admirably and deftly captured. I wished bitterly that my own children were with me to see it; it would have given them a strange aftertaste of their own daydreams. They would have recognized it inside themselves as something far more truthful than any Disney fantasy. A *real* childhood accords full reality only to visions, and respects them. Here was the Postman's vision in stone.

Here and there dotted about the old Postman carved up aphorisms in order to encourage himself, to freshen up his nagging forces, no doubt. Some are mere cracker mottoes, some little verses, some quotations from Holy Writ: some are free verse poems. It is like riffling the artist's notebook, or looking over his shoulder as he works.

> Sous la garde des géants
> J'ai placé l'épopée des humbles
> Courbé sur le sillon

La vie est un océan de tempêtes
Entre l'enfant qui vient de naître
Et le veillard qui va disparaître

Finally, when the whole work was complete down to the last inscription he even built a tomb for the faithful wheelbarrow which had been his constant companion for so many years. More than that, he permitted the wheelbarrow (which appears also to have been endowed with an aphoristic turn of mind) to write its own verses, its own funeral inscriptions. This is how the barrow expresses itself:

Je suis fidèle compagne
Du travailleur intelligent
Qui chaque jour dans la campagne
Cherchait son petit contingent.

Maintenant son oeuvre est finie
Il jouit en paix de son labeur,
Et chez lui, moi, son humble amie,
J'occupe la place d'honneur.

Together with the wheelbarrow in its quiet niche lie the tools with which the Ideal Palace was constructed.

But the path of genius never runs smooth; at the completion of his grand work the Postman Horse announced that he proposed to be buried in it; he had prepared his own tomb. Here he ran into opposition from the Church which has always been against permitting people to get themselves buried in their back gardens—I have never understood why. . . . A long argument ensued, but finally the Church won. The Postman Horse must, like everyone else, be buried in the village cemetery. Whatever his feelings he accepted this fiat at last and bought himself the requisite site. But here his artistic feelings overcame him. The indomitable old man set about building himself a tomb which is like a small annexe to the Ideal Palace, identical in style and inspiration. It took him ten years to complete it, but complete it he did; and that is where he lies today, under a simple inscription which might well have been carved over a Greek tomb containing the bones of a Heraclitus or an Epicurus.

Le tombeau du lilence et du refos sans fin.

We motored slowly out of the beautiful village of Hauterives, across the bridge which spanned the rushing trout-stream, in a pleasant silence—the only sort of tribute one can pay to artistic experience. Along these leafy green lanes I seemed to see the little postman tramping along, wheeling his choice stones back to the quiet house, talking quietly to himself as he walked. A plump pheasant walked across the road and Lejoie said: 'We shall reach Chabert's in twenty-five minutes.'

It was only, after all, a switch from one art-form to another, for Chabert we found to be almost as much of a visionary as the old postman. His little hotel stands in the main street of Tain l'Hermitage which has the air of being a little market-town running to urbanization. Like nearly all good eating places in France the exterior is unprepossessing. It is simply a pleasant old-world bar attached to a restaurant. The Hotel is a private one, a mere diversion you might say, for there are only seven guest rooms. You can only stay there if the master invites you, and he only invites a special race of men—*les gens qui vraiment aiment manger.* I could see him anxiously scan my face to see if really I merited his hospitality.

The great Chabert was a small compact man with greyish hair and finely cut features; he gave off a feeling of unhurried calm, of gentleness. He was obviously someone who could watch a pot boil without getting rattled; every movement of the hands was eloquent. They were the hands of a musician, of someone who was sure of his effects.

Of course there was a good deal of hubbub, introductions, explanations, when first we arrived. Lejoie's mother was delighted to see him; it was nearly six months since his last visit. He had brought characteristic presents for them both in the form of a rare cheese from Gascony and a bottle of liqueur. Our luggage was unloaded while we had a stirrup-cup. Chabert popped in and out of his kitchen where half a dozen white-capped young men juggled with the pots and pans under his watchful direction. The promised dinner was already on the slips. It would be ready within the hour. But first, said Chabert, he would like to convey some general information about the wines of the district and to this end we could profitably kill an hour or two before dining, combining information with pleasure. Chapoutier? Where had I heard the name?

As a matter of fact it is written in letters a mile high right across the hillside behind Tain l'Hermitage; you can read it four miles off. It signals the ownership of the best vineyards of the region. As we set off down the darkening street Lejoie refreshed my memory on this point. It was only two streets away from Chabert.

Chapoutier himself was seated before his desk in the imposing central office of the firm, waiting for us; before him stood a magnum of champagne. From time to time he touched it and turned it in its bucket with the air of a doctor taking its pulse. He was a young man, gay and spirited as became a wine-specialist. The keys to the great cellars lay before him.

Lejoie was an old friend, of course, which got conversation away to a merry start. Pouring out the champagne Chapoutier said deprecatingly that it should not be taken seriously; it was a mere *rince-bouche,* a mouthwash, in order to clear the palate before we tasted the wines in the cellar. I tried to regard it in this light, purely as a medicament, but I could not help enjoying it just a little. It had an exquisite flavour. In fact I could have gone on rinsing my palate all night with this admirable stuff.

But at last the bottle was finished, and deeming us all suitably clean-palated, Chapoutier pressed a tall goose-necked wineglass into each hand, and taking up his keys and his pipette he led us out into the dark street and across to the great cellars.

The night was clear and fine; the cellars deep and immense and secret. As the lights were switched on here and there they showed bins and barrels and *tonneaux* stretching away on all sides, into the darkness, around us, symmetrically ruling away perspectives into infinity. Keen-eyed, clean-palated, we followed our host slowly from bin to bin, accepting a squirt of each of the vintages from his hospitable pipette, and sitting down to savour it on the nearest cask. There is no need to go into the details of all we tasted. Chapoutier's wine is too well known and has been the subject of numberless essays and studies. It is, however, important to record that his conversation sparkles every bit as excitingly as his most sparkling wine. But then the object of good wine is, and always has been, good conversation. The eleventh commandment has always been, 'Drink well to talk well.'

In those cavernous cellars, their walls covered with a deep lichen-coloured fungus—the bloom you get on an over-ripe peach—in the semi-darkness, voices muffled by the thick medieval walls, we found conversation take wing. By the time we had broached the twelfth white bin and the fourth red we had discussed as well as toasted Rabelais, Mallarmé and Stendhal; we had sent Marxists about their business, decried religious bigotry, deplored the French Revolution, denounced the Bourbons and the Jesuits, flung defiance at nuclear physics, vaunted Byron, Poe and Rimbaud, rapped Henry James over the knuckles, and sung a few staves of Georges Brassens. Intellectually speaking we left no glass unturned.

By the time we staggered out into the night, somewhat dishevelled but still keen-eyed and burning with intellectual zeal, I felt as if I were moving on castors.

The night air was cool and soothing to our fevered heads, however, and while our tongues had been loosened by these excellent snecks of wine they were still attached to our brains. At any rate that is how it felt. Under a street lamp we all embraced ferociously like French generals conferring decorations upon each other, and swore undying blood-brothership. 'Come again,' cried Chapoutier with warmth. 'Any time at all. It is a pleasure to have some good conversation.'

By the time we reached Chabert's the cozy table had been laid in a private corner of the restaurant, and the master watched us enter with a quizzical eye. 'Ah, you are just in the right mood,' he said approvingly. 'Often people are knocked silly by a visit to the cellars and run the risk of not appreciating their dinners. Then I have to let them wait an extra half-hour—and of course I risk the quality of the dinner.' Everything is very finely calculated in France—according to a graduated scale.

Now began one of those famous Chabert dinners, gathering its way slowly like a Bach fugue, moving through scale after scale, figure after figure, its massive counterpoint swelling and gathering. And yet without any pomp whatsoever; quietly, deprecatingly the great Chef himself attended to the dishes, getting up from the table to make some minor arrangement with his own hands, and sitting down again to reminisce quietly over his early life in the French navy. He had started as a sea-cook when he was thirteen; slowly he had worked his way up the scale into what he had now become, a master-chef, an artist. His wife smiled as she listened, chin in hand, to these early adventures, and then she in her turn spoke about the Facteur Cheval whom she had seen when she was a little girl. 'An irascible quick-tempered little man,' she said, nodding her dark Mediterranean head and smiling. 'He was very much on the defensive because everyone said he was a fool. He defended his own genius to the death.'

'He was right,' said Chabert approvingly.

'He was right,' said Lejoie.

'He was right,' said I.

Meanwhile this memorable dinner was slowly gathering form and momentum before us. Later that night on my way up to bed I asked Chabert to write it all down for me in his own hand. I wanted an autograph as well as the Menu. It is perfectly useless to describe good food. The thing escapes words, as poetry does, and indeed all good art. Here, then, is what Chabert wrote down in his fine nervous hand.

> Les Quenelles de brochet à ma façon
> Le vin St. Joseph Rouge
> > Côtes Rôties 1952
> Pâté de Canard truffé avec des petits
> oignons à la Grecque et à la mode de chez-moi
>
> Pintadeaux nouveaux aux bananes
> (Sauces avec Madère, Porto, Crème, Glace de
> Viande etc.)
> > Petits Chèvres de Chantemerle
> > Coupe de Fraises Melba

The reader will notice the phrases 'à ma façon' and 'à la mode de chez-moi', and imagine that like all great chefs Chabert is keeping his trade secrets to himself. This is not the case; it is simply his modesty which prevents him from adding his own name to the dish, as he would have every right to do—as every great inventive chef does in France. He deplores this habit and says that it smacks of pretentiousness. For his part he believes that a great chef should do everything well and a few things of his own choice superbly.

'You see? He is another fanatic,' said Lejoie as he listened smiling. We were all sitting together over a glass of fine brandy listening to the clock chime midnight. Soon I would be comfortably tucked up in bed, my drowsy brain packed with dazzling impressions of this visit, trying in vain to sort them out. 'I hope you'll write something about it,' said Lejoie suddenly, as we were all saying good-night. 'I would feel the visit had been worthwhile.'

We lagged upon the staircase, slowly talking our way up into the darkness of the first floor.

'If I did what would I call it?' I said.

' "In Praise of Fanatics," of course,' said Lejoie.

So I have.

Laura, A Portrait of Avignon
(1961)

The psycho-analyst incautious enough to ask me to associate freely on the word Avignon, or indeed to riffle through my travel diary, would not I think be too surprised by the word Laura as an opening gambit. Literary men are supposed to be literary. But what would he make of the other entries, I wonder? They run like this. (I always use the laws of free association in my diaries. It saves time and keeps them fresh.)

> Bringing Laura!! back.
> Plumber, water-tap, Gargantua.
> Edgar Allan Poe.
> 'If her ragoût is good . . .'

Mysterious enough to baffle an analyst I think, but really quite simple. The truth of the matter is this, that I went to Avignon with a plumber called Raoul to find a water tap and bring back a bride called 'Laura'. There is nothing more Petrarchian than a girl called Laura, living in Avignon, who advertises in the Marriage section of *Midi Libre* saying, 'Lasse d'être seule, je veux me marier.'

But let me begin with the plumber called Raoul. He was, as plumbers go, one of the most careless and destructive men I have ever known. He had one hand rather bigger than the other, which may explain it. I don't know. But the fact is that if he tried to take a pipe out of a wall the whole wall came; whatever he tried to bend broke off short. He would stand with an air of dribbling amazement looking at the smashed object, blushing. He didn't know his own strength and seldom looked where he was going. When he fell down the earth shook. He had a high foolish neighing laugh which he used continuously. I imagine the damned in hell laugh in just this way. In fact I cannot think why I ever liked him. I think I was curious. He was so like an infant Gargantua, so typically Provençal, that I listened to his accounts of what he ate and drank like a man in a dream. Barrels of oysters, drums of red wine, whole oxen fresh from the spit. Often he ate so much that he was indisposed and this affected his work. His clients never knew at such times what might not come out of the kitchen tap. It was safer not to turn it on.

Now this absolute fool of a man had a mate, a silent morose little man who looked like Schopenhauer, whose job was to trot behind him and pick up the remains. He never spoke, the mate. It was hardly necessary. He wore a soiled beret and had a cigarette stuck to his bottom lip. When Raoul got playful he often threw pieces of pig iron about, and I think the mate kept all his energies for side-stepping. Anyway between them they broke the garden tap, a rather fancy one with a sort of key-shaped handle which could be removed in order to foil marauders. (In the summer a good deal of water-pinching from the neighbour's well is quite fashionable. You wait till your neighbour goes out and then swiftly water your geraniums.) The tap itself came from Paris, and it wasn't replaceable (so Raoul said) unless he went to the whole-saler in Avignon. This meant a journey of about seventy miles. 'Why,' he said, 'don't you come for the ride?' The idea didn't seem a bad one. Raoul added suddenly, blushing to the roots of his mane—he grew his hair half-way down his back—'I have got to go there anyway soon to arrange for my marriage.' Then he showed me the advertisement in the paper. He had been in touch with the girl and she sounded rather promising. They had agreed to meet. Then he added hoarsely, 'Her name is Laura.'

Laura! I thought of the honeyed sonnets of Petrarch, of the long years of his agony (was it contrived?). I thought of the splendid simplicity of the old anonymous Abbé J. T. who described the meeting in his smoothly turned French. I have an old biography of Petrarch which I picked up on the banks of the Seine. 'Le lundi de la Semaine-Sainte, à six heures du matin, Pétrarque vit à Avignon, dans l'Eglise des Religieuses de Saint-Claire, une jeune femme dont la robe verte était parsemée de violettes. Sa beauté le frappa: c'était Laura.' It was as simple as that. Love at first sight! And now Raoul was going to get his. He looked quite dazed at having confided in me. For my part I had a sudden feeling of apprehensive sympathy for the poor girl. With such an infant Gargantua for a husband anything might happen. She would have to be as stoutly built as a camel-backed locomotive, I thought, not to run the risk of being overlaid or hit by the odd piece of pig-iron.

I said I would go.

I have always been a rash, foolish, intemperate and hasty man. Raoul was delighted. 'In that case,' he said, 'I will drive you, and you will pay for the petrol.'

I said I would. Raoul appeared one afternoon in the strange old covered wagon which he drove round the countryside full of twisted taps and pig-iron. His mate sat behind nursing a large demijohn of a wine he called Picpoul. As we snarled among the white roads he decanted it precariously into a blue mug which was passed around, each taking a ceremonial sip. It was rather fortifying, though it did not loosen the little man's tongue. Raoul, on the contrary, was extremely talkative and was pleased to expound some of his philosophy of life to me. 'Now I would never have gone for a girl from one of those agencies,' he said confidentially, 'You never know what you get from an agency. But a girl who bothers to pay for her own advertisement is clearly serious. They cost a good deal, those private ads. I let hers run for over a week before I answered. It must have cost her a pretty penny. Of course one can easily be mistaken, though I must say she sounds all right from her specifications.' He sounded as if he were thinking of buying a barge. 'First of all,' he said, clearing his throat, 'she is religious and of good family; her father was a well-digger and she has a vineyard. She is strong and capable of a child or two, which would be fine. Lastly she is a Cordon Bleu. This is the only point on which one has to be a bit careful. Sometimes one passes these cooking exams through a bit of *piston*. So I'm going slowly until I know. We'll try her out on a *ragoût* first. It is my favourite dish. If her *ragoût* is good . . .' Involuntarily we all licked our lips and passed the blue can of wine. It seemed to me such a healthy, such a practical attitude.

'Mind you,' added Raoul, 'one can easily make a mistake. It comes from lack of detail in the advertisements. It is so costly that you have to abbreviate everything. And nobody confesses to the sort of faults which make or mar a marriage. For example in a woman one would expect to find a list of the dishes she really does well, and whether she nags. But what woman would confess to nagging? Similarly in a man a woman should know if he snores, is bad-tempered in the morning, and if he leaves a razor and brush unwashed after using. Such small questions sometimes make or mar a marriage. And you cannot put them all into a two line advertisement. A friend of mine who was unwise enough to get his wife from an agency only found out too late that she liked the music of Chopin. All day long she was glued to the radio. She would not play bowls, and she hated the smell of drink on his breath. Naturally they are divorced. Now as for Laura, she confesses that she is often melancholy and lonely, but I think it is due to being alone.

Her parents are dead. She works part-time in a mercer's shop. All this will have to be gone into very carefully before I decide anything. Also she says she does not dance very well, which makes me doubtful, for I love a good dance. However we shall see.'

Surprisingly his mate opened his mouth in the back to say, in tones of melancholy resignation, 'Ah she is probably a whore.' Raoul shook his head sadly; as one who deplores such a lack of faith in one's fellow man. 'You,' he said softly, 'never believe anyone. Pass the wine.'

We passed the wine, and I watched the slow Provençal roads unwinding among the foothills to right and left of us. Raoul's car stank horribly of burning rubber and hot steel, but it seemed to go quite well.

'Will you bring Laura back?' I asked and Raoul shrugged an elephantine shoulder as he replied. 'First we must settle this matter of the cooking. Then I have to show her my papers, all duly certified by the notary so that she can see how much property I have. A girl has to be cautious too.'

'And if she is ugly?' I asked. The thought surprised him. He had clearly not taken into account any question of personal attraction in the matter of marriage. 'Well she looks all right from her photograph,' he said. 'Not beautiful but nice.'

The little pessimist behind us said: 'You can tell nothing from photographs. Do photographs show wooden legs? She may be a hunchback for all you know.'

'In that case I shall withdraw from the deal.' said Raoul with simple dignity. 'I do not want a wife that one unscrews and hangs up from a nail each night. Naturally we shall have to examine every possibility.'

The little man belched.

With the warm sunlight and the pleasant though slightly

tainted breeze that came in through the side-windows I fell into a comfortable daze. Northward glittered the Cévennes foothills. We were running down on the long straggling net of roads which leads to Uzès and the Pont du Card. Raoul was in talkative mood and was discoursing on the life beautiful, with all modern conveniences naturally. 'Avignon,' he said, 'is so old and so ugly. I could never think of living in such an old barrack of a place. Now give me a town like Alès.' I did not say anything, for there was nothing one could say. Alès is a hideous little mining town full of concrete brick modernities. The plumber's dream—every plumber's dream. 'In Avignon I should go mad,' said Raoul 'though I must admit,' he added, 'that the state of the plumbing is so bad that I should have work for life. But those old buildings are so ugly.'

I thought of the crumbling violet palaces of the vanished Popes, of the Rhône's green swirling current around the smashed bridge of St. Benezet, and sighed. 'I can't think what they see in them. I myself would have the whole lot down and some decent modern apartment flats put up. Do you know that part of the town is still built on piles, and lots of the old houses have a trapdoor in the basement which gives directly onto the river? It's weird. That is why such a lot of murders are committed. You just push the body through the trap and it's found later right down-river. It's easy. No, I shouldn't care to live there. It's unhealthy.' He talked as if the river were choked with corpses.

'And the tourism?' said the little man in the back, 'what of the tourism? Foreigners come for the ancient things. They have their own apartments at home. They come to see the monuments. In this way Avignon gets rich.' Raoul admitted that he hadn't thought of that. 'One must live,' he admitted, though rather doubtfully.

After Uzès he surprised me by suggesting a detour by the Pont du Card. 'But I thought you hated old monuments,' I said. Raoul looked at me scornfully. 'That is science!' he said coldly. 'It is not art but science, sir. It is a Roman triumph of the plumber's science. I always take my apprentices out there. It is their first lesson in plumbing. Now the Pont du Card I love and know well.'

'But it is beautiful, no?'

'It is practical, sir,' said Raoul firmly.

I was surprised that this unromantic soul was capable of such intellectual distinctions. I was even more surprised to find that he was not boasting, for as we entered the magnificent defile, which is so reminiscent of the gorges of Syria, he slowed down in order to drink in once more the beauty of this fantastic ruin. 'What do you tell your apprentices?' I said absently, letting my eye span the gorge to follow the harsh but sweet lines of the noble aqueduct. From whichever angle one comes upon it, at whatever time of day, that Pont du Gard is lovely. Raoul was talking. 'I always stop the car here and make them descend. I say to them quite simply: "This is the noblest Roman monument in the world, built by Agrippa to carry the waters of Eure and Airam to Nîmes. Note it well, my children. It has three tiers of arches. At the bottom there are three, in the second tier eleven of equal span, and in the last thirty-five. Though of such gigantic size it exactly reproduces the side of a Romanesque cathedral—so I have read. It supports a canal five feet high and two wide. At the top its length is no less that 873 feet."' He broke off proudly. His erudition floored me.

'And what do they say?'

'Usually they are silent. After a moment I take them up like this onto the bridge to see its reflection in the Gardon. Is it not wonderful?'

'It is very beautiful.'

'But that is because it is useful.'

We did not pursue the argument. Besides in such a place aesthetics should be left to look after themselves. We idled about for twenty minutes or so among the great bronze arches, chatting in desultory fashion, awed by the spirit of place. Then once more we took the curling road into Remoulins, and so outward across the plain to where, beyond the shallow range of blue hills, the old town of Avignon lay waiting with its modern Laura.

'What will you do while I am busy?' asked Raoul a trifle anxiously for he did not wish to appear as failing in hospitality. 'I could find you a nice café. It won't take me long.'

'Don't worry about me. I have an introduction to someone. I'll go along and see if they are at home.'

'But we must have a point of rendezvous,' said Raoul. 'I will put you down at the Grand Café in the Place de la République. It is perfect. You will see all the actresses.' He licked his lips. I did not quite know the importance of this remark about actresses.

We were now rumbling through Villeneuve-les-Avignon on the right bank of the Rhône, the road climbing and curving into the sky, to descend headlong to the bridge which spans the river. At the last corner before you take the plunge you can see, misty across the long flat expanse of the smooth-flowing river, the conglomeration of towers and belfries which has made Avignon one of the most beautiful of the southern French towns. Beautiful and yet somehow barbaric (I was thinking of Raoul's emphasis on utility) Avignon is a colossal fortress, with its long crenellated ramparts (now burning rosy and honey-gold in the afternoon light) built for defence. For a hundred years it was a Rome in exile, and the proud Popes who inhabited it saw to the matter of defence with practical thoroughness that left nothing to chance. Less formally perfect than Venice, less symmetrical in organization than

Carcassonne, it is nevertheless quite as magnificent with its muddle of towers and steeples and belfries as it rides, like a galleon in full sail, across the mistral-scourged plain. Today the sky was blue, with no wind. When the mistral gets up the blue skies of Provence turn white as a scar. 'Well,' said Raoul. 'There she is. And the famous Pont d'Avignon. It looks silly all broken off like a tooth. I would have it down and build something nice with a railway across it.'

The big bridge which spans the island is an ugly one. In fact most of the architecture being executed in the south of France today conforms to type. We are destroying our monuments piecemeal in England, too. Nevertheless Raoul liked it. It was a step in the right direction, he thought. I reflected sadly that while each town has a Committee of Beaux Arts which is supposed to (and effectively does) protect the ancient monuments it has no powers over new buildings. Avignon is sliding down into urbanism like all the rest of the medieval towns. In fact Raoul gave a cry of delight at the sight of a giant crane poking up from behind the machicolated walls, and the glimpse of a new apartment block. 'Good,' he cried, 'there is something modern.' I wondered if in five hundred years from now these modern blocks would attract sentimental and wondering pilgrims as do the old palaces and churches today. Perhaps we are wrong and Raoul is right. But at any rate it was pleasing to see that urbanism was being strongly resisted in the vacant lots around the walls, for here were several large gipsy encampments, and all the apparatus of a great country fair—the stalls set up along the outer ramparts, buzzing with insanitary but effervescent life. We swerved into the shadow of the great walls and found ourselves inside the town with its cramped medieval streets. Here all traffic is slowed to the pace of a bullock-cart. Abuse, bad language and gesticulation reign supreme. The policemen give the impression of having surrendered completely. They shrug and smile and playfully wave you down streets hopelessly blocked by drays and handbarrows and lorries. Everything (this is part of the policeman's private sense of fun) everything is marked ONE WAY. If one were foolish enough to observe these signs one would go round and round forever. Raoul knew this. He ignored the traffic signs and wherever he saw a NO ENTRY sign he took it. Even so it was slow work, though from his point of view spiritually uplifting. The arguments! The oaths! The invocations to Our Lord! We literally swore our way across the town to what he thought was the Place de la République but which turned out in fact to be the Place Clemenceau. Here I got down at last, somewhat shaken but glad to feel terra firma under my feet again. It was a good place of rendezvous. A beautiful square with a shady café just by the theatre, outside which brooded the statues of Voltaire (to judge by the foxy look) and Molière: both much weather-eroded and pigeon-bespattered. 'Now,' said Raoul, 'let us meet here. If I don't come, you keep coming back to it, say every hour. If you don't appear by midnight I shall assume that you have gone off with a girl and return home. You can come on by train tomorrow. I promise to remember the tap.' The tap! I had forgotten it myself by now.

I walked about a bit down the twisted streets in the violet shadow of the Palace of the Popes. I had an introduction from a man I had known in Paris to a Count who lived in Avignon. It took me a little time to find the Count's lodgings. I had despatched a telegram the day before asking if I might pay him a visit. Unfortunately he was away. His housekeeper however had a letter from him in which he apologized for his absence on business and then, with characteristic southern hospitality, added: 'However I will not fail you entirely, for I have asked the Provençal poet Robert

Allan to keep you company for the few hours you are here. You probably know his work. Curiously enough he is a descendant of Edgar Allan Poe.' Curiously enough! It is, appropriately, the most popular of phrases in the French Midi, and justly so. Everything that happens is curious, unexpected, out of the way.

The rendezvous arranged by the Count was happily the café which I had just left, and I returned towards it at a leisurely pace, deliberately taking a turning or two out of my way in order to enjoy the sinuous windings of the little streets. Now, at twilight, the little square was humming with life. Waiters were setting out supplementary tables and all the bon ton of the town converged upon them; the lights had begun to go up, outlining the leafy trees and throwing into greater relief the violet sky against which the huge architectural lumber of the palaces loomed with an air of solitary abandon. Avignon at evening is like a rook's nest. The Grand Café was bursting with life, its mirrors were swimming with colour. This was partly due (here come the actresses!) to the fact that it was a stage pub, situated hard by the stage door of the theatre. Consequently (stage people being the same all over the world) it was crowded with actors waiting for their cue, and actresses waiting for the call boy—and all in full make-up. At a glance it was clear that the piece was a Provençal epic, perhaps *Mireille,* for the mirrors threw back from a dozen corners of the room the costumed figures of Old Provence—figures which must have been familiar to Van Gogh and Gauguin during their ill-fated stay at Arles. High-coiffed Arlésiennes with their coloured bodices, and leather jacketed and booted *gardiens.* In the midst of all this swimming colour a youngish, dark man rose and came towards me with outstretched hand. It was the poet. In fact it was a rook's nest of poets. As he murmured an introduction to verify my identity he said: 'We are entertaining a poet from Spain. Please join us for a drink. Afterwards if there is anything you wish to see . . .' His resemblance to the author of 'The Raven' was striking.

To most tourists Provençal is an obscure dead language of the past, something once used by the troubadours and now forgotten. Quite the contrary is the case. There are more people who read and speak Provençal today than there are who speak the Portuguese language. Geographically it is distributed over the whole of southern France, though it varies slightly with the district. The language found its Burns in the poet Mistral who used it for his great epic poems, and who indeed founded the poetry of Provence. It stemmed from a small group of poets in Avignon who called themselves 'The Félibres'. No one knows what the title means today, but the poets have maintained their distinctive look. They wear a narrow tie of coloured wool. Young Allan was typical of them with his hair grown rather long at the back and his pronounced side-whiskers. He wore a shirt of cowboy check. Of course he was a youngster. In later life he would doubtless graduate to rather long Victorian coats with a tail and a sombrero. The modern Félibres are as proud as the Scots of their tradition, and while they are all Frenchmen who could as easily write in French they prefer to keep the native tongue of the Midi alive. As Allan said: 'The proof of a language's existence is its poetry. So long as a language is "worked" by poets it never dies.' He used the word 'travailler' which is a happy one, for it is used also for tilling the earth. I was introduced in rapid succession to three other poets. (I began to have a sneaking feeling that everyone in Avignon was a poet.) Two were mildly bearded. One was extremely self-assertive and flamboyant and wore a sort of long-brimmed Homburg. I think he had had a drop or two for he was declaiming something with gestures, and casting hot side glances at a bevy of Arlésiennes who were waiting for the call boy in their pallid make-up. They at least were drinking coffee. Women are so rational. We poets were well away on some kind of local fire water. The assertive one in the hat was, I was told, the best bull-fighting poet of the age. His only theme was the bullfight, and at every Easter *corrida* his ode usually won the prize.

It is perhaps foolish to imagine that a group of people around a café table can give you any sort of insight to a place, and yet it is true. Just as you can smell the whole of London in one pub, or the whole of Paris on the crowded *terrasse* of a little student-quarter café, so Avignon became much more real to me as I talked to this little group of soberly dressed people. It was not their present con-viviality either which suggested to me that the keynote of the place was gaiety. It was something about the smell of it all—the evening sinking behind the squat buttresses, drenching the plain and the long green curve of the Rhône with its successive washes of colour. And inside these walls, which one day enclosed the hopes and fears of all Christendom, lay this brilliantly lighted little square with all its colour, movement, and animation. I asked Allan if Avignon was gay. His eyes sparkled and he nodded. 'It is strange isn't it? I mean that we have a wretched climate. It is cold in winter and the river makes the air humid. And then the blasted mistral when it comes plays havoc. I think the town is probably the most exposed to it in the whole south. Talk about dancing on the bridge! Why, when the mistral gets up they have to stretch ropes along it for people to hold on to as they cross. Without the ropes you'd have to crawl on all fours. Yet, in spite of these apparent drawbacks, it is gay. Yes, You know that it is really the second town of France for the intellectuals. It is to Paris intellectually what Lyons is industrially. The visiting theatre companies adore playing here and the big festival is quite something to attend. There are quite a crowd of painters and writers living here. And then the gipsies. They can't get rid of them. They camp outside the walls.

And then of course all the gangsters and white slavers from Marseilles come here for week-ends to cool their minds. It's quite cosmopolitan though it's so small.'

'I suppose you could say that of Aix.'

'No. Aix is essentially a town for artists and tourists. But Avignon is like a small capital of a province. All the young painters in Aix want to get to Paris. Nobody ever wants to leave Avignon, and very few people do. As for the gangsters, if they do go to Aix it is with the intention of robbing some rich foreigner. But they come to Avignon to relax. Some of them are very stimulating indeed. There are one or two intellectuals among them. Last week I met one who owns a chain of bawdy houses and he turned out to be a book-collector. He has the finest collection of fourteenth-century books in the whole of France.'

So we spent the time in pleasantly convivial chatter while I waited for Raoul. A cool river-breeze had begun to shiver the awnings of the lighted shops and a young moon was struggling into the sky. The cast of *Mireille* came and went about their business, responsive to the sharp cry of the call boy, plunging into the darkness like divers into a pool. I was wondering whether to propose dinner to my host when the plumber materialized suddenly at my shoulder. He wore a vast smile of complaisance which hovered as if suspended by his pink napping ears. 'Eh alors,' he cried jovially. 'She is all I thought and better. We have been talking before a notary. And I have your tap.' He flourished it as he spoke.

'Is she coming back with you?'

Raoul shook his head. 'She will come day after tomorrow by train. She had some things to attend to. But first, before we leave we must visit her family house and have a drink. She promised that to her father's memory. You will come won't you? She is outside in the car.'

Reluctantly I took my leave of Edgar Allan Poe, promising him to return one day with more time at my disposal. The poets bade me goodbye with the delightful civility of the south, removing hats and berets before shaking hands, while the convivial ones added a thump on the back for good measure. I made a feeble attempt to pay for the drinks I had had, and was shouted down and all but pushed out into the street. Raoul was waiting in the shadow waving his tap. He had parked his wagon down a side-street. Laura was sitting in the front seat and Raoul introduced us with a sort of shambling nervousness which he tried to offset by giving his nerve-shattering laugh. Laura was all that I hoped she might be, tall and strongly built, with great peasant hands. A sculptor would have caught his breath to see the way her square head was set on her spine, thick and true. She had the kind of beauty which comes from being perfectly designed for a traditional purpose—like a spade, say; she was the perfect peasant in a state of nature. She had very good grey eyes well set in her face, a short rather beautifully shaped nose, and high cheek-bones. Her hair was done in a bun. It was thick and lustrous in its darkness. Good teeth. Raoul really was in luck. I climbed into the back beside his mate and sat down on a box. The little man appeared to be half asleep. We started to negotiate the rabbit warren of streets, edging towards the river, and Laura politely apologized for detaining us. 'I promised my father that if I married I would offer my intended a drink in our house on the first day of the meeting,' she explained seriously. Raoul chuckled. 'And I want to see the house.'

Laura settled her shawl round her shoulders and said: 'The house is not very much to see. It is on the island, and the garden is always flooded in autumn and spring. Nevertheless we lived there.'

The lights of the gipsy fairground twinkled like fireflies against the piecrust gold of the old wall. The moon picked up its own misty reflections in the swift flowing river. By night the hideous modern bridge did not look so ugly after all. We swooped across it like a swallow, to turn right and roll steeply down to the low flat Isle de la Berthelasse with its shady ribbons of tall willows and planes and poplars. On the other side of the river the beautiful fortress of Philippe le Bel rose clear and incisive from the shadowy ramble of buildings which marked Villeneuve-les-Avignon. The little island which divides the great river is low lying and always half shrouded in river-mist. Despite the fact that it is so frequently flooded when the Rhône is in flood, the peasants still keep their tenacious grip on it, for the soil is the richest hereabouts. Indeed as you roll down its narrow willow-fringed roads you have the sudden illusion of being in Normandy rather than in Provence. Cows graze peacefully in green fields. Yes, it is a landscape by Corot. This effect was much emphasized by the weak moonlight which hazed in every perspective. Across the river the strange crocketed steeples and fortresses had receded into dark anonymity, their outlines along the ceinture of medieval wall being marked only by the lighted booths of the gipsies. We turned at last into a dim gateway. Laura's house was a modest one built on the typical Provençal pattern over a magazine where one might store barrels of wine or other produce. It consisted of one large room approached by a flight of steep steps. She led the way and after a struggle opened the door for us. We stood outside on the porch while she busied herself in the dark interior to find a lamp and matches. 'This is all,' she said at last, holding up the yellow lamp to let us see the forlorn and deserted room, unceilinged and apparently undusted for long months. 'It is dirty now. I live in the town and only come here for my free Sundays. Afterwards, how-ever, you may get a good price for it,' she added, turning to Raoul who stood on one leg picking his teeth. 'There is a little land, and on the island land fetches a good price.'

She busied herself once more to make preparations for the ceremonial drink. Raoul and his mate started poking around down below, peering into the barn. Finally they settled themselves on a fallen tree-trunk. Laura came softly deftly down the stairs with some tall-stemmed glasses on a tray with a bottle of spirits. She trod carefully holding the lamp in her left hand. In the strange mixed light—half pale moon and half butter-yellow lamplight—she looked more than ever a fitting mate for an infant Gargantua. I thought suddenly of one of those large-bosomed Pomonas of Maillol which seem to express all the fruitfulness and happy sensuality of the Mediterranean. How he would have loved to sculp this young peasant girl with her strong hands and shapely arms. We took our glasses and she filled each one with a dose of the Vieux Marc of the region. It is raw and powerful and catches one by the throat. We stood and Raoul raised his glass, saying: 'To the memory of your father.' Laura herself did not drink, but stood there quietly smiling. 'I promised him,' she said simply. With the ceremony completed everyone relaxed and a second dose of Marc was gratefully accepted. Raoul jogged my arm. 'Look at the boat,' he chuckled. 'That is in case of flood.'

It was a small wooden coracle such as fishermen use on shallow lakes, and it lay on its side in a corner of the yard. I was intrigued to notice that the long iron chain which was attached to the prow was fastened to a staple in the house-wall outside the first-floor window. Laura noticed the direction of my glance and smilingly explained: 'Sometimes the flood comes so suddenly that you don't notice it. You awake and find that it has reached the bedroom window. But when you have a boat attached high like that it floats up and so you step into it from the first floor.'

'Clever,' said Raoul, giving his foolish neigh of laughter. We had one more drink and it seemed time to depart. We planned to stop somewhere on the road to Béziers and have a bite of supper—Raoul knew a little place patronized by the routiers. So, locking up the house, we ran Laura back over the bridge and dropped her at the ancient gate. She shook hands with us all and with her new fiancé with a grave and pleasant composure. 'Then day after tomorrow,' she said and Raoul nodded. 'I shall be waiting for you at the station.'

'Everything will be as arranged.'

'Everything will be as arranged.'

She turned quietly on her heel and was gone through the great stone portals. Raoul sighed as we climbed back into the covered wagon and edged our way out through Villeneuve towards the dark hills. The little man in the back was definitely asleep now, I could hear an occasional snore. Raoul yawned luxuriously and lit a cigarette. 'What did you think of her, eh? Isn't she fine? Just what I needed.' I agreed, and indeed wholeheartedly. It was a great stroke of luck for him; there wasn't much romance about the modern Laura, perhaps, but perhaps this was just as well from Raoul's point of view. Instead of spending twenty years writing passionate sonnets he could get on with the work of the world and raise himself a brood of children shaped like spades, with red knees, huge hands, and grey eyes. . . .

'You look surprised,' he was saying, 'but actually as I told you it is all a matter of scientific judgement. The golden rule is never to trust an agency in a matter of real importance.'

I told him I never would.

ACROSS SECRET PROVENCE

(1959)

THE IMAGE EVOKED BY THE WORD is of course a map, but not the conventional map such as tourists obtain from a travel agent. No, it is a highly selective personal map, rich in pictorial data, and the skilful needles of an Algerian tattooist have pricked it out nobly, grandiloquently, like a musical score, upon the chest and abdomen of my friend Pepe. This map enables him, when over-come by national patriotism or simply by the desire to discourse on some elementary point of local geography, to make the ges-ture of a Napoleon returned from Elba—throwing open his shirt in order to growl: 'This is the true Provence! I have it all engraved upon my breast!' Then he gives a bray of laughter. But of course you have to be an intimate of his first, to have shown yourself worthy of the secret country which the map depicts—Pepe's pri-vate Provence.

A series of lucky accidents admitted me to the great man's company on a blazing June afternoon when the red dust was rising like smoke under the hooves of the bulls in the bull-rings of Orange. He admitted afterwards that he was intrigued in the first place by the dog-eared copy of Mistral's poems which was sticking out of my knapsack. (Would not an American be touched to see a copy of *Leaves of Grass* sticking out of a hobo's pack?) But sitting jam-packed in that thirsty throng on such an afternoon was something of an ordeal for a mere foreigner; and clearly I was a person of some discrimination—for had I not come to cheer the exploits of 'Gandar', the greatest cockade-carrying bull of the age? Our hoarse cheers mingled in the dusty air as those famous black hooves rumbled on the arena floors, as if on the vellum body of some mighty drum. Two of the seven *razeteurs,* as they are called, had already been disposed of—one being carried out on a stretcher, and the other helped limping from the outer ring by the gendarmes. Twice in the bull's honour the loud-speakers had grated out the triumphal march from *Carmen* which is the formal accolade granted, not as an honour to human bravery, but to the power and tenacity of a champion bull successfully defending the red cockade which nestles between his curved horns and may be plucked out only by the white-clad fighter with courage enough to run across him as he charges. This peculiar form of bull-dusting is, according to Pepe, the heart and marrow of Provence. ('Provence is where the cooking is based on garlic and olive-oil, and where the *course libre* flourishes.') I do not think he is wrong about this, despite the greater publicity given to the Spanish form of bull-fighting in the newspapers. That is, at best, he says, a picturesque form of ritualized murder; but the *course libre* is an exciting and extremely dangerous game, a test of strong nerves and speed. And the bull is the darling, the hero of the crowd, never the man. . . . Some of these facts he growled at me during that first blue afternoon while the little knot of sweating bullfighters in their white clothes and coloured sashes edged softly and circumspectly around the ring, hoping for the vital half-second of distraction on the part of the bull which would enable one of them to make his temeritous curving run in under the horns to snatch at the coveted cockade with his short metal comb (*lo razet*). The prizes mount with the danger, and 'Gandar's' cockade and horn-strings (which must also be snatched) have seldom been worth less than fifteen thousand francs. It is dangerous a way of earning a livelihood—for as you turn to snatch the cockade your feet must have got up enough speed to carry you like a swallow over the barricade to safety: beyond the reach of those slashing horns. Moreover it is only at the very moment when the bull lowers his crest for the toss that you can snatch at the cockade he wears! One false step here, a miscalculation in your timing . . . Four or five *razeteurs* are killed every year, and more hurt; yet the tradition lives on.

Yes, the odd thing about it is that the official hero of the *course libre* is the bull. His is the name traditionally printed in scarlet poster-type on the placards, and his the applause when a *razeteur* is sent sprawling over the barrier with a broken rib or tossed in a crumpled heap against the stockades. 'And that is how it should be,' says Pepe roundly. 'In Provence the bull is king! And that is how you will see it depicted on the Cretan vases from which our game derives.'

I have mentioned the copy of Mistral's classic poems in the Provençal tongue. This Pepe certainly eyed with guarded approval; but his old eyes really kindled when I confessed that I had come down the Rhône to Avignon in the traditional old-fashioned way (forgotten today by the rushing tourist)—by river-barge. Yes, I had woken at dawn under those rosy battlements to watch the pearly mist lifting and to hear the lazy jackdaws calling from the abandoned Palace of the Popes; I had tasted the river-winds with their eddies of honeysuckle and rosemary bruised by the hooves of riverside cattle, and had drifted in a labyrinth of trembling stars in which, sights and sounds all mixing, I heard the background of nightingale-song interrupting the hoarse distant singing of boatmen and the heart-tugging moan of barges up-river. . . . This in a sort of way proved I was 'genuine'. His wrinkled old face wore a smile of unwilling admiration. 'She must have been a beautiful girl,' he said at last in his growling voice. I understood the allusion. In the old days Provence was the recognized

cure for northerners with broken-hearts—just as the more taci-
turn British went off to East Africa to shoot big game! But here
alas! I could only disappoint him, for my visit was of no such
romantic provenance. I was simply hoping to unstick a novel
which refused to get itself written, by taking a brief holiday; sometimes it is the only way. So I had idled my way south by bus and
train, stopping off here and there to buy a child's *cahier* in a village
stationery-shop, and to sit for a while on some shady *terrasse* by a
meandering Roman river, pen in hand, 'just to see' if that missing
chapter would come. . . .

I told him some of this, but not all. He shook his head slowly
and understandingly and then grabbed my arm in the grip of the
Ancient Mariner himself. 'We will be friends,' he said. 'For I can tell
you many things.' I smiled at the resolute brown figure with its
square hands. He wiped his flowing moustache with a silk handkerchief and nodded sharply. 'You will see,' he said. And then we
both dutifully rose to add to the storm of clapping and cheering
which greeted 'Gandar's' return to the pen. The bull's sweat
starred the red dust like raindrops.

Pepe wore, if I remember rightly, a brown hat with a very wide
brim, and more than a touch of toreador about its design, which I
was afterwards to recognize as the Stetson of the Camargue (a
miniature Wild West, devoted to horse-breeding and bull-raising,
which extends across the shallow alluvial delta where the Rhône
reaches the sea). He wore this with a distinct tilt and an air to match
it. Then a leather waistcoat with beautifully stitched pockets over
a ferociously checked shirt with sleeves fastened by expensive-
looking cuff-links. His tie was a narrow black ribbon. His gaberdine
trousers were strictly tapered into a shape which suggested riding-
breeches, and their ends fitted snugly into an ancient pair of soft-
leather jack-boots. His appearance was flamboyant in a reserved

sort of way, though not eccentric. His head was magnificent, and his smile somewhat costly—for many of his teeth were gold. His voice was pure gravel, and every enunciation of his was a challenge. One felt that he was prepared to strip and fight for the least of his opinions—even those in which he did not believe. . . . What else? Yes, he snuffed instead of smoking—snuffed vigorously with great inhalations and magistral explosions into a green silk handkerchief which he wore in his sleeve and waved about a good deal to illustrate his observations on bulls and human nature in general. Oddly enough, for one so elegant, he carried no snuff-box but a twist of brown paper filled with what looked to me suspiciously like unrefined sulphur. He offered this about liberally to all and sundry, confident perhaps that nobody but himself snuffed in the whole of Provence. He regarded my packet of *Gauloises Bleues* with a commiserating air. Perhaps he had heard of lung cancer? I did not ask.

His opinion of 'Gandar' was high on that sultry afternoon, I remember, but his opinion of human nature low. 'They call themselves *razeteurs*,' he growled. 'Why, in my day a bull like Gandar would have been stripped of his prizes—*dépouillé*—in under a minute.'

As I was no specialist in the matter it was not my business to contest his view; I contented myself only by murmuring that already that afternoon two of the fighters had been carried off, one with a rent in his thigh and the other with a broken rib, if nothing worse. Pepe snorted: 'Pouf! That is nothing for Provence.'

Our friendship survived this small disagreement, and indeed gained further ground when he found me drinking *pastis* at the refreshment booth—the aniseed drink so beloved of Provençals, which turns white with the addition of water. 'Good!' he cried. '*Moi aussi.*' We seated ourselves on a fragment of Roman column under a tree, and it was now that he gave me to understand that

he regarded my intentions as honourable—that I was hencefor-
ward to consider myself his familiar. 'You wish to see Provence!' he
said, as he slowly unbuttoned his dramatic shirt. I was to be
vouchsafed a first view of his private map. I confess I thought for a
moment he was taking off his shirt in order to challenge me to
mortal combat, and was relieved when the proud gesture revealed
only this splendid piece of *art nouveau*. 'It is all here,' he said simply,
proudly. I gazed rapturously at this copyright map printed on his
body by a devoted Algerian artist. 'I was homesick,' explained
Pepe. 'I bade him make me a map of the true Provence.'

Roughly speaking it was diamond-shaped, pinpointed in the
north by Montélimar and in the south by Marseilles, and it followed the whole romantic valley of the Rhône with its fantastic
gallery of historic names. In the West it stretched beyond Nîmes,
in the East as far as Apt.

'*Tiens,*' I said, 'it's a beauty,' and Pepe glowed modestly. Montélimar started high on the chest, while Marseilles was all but lost
in the folds of the abdomen, unless Pepe held his breath, which he
was doing now in order to let me feast my eyes on this treasure. 'I
had to stay tight as a drum while he did it,' he explained hoarsely.
'And it was painful. But I was young. I stayed drunk on *arak*
while he worked.' It was true that with the spread of middle age
and the growth of a comfortable bow-window the southern
ends of the map had begun to spread a bit. The *Etang de Berre* waxed
and waned in size with his breathing. But when all was said and
done it was a most original production, though of little use perhaps to motorists. He gazed triumphantly at me. I gazed at his
stomach. I had realized at once that the map illustrated his main
contention about Provence, for it covered roughly the area he had
already described—the garlic and cockade belt, so to speak; I
had also recognized by now from his appearance that Pepe had

a particular intimate connection with bulls and horses—he was a mixture of Spanish landed gentleman, Southern Colonel, and the 'Horsey Gent from Newmarket' beloved of Surtees. But he was quite unmistakably representative of a tradition which was original, was none of these things. 'Do you notice the bullet-holes?' he said, after a pause, with an air of opulent complacence. 'I had him paint in a few bullet-holes in order to charm the ladies. Women love a man of action. I have always tried to please, though in fact I have never been in action.' They were extremely cunning bullet-holes, most vividly executed, and I said so with conviction. He winked and grunted. 'Then you will notice something else. My home-town is the belly-button. Centre of the world for me. Centre of the Universe. *Gaussargues!* I bet you have heard of it.' I had not. He frowned as he rebuttoned his shirt. His face wore a disapproving look. '*Gaussargues,*' he said in his deep voice, 'is the greatest little village on earth.'

These words, I realized, were in a way an adoption formula. So long as I stayed in Provence, he added, in a voice which made it sound as much a threat as a promise, I was to be his guest. I would learn to imagine as well as to see this hallowed ground through his eyes. Indeed, could anything have been luckier? For I had tumbled upon an initiate both knowledgeable and completely drunk on his native country. The old platitude about not being able to appreciate a place in a short time is far from true; everything depends on the company you keep. All told I was only a few weeks in Provence, yet thanks to Pepe I know it better than many other places where I actually lived—in some cases for years.

I think the secret of the matter is one of attitude; for Pepe it was only the 'sights'—the mouldering copper and violet ruins of Roman amphitheatres in places like Nîmes, Orange and Arles; or the parched buttresses and crenellations of medieval palaces snoozing away the centuries under that ripe old sun; these set-pieces we visited to be sure—but always *en route* for some contemporary gala, be it a bull fight, or a battle of flowers, or a cattle-branding, or a carnival. Who else can have seen Daudet's windmill through a glass of *Tavel rosé*—that magnificent topaz-coloured wine which shares with *Châteauneuf* a comfortable dominion over the southern vineyards? And if we paid passing homage to the Nîmes arena (which Panurge built in three hours!) it was while we were hunting for a particular Provençal dish—*bran-dade*—which must be tasted if my initiation was to be completed. Indeed, to be truthful, the wines and cheeses of this region have worked their way into the landscape, so that my memories of it are shot through with the prismatic glitter of them. They are, so to speak, the living score upon which the reality of the place is written, and they gave colour to those romantic names of the region's heroes—from Rabelais, Nostradamus, and Van Gogh up to Paul Valéry. (At Aigues-Mortes, Van Gogh's coloured boats still idle up and down the green canals among the dragonflies; it seems less than a moment since the painter folded up his easel and left.) Tarascon, Beaucaire, and the Stes. Maries (the headquarters of all the Gipsies in Christendom). . . . And where Petrarch mourned his beloved Laura, we had an obstinate but lucky puncture which enabled us to pledge the lovers in a decisive little Blanquette which Pepe had provisionally decided not to open till the following day. But the heat and effort made him recant. ('By God,' he said reverently, 'what a wine. And nameless yet! They should call it Laura's Tears.') Neither of us could remember a line of Petrarch to recite in memory of that virtuous and star-crossed shade; but we felt a sense of kinship with her as we drank to her in that memorable defile, by the cold clear water. ('I once loved a girl from Avignon called Laura,' said Pepe. 'But she was far from virtuous like her namesake.

As a matter of fact I prefer them that way—though I yield to none in my admiration of Petrarch's lady-love.')

For a whole week we wove backwards and forwards thus across Provence, like spring-intoxicated dragonflies; and yet this for Pepe was a business trip, for several of the bulls he owned were fighting. There were long shady confabulations in taverns, under trees, in stifling offices. There was money to collect and staff-work to be done before we could return to the navel of the world which (he promised me) would cap everything. Meanwhile . . . the familiar prospects of vines, olives, cypresses; one comes to believe that they are Platonic abstractions rooted in the imagination of man. Symbols of the Mediterranean, they are always here to welcome one—either trussed back by the winter gales in glittering silver-green bundles, or softly powdered by the gold dust of the summers, blown from the threshing floors by the freshets of sea-wind. Yes, the great wines of the south sleep softly on in the French earth like a pledge that the enchanted landscapes of the European heart will always exist, will never fade against this taut wind-haunted blue sky where the mistral rumbles and screams all winter long. Yes, even if there were no history here, no monuments, no recognizable sense of a past to indulge our twentieth-century sense of self-pity, the place would still be the magnet it is. These Emperor cheeses, these magnificent unworldly wines still attest to the full belly and the rugged physical contents upon which Rabelais built his view of the ideal world of laughter. They are the enemies of literary nostalgia. The existence of Laura, of Tartarin, of Cézanne—the continuity of the world of the imagination—they are simply the proofs, so to speak, that some spots on earth are the natural cradles of genius. Provence is one. So long as the wines and the cheeses hold their place, such immortal company for the imaginations of men will never fail us. . . . Idle thoughts, drifting through the mind as we sit on a shady *terrasse* near Arles drinking *Côtes du Rhône Gigondas* with a prime St. Gorton cheese and fresh bread (Pepe winking derisively at a Coca-Cola sign on the wall opposite!). So we worked our way south to where at last the Rhône slows down like a mighty pulse to push its massive way across the flat Camargue to the sea, and after a final sunset-cup under the little church of the Saintes Maries we turned back to cross the plains and foothills to *Gaussargues,* the navel of Provence, the belly button of the world, Pepe's personal omphalos. . . .

Here again he was right—or was it simply the deceptive sense of repletion and content in that green-rayed dusk, travelling along the dense plumed avenues of planes as if under a green tent of coolness? No, the little Roman town with its graceful bridge and ambling trout-stream was certainly somewhere to linger. It figures in no guide-book—its time-saturated antiquities are considered unimportant beside those of its neighbours. But it is a jewel with its tiny medieval town and clock-tower; its rabbit warren streets and carved doorways with their battered scutcheons and mason's *graffiti.* Rooks calling too, from the old fort, their cries mingled with the hoarse chatter rising from the cafés under the planes. *Gaussargues!*

And here Pepe somehow came into his own—on the shady water-front café before the tavern-hotel called 'The Knights' where I was lodged, and where the affairs of the world were debated to the music of river-water and the hushing of the plane-fronds above us. Yes, if it was not entirely a new Pepe it was an extension of the old flamboyant figure in new terms—for here he was at home, among his friends, these dark-eyed, keen-visaged gentry wearing black berets and coloured shirts and belts. Their conversation, the whole humour and bias of their lives revolved about bulls and the cockades they carried, about football matches against the hated northern departments and the celestial fouls perpetrated during them; and more concretely about fishing and vines and olive-trees. Here too one entered the mainstream of meridional hospitality where a drink refused was an insult given—and where travellers find their livers insensibly turning into pigskin suitcases within them. Such laughter, such sun-burned faces, and such copious potations are not, I think, to be found anywhere else outside the pages of Gargantua. At times the rose-bronze moon came up with an air of positive alarm to shine down upon tables covered with a harvest of empty glasses and bottles, or to gleam upon the weaker members of the company extended like skittles in the green grass of the river-bank, their dreams presumably armouring them against the onslaughts of the mosquitoes. Those of us who by this time were not too confused with wine and bewitched by folklore to stand upright and utter a prayer to Diana, managed to help each other tenderly, luxuriously to bed. . . .

Murier the dentist, Thoma the notary, Carpe the mason, Rickard the postmaster, Blum the mayor, and Gradon the chief policeman: such an assembly of moustaches and expressions as would delight a Happy Families addict. Massively, like old-fashioned mahogany furniture, they sat away their lives under the planes— village characters belonging to the same over-elaborated myth which created Panurge. They were terrific and they knew it! And such vaunting, such boasting, such tremendous feats of arms: as when Pepe fought a duel with the dentist. I forget how it all began—doubtless over some trifling disagreement about who should stand who what to drink. But the challenge was given and taken up at once. Followed a grave choice of seconds and an even graver choice of weapons: which in the end proved to be open umbrellas. The duellers faced each other with a full wine-glass in the left hand, umbrella in the right. 'On guard,' cried Murier hoarsely, and the battle was joined. It was clearly to be a fight to the death, with no quarter given or asked.

I wish I could say that thrust and riposte flashed back and forth as quickly as sheet-lightning. It would not be true, for both contestants were somewhat unsteady and attacked each other with the sort of unhealthy expression that one sees on the faces of chess players. In this stately but relentless fashion they moved up and down the main street until a balcony window opened and an old lady in curl-papers menaced them with a loaded chamber-pot if they did not desist; this had the effect of causing a momentary diversion when, taking advantage of Murier's lowered guard (he was under the balcony), Pepe drove his umbrella home to the hilt, upsetting his enemy's wine all over his trousers. Prolonged applause, and a return to the *terrasse* where Gradon moodily suggested arresting the whole lot of us and putting us in irons.

These were good, informative days, for during them I saw Provence standing at ease, as it were; saw it from the narrow aperture of ordinary village life which does not blind one to defects but shows everything in its true proportion. I understand, too, why it has remained so fresh and unspoiled to this day, for its comforts are few and its hardships rugged ones—such as the almost total absence of main drainage and bathrooms in the hotels, which would be enough to discourage the tourist even if the word 'mistral' did not exist.

Mistral! There is something of Olympian Zeus about the way it roars and rages down from Mount Ventoux, always unexpectedly and always at full force, rolling boulders and dust ahead of it and whistling down the river-valleys like a herd of mad bulls. In the dusty plain of the Crau the trees are all hooked into weird shapes, twisted and bent by its force. It is upon you at a moment's notice, cramming the words back into your throat, sending the dust-devils spinning and whirling like so many dervishes among the vineyards. But it belongs faithfully to the landscape, and matches it as the dragon matches the fairy-tale; your Provençal treats it with a boisterous contempt despite the feverish headaches and general malaise it brings with it—due probably to the tremendous drop in temperature which accompanies its appearance. 'Somehow one would not be without it,' says the Count de C.-J. as we watch it racing across the plain towards the château. 'Every rose must have its thorn.'

The Count, who is one of France's best essayists, lives virtually the life of a recluse among his magnificent vineyards. He is a good-looking and somewhat reserved man in his middle forties, with a withered arm. Quiet of voice and seldom smiling except with his expressive dark eyes, he dispenses a less boisterous but equally warm hospitality beside his own quiet lily pond, seated under a shady pergola of vine and plumbago.

Once, they say, he was a great figure in Parisian society, but some early tragedy led him to abandon *la vie mondaine* and retire to a life of unbroken seclusion upon the family estates. Exactly what the tragedy was no one would tell me—though everyone seemed to know. Was it too painful for the village to mention—or was this simply an example of supreme tact? I shall never know. But I can guess why he was so admired: for though he was every inch a *seigneur,* and though he never set foot outside the grounds of the château except to labour in his fields, he was somehow still part of the active robust life of the community. Fishermen caught poaching or families in distress knew that Pepe had only to carry their story to him for help to be forthcoming. Nor was there a café-reveller who thought twice about invading the château after dark for a 'stirrup-cup'. In this, I suppose, Pepe was himself the worst offender by far, and several times he led me scrambling and blundering up the dark paths at midnight to ring the bell on the great oak door. He was always sure of his welcome, and always with the same unsmiling politeness the Count would appear, often pyjama-clad, to light a lantern and (if the hour was late and his housekeeper in bed) to hunt out drinks for us from his vast cellars. I think he shared some of my own amused admiration for the flamboyant Pepe; at any rate they addressed each other comfortably in the singular like old intimates. 'Ah! the devil,' he would say as Pepe recounted some dark triumph of skill or business acumen. 'Ah! what a trick to play on a fellow creature'—with his smiling affectionate eye upon the face of his friend glowing rosy in the lantern's light. Blundering homewards down the dark path after such an evening, Pepe would explain. 'He himself leads the life of a blasted nun, but he enjoys visitors up there. But he has never set foot in the town and never will.'

So the days lengthened quietly into sunburnt weeks, and gradually those missing chapters (the quest for which had first led me south into Provence) began to take shape in my mind. A curious process like pack-ice breaking up. I did not dare to ascribe it only to the wine! But one fine morning I found my child's *cahier* had begun to fill up and I realized with a pang that it was time to make tracks, to get back to Paris and my dusty typewriter. My decision, so firmly announced over *pastis* on the *terrasse* of 'The Knights', was greeted with a chorus of disapproval. I had as yet seen and heard nothing, they said. I knew nothing as yet of Provence—as if this immortal hangover were not experience enough! Pepe himself was almost in tears. But I stuck to my guns. I had to leave, and in order to nail my resolution to the sticking-point, I actually chose a date of departure. A long and pregnant silence fell over those vintage characters as they sat before their drinks. Softly the river ran, softly the dark fronds of the planes hushed above us.

'It is the day,' said Pepe sorrowfully, 'of the Anciens Combattants. We have a memorial dinner every year for the class of '34. We had planned to make you an honorary *combattant* for the evening. Wait till you see the menu—it is pure trigonometry, *mon vieux*. You will feel quite faint. No, put it off, this rash decision. Put it off a week or two, my dear friend.' It would have been easy to put it off perhaps for ever; but I remained adamant. The silence of perplexity fell once more. Murier suddenly sat up and said: 'But the last train does not leave until midnight. There would still be time to dine with us and catch it. It would be some sort of a send-off for you. Otherwise we would be wounded in our *amour-propre* for in *Gaussargues* we always try to do the right thing by our visitors.'

As it turned out it was one of the most memorable send-offs I have ever had, thanks to two factors whose importance I could not then foresee. The evening in question turned out also to be the duty evening of the Voluntary Fire Brigade, whose relief commandant was Pepe. But this little fact only dawned on him as we actually sat down to dinner by glossy candlelight in the medieval cellars of 'The Knights', our tables flanked appropriately by barrels, bottles, butts and bins of wine against which we could lean if overcome by the fumes of the . . . but no, I will not give the Menu. I will always keep it a secret, locked in the recesses of my heart. I will not even give the wine list. . . . We were regaled by the music of a Spanish guitar played by Porot, the hawk-featured sacristan of the church, and served by two twinkling dark Provençal girls whose ears (though tanned) flushed increasingly as they listened to the highly robust quatrains which poured from the good Porot's lips. It was in the middle of the first toast that Murier turned pale and cried: '*Pardi,* there are six relief *pompiers* here tonight—and it is the Voluntary's duty evening. If the widow Chauvet should become lonely . . .'

Here I should explain the immediate roar of laughter which went up, and the rueful growling annoyance of Pepe who was obviously the target for it, to judge by his grin and the way he slapped his thigh and said 'Damn the widow!' More laughter.

Now the good widow Chauvet was a delightful old lady in her late seventies who lived a life of studious eccentricity in a tiny villa on the hill. In appearance stately and decorous she was nevertheless rather a flamboyant character too, in her own quiet way. Her hair for example. . . . It was as good as a firework display. It was clear that some local illusionist posing as a hairdresser had subjected her to the worst indignities. Yet she was proud of it, and proud that it was her own. In parts her coiffure resembled a Maclaren tartan, fading away around the sides to verdigris, kelp and bistre. In other parts it spanned the whole spectrum from high violet to a brilliant, ringing gold which suggested that at some time she had been subjected to electrolysis. Twice a week her advertisement appeared in the personal column of the *Courrier du Sud*. It read as follows:

> Charming gifted widow, 45, with furniture worth nine million and small annuity, seeks distinguished Catholic husband who will appreciate and share august but dignified country life. Agents please abstain.

Whether she ever received any replies to this appeal nobody knew; but for years now she had been quite determined to find another husband to replace number three ('parce qu'il faut faire une vie quand même'). This was all very well, and indeed she was rather admired for refusing to give in to old age, but the trouble was that latterly her choice tended always to centre on poor Pepe, who certainly had other fish to fry. It had become a joke: one of those long-winded village jokes which make life so delightful in places where the atom bomb as a subject for discussion has not been heard of. Yes, she was a *brave fille,* this widow Chauvet. But sometimes, on a duty evening, she would deliberately set her chimney on fire, overcome by what was described as a *faiblesse* (due to the Tavel *rosé* she took with her meals?), and in this way secure a certain modicum of male company in the form of the gallant brigade of *pompiers* led by Pepe, who would rush up the hill to the rescue in their fire engine. It was rumoured that such was her love for Pepe that she kept a duty roster of voluntary *pompiers* pinned to her kitchen wall, so that she would know exactly when to set the chimney alight. At any rate she had never done this on an evening when the gallant Pepe was not himself in charge. The inference was clear.

This interruption, then, was very much to be feared; and for a moment the knowledge that the widow might strike cast a gloom over the company. But the food was so delicious, the candlelight so charming, the songs of Porot so clearly demoralizing to the two young serving-girls, the wine flowing so strongly . . . that everyone settled down at last to this memorable banquet in good earnest. I kept an apprehensive eye on a wrist watch and wondered whether I should have to be taken aboard the train on a stretcher.

It was a quarter to twelve when the siren went; just after the thirteenth recitation and the fourteenth comic song. Murier had stood on his hands 'just to prove' something or other; Thoma the notary had sung a selection from an unidentifiable opera; Gradon had done the can-can and sung a little song which had for chorus the refrain: *'Merde Merde Merck au flic'.* It was clear that he was due for a court martial if he went on like this. I was just about to recite (on request) the speech 'from *Hamlet* by Laurence Olivier' (sic) when the first haunting moans filled the air.

'The siren! It must be the widow,' cries Pepe tearing his hair and gazing wildly around him as if hunting for his sense of duty. Clearly I had just time to get to the station. The telephone began to ring slowly, painfully in the little vestibule of 'The Knights' where my rucksack already lay, its straps adjusted against my departure. One of the duty *pompiers* clattered up to answer the call, and clattered down again grinning. He did not need to utter the words, for they were taken out of his mouth by the company which intoned fervently: 'The widow Chauvet is on fire again,' before breaking into croaking guffaws like so many bull-frogs on a lily-pad.

But they were also racked with an apologetic sense of hospitality steadily floundering in that slow insistent wail. Pepe, like the captain on the bridge of a sinking ship, cried: 'Fetch the machine and the *casques*,' and four of the guests left at the double.

'Listen,' says Pepe to me with anguished deliberation. 'Fear nothing. All is in order. We will drop you at the station on the way to the widow's house.'

That is how I came to find myself perched on the *Gaussargues* fire engine, surrounded by grim-faced gentlemen in formidable *casques* of gleaming brass, while Murier piloted us down the main street at what seemed to me to be the speed of sound itself. Sound! The horn of the machine honked dolefully like a series of dying swans as we swerved across the esplanade and over the bridge, and out along the road to the railway station.

'Fear nothing,' said Pepe, himself by now accoutred in huge rubber boots and an axe. 'All will be well. You will see.'

The functionaries of the railway were clearly under the impression that I was pretty important as visitors go—perhaps an atomic scientist or mad oinologist. I was rushed on to the platform by a posse of gentlemen in tremendous brass *casques* with such impetus that the stationmaster bowed from the waist. It was not a moment too soon; our watches must have been bedevilled by the town clock—a not uncommon thing in *Gaussargues.* Doors were shutting and flags were being waved. A dozen brown hands were flung out to clasp mine. 'Goodbye,' I cried inadequately. 'You had better hurry.' Up there on the hill there seemed quite a fire; it looked as though the widow had done it properly this time for the roof itself was alight. Pepe drew a deep breath as we shook hands: 'You will come back?' he asked. I nodded. 'As yet you know nothing of Provence, nothing.' I admitted it. The train jerked once, twice, and began to slide. 'Good luck,' I said, 'and good weather in *Gaussargues.*' Pepe waved his *casque* in stately fashion; through his shirt I caught a glimpse of his tattooed hide—Montélimar to Avignon, unless I am mistaken. 'We'll always have a place for you at the *Anciens Combattants,*' he yelled suddenly as the distance widened, and then we turned a corner and he vanished.

It is some months since I left *Gaussargues.* I am writing these words in Paris. I have seen and heard nothing of Pepe since I left, and though I occasionally scan the meridional press for news of my friends in the Midi, *Gaussargues* itself is never mentioned. It is a pity. It would be nice to round off the story in some way, perhaps even by being able to report Pepe's marriage to the widow Chauvet; but I think he is not very much interested in furniture worth nine millions.

OLD MATHIEU

(1958)

HE MUST BE IN HIS EARLY SIXTIES, yet though his hair is white and his face as wrinkled as that of a tortoise he is still sprightly of step. He swings up the hill to his holding of vine and olive with the air of conqueror and is prodigal of good-mornings. His greeting sails over the garden wall like a thrown flower. On his way back at dusk he occasionally stops for a gossip. Yet somehow this year he has become less cheerful, less confident—and indeed his concern is understandable, for it matches that of his fellow *vignerons*. The failure of the '57 harvest was a blow whose full effects are only now beginning to be felt with the appearance of imported Spanish table wine and the hushed incredulous talk of wine-rationing by next August. In France! 'Yes, the Spanish wine has come,' he admits with an air almost of self-reproach. He is not critical of its quality—everyone admits that some is even superior to the local *gros rouge*. No. He utters the words with the hangdog air of a cricketer who might say: 'We have been forced to invite three American baseball players to join the Test team!'

Wine for Old Mathieu is neither a cult nor simply a business; rather is it something between a livelihood and a vocation. Talking of it he sounds rather like old Wilfred Rhodes discussing famous spin-bowlers of the past. The little soiled and folded copy of the trade paper peeps out of his pocket—*Le Vigneron*. Sitting down on a stone he unfolds it slowly and reads out the report of the last harvest with the wounded and shrinking air of a soldier studying a casualty list. 'C'est bien grave, monsieur.' And indeed it is. On his lips the famous names sound full of the regional poetry of old county regiments or county cricket teams decimated in a year of bitter crisis. 'Bordelais. N'a que la moitié d'une récolte normale. Nettement inférieure à '52, '53, '55, sauf quelques rares crues. Bourgogne. 1957 ne représente guère plus que la moitié d'une récolte normale.' Here and there, however, there are frail gleams of hope to mitigate this terrible casualty list, and over these few items he lingers. In the Bourgogne report, for example, satisfactory production was signalled from several points on the battlefront, notably in the Côte de Nuits—at Gevrey-Chambertin, Morey, Chambolle-Musigny, Nuits St. Georges; but 'très faible' production on the Côte de Beaune, notably Le Mâconnais and Le Beaujolais. Nevertheless on the Beaujolais front (his voice picks up) there are *bonnes cuvées* to be signalled from Fleurie, Moulin à Vent, Côte de Brouilly, Morgon and in the Beaujolais villages. 'Mais le Beaujolais '57 est bien loin d'être un grand millésime.' Sighing he turns a page, first carefully picking his finger and peering short-sightedly at the small newsprint. 'Vous voyez? C'est bien grave, monsieur.' The news of Champagne is nothing less than calamitous—160,000 hectolitres against a normal production of 350,000—and this only of 'qualité moyenne'. The news from the Alsace and the Jura is equally sad with production tumbled down to below half and all the qualities indifferent. The production in the Loire region down to six-tenths of its normal size with some total failures to be recorded after the bitter spring frosts of last year. 'Récolte presque nulle à Pouilly sur Loire, très faible à Sancerre, Vouvray, Savennières. Mais . . .' and once more the old voice rises hopefully as he records, 'une bonne qualité dans les Côtes de la Loire'. But it is quality against quantity. On the home front, so to speak, things are not quite so bad. The Côtes du Rhône and Provence production was up to three-quarters of normal with some superior wines to be signalled, notably from Châteauneuf-du-Pape. Also the Vins Doux

Naturels show a silver lining with production standing at well over half the normal and quality relatively high all round. But in the South-west once more the tale of disaster is repeated, with production whittled away to under half—vine-regiments decimated by the frost. How marvellous their names are! Montbazillac, Rosette, Pecharmant, Montravel, Bergerac. Côtes de Duras. Jurançon, Madiran, Pacherenc, Du Vic Bilh. 'Le vignoble de Monbazillac fût particulièrement éprouvé par les gelées. Qualité moyenne.' An epitaph for a famous vineyard.

He folds up the little magazine and tucks it carefully back in his pocket. 'The Vines!' he says reflectively, shaking his head as if over their beloved incorrigibility. Indeed in this anxious year they have become presences standing out there in the rain. And the weather reports for April and May have deepened the gloom everywhere with their talk of snap-frosts and rainy spells to come. Are the vines to fail again this year? I am beginning to see them through the eyes of Old Mathieu. They are planted from end to end of the wintry horizon in regular symmetrical lines, as if on a chessboard. In the landscape foreground they look like small pagan headstones in some huge cemetery; and as they fade back into the hills in diminishing lines they dot the fields of tobacco-coloured earth like cloves.

And the plants themselves . . . hairy as the thigh of a village Pan they writhe out of the dark ground, ash-dark and swollen with the promise of leaf and fruit, but nude now; and everywhere by March there are men in blue blouses bending over them as if over street casualties, binding a limb, setting a splint, tending them. All the silences in these white villages are full of the snap of sécateurs, and carts trudge round in the mud collecting the dead vines—or those which for one reason or another have failed to bear. Spades dig them coarsely up—extirpating them like rotten molars and tossing them into the carts which soon brim over with these little brown statuettes, arms raised on high, primitive woodcarvings of Dionysus himself; each a small figure with raised arms, knotted, tumescent, as if from the pressures of the soil itself—a strength cut back, contained, muzzled by the surgeon's sécateurs. The April rain hisses down among them, condensing in great glistening beads on their shaggy skins, like sweat—sweat and tears from the drawn-out agony of growth.

Each elbow of vine is left with two points, two dry points of contact with the sky like terminals. Each shaggy little statue raises two arms, each arm has two fingers. And then, as the slow spring advances, a leaf appears on each of the fingers—a frail yellow pilot-light. It questions the air delicately, timidly, like the horns of a snail. Another follows and another. So the great hairy thigh of Dionysus blossoms in yellow leaves which advance with a downward-pressing movement, wriggling along between earth and sky as if uncertain which to seek; a curious snake-like downward movement.

But by the time June comes the whole valley will be in leaf, plum-dark, transformed. The dry brickdust and tobacco-veined earth will have become smothered by the new heraldic green of the vines, manufacturing the shade in which the fruit is to ripen.

It is Old Mathieu himself who taught me how to trim the vines in the neglected and abandoned vineyard in which this old house stands and which we will soon be leaving for good. In a single year of neglect the vine can throw out a four yard withe which sprouts upon it like those long and silky antennae upon the heads of certain nocturnal beetles. These must all be trimmed back to 'make the vine push', in the words of Old Mathieu. He brings up his sécateurs on two successive Sundays and patiently shows me how the operation must be conducted. It is not unlike a spell at the nets under an exacting yet patient coach. Holding the long-shanked cutters you straddle the vine, cutting downwards, having first chosen your trimmings. Gravely he instructs you: press down and keep the sharp side of the cutters against the body of the vine. 'Il faut tourner doucement avec la souche.' (I am reminded of a difficult shot to cover-point—or of a glide through the slips.) 'Tourner,' he cries softly. 'Il faut tourner, Monsieur.' It has its own rhythm, this downward cut with the sécateurs, but it is not too difficult to learn. Together we work slowly through the orchard in front of the house. 'The one at the back you shall do by yourself,' he says with a smile. 'And when I pass up the hill in the morning I shall see if it is properly done or not.'

One can trim about sixty or seventy vines in a day, and it is absorbing work. First the choice of the shoots to be cut away, the cleaning and barbering of the trunk, and then the operation which will leave two fingers upon each branch, and not more than six upon each single vine. 'Il faut de la patience. Il faut bien le juger.'

Working with the invisible presence of Old Mathieu at my elbow I complete the job. Anxiously as a student I await his early morning passing. Presently I hear his cheery good-morning on the road below. I find him standing with his critical and friendly eye upon the vineyard. 'C'est pas mal,' he says. For an amateur *vigneron* this is an accolade indeed.

Delphi

In 1964 Durrell returned to Greece for the first time in nearly two decades. He published this essay the following year.

DELPHI

(FROM SPIRIT OF PLACE)

TO WANDER ACROSS THIS COUNTRY of stone fables, shattered mythologies, blunted statues which have been passed (like wax in a flame) across the sun's burning-glass can be both frightening as well as inspiring. How different from Italy, where the beauty comes out of domestication—the touch of the wise human hand is everywhere. Everything has a history, can be traced, decoded, understood. But Greece . . . everything is confused, piled on top of itself, contorted, burnt dry, exploded; and the tentativeness of the scholar's ascriptions is a heartbreak. It is as if nothing were provable any more, everything has become shadowy, provisional. The scholar begins to stammer; he can hardly tell us anything without using the words 'probably', 'possibly'. Sometimes, greatly daring, he advances towards a phrase like 'it seems likely that. . . .' One feels that one has arrived too late; after all, most of what we know comes from so late a traveller as Pausanias, for whom Greece was as much of a tourist centre as it has become today. But long after the ravages of Sulla, the Emperor Hadrian had tried to revive Greece with gifts and temples, and superficially it must have seemed busy and prosperous enough. But this Neo-Greek revival was a hollow thing.

Yet if this disappointment persists for the traveller today there is something more certain upon which he can base himself; the landscape remains as unchanging, uncompromising, ravishingly pure and vertical. And each of the ancient sites has its own flavour—expressed from the very ground, it seems. I use the word 'express' since it suggests also the extraction of precious oils from a fruit like the olive. The rareness of Greece lies in this singular purity of landscape-awareness; the historic memories echo on, drone on like the bees that once droned in the tomb of Agamemnon. (Alas, they have been killed off by the injudicious use of a modern chemical spray on the fields of corn and barley around the tomb, where they fed.)

Among these ancient sites Delphi is the most grandiose, as well as the most sphingine; the long winding roads leading away north from Livadia coil like the sacred serpent. The landscape, curled inwards upon itself, reveals itself only in snatches; the mountain ranges come up and recede, recline and rise up. It is almost as if the dose had been one measured by the ancient physicians who built this road towards the centre of the earth—towards that mysterious omphalos which I first found as a boy, lying in an open field above the road. I still have an impertinent picture of myself, leaning negligently against it as if at a bar. . . . But among so many visits to Delphi I have never found the slightest variation in the impression it makes on me; the latest was last year, after an absence from Greece of nearly twenty years. What is this strange impression? As I have said, each site in Greece has its singular emanation: Mycenae, for example, is ominous and grim—like the castle where Macbeth is laid. It is a place of tragedy, and blood. One doesn't get this from its history and myths—they merely confirm one's sensation of physical unease. Watch the people walking around the site. They are afraid that the slightest slip and they may fall into a hole in the ground, and break a leg. It is a place of rich transgressions, tears, and insanity. A few miles away lies dream-saturated Epidaurus, so lax and so quiet; one would not dare to be ill for long if one lived there. Its innocence is provoking. But Delphi . . . The heart rises as the road rises and as the great scarps of mountain rise on either side; the air becomes chill.

Finally, round the last corner, there she is in her eyrie like a golden eagle, her claws clamped around the blood-coloured rock which falls away with vertiginous certainty to the dry bed of the Pleistos. The long thrilling sweep of the olive groves—greener than anywhere in Greece—is like the sudden sweep of strings in some great symphony. And then the ribbon of sea, the small port; for once the sea seems diminished. Behind one the rock climbs, the paths climb, the trees climb with one, until all is bare rock and blueness once again. Up there an eagle flies—one thinks of Zeus! But the atmosphere is so pure that one can hear the stroke of his great wings as he frays the air. A slight wheezy creaking, like a man rowing across water.

Aesthetically there is nothing much to see at Delphi except Delphi itself: would you go to Lourdes to study modern sculpture? Once again the fragments belong to different epochs, different cultures. Moreover they are all votive objects, mere genuflections in stone or terra cotta. Even the famous charioteer is of a poor provenance and hardly gives one an echo of Plato's metaphor.

But the place itself; it is built upon two enigmas and neither of them is easily decipherable—the omphalos and the oracle. In an age looking for both physical and intellectual points of reference these two symbols stand for something important, even momentous. Somehow in Delphi while one is uneasy it is not with a sense of fear so much as a sense of premonition; what is here, one feels, is *intact* in its purity. The force is still there buried in the rocky cliffs. It could speak if it wished and overturn everything with one reverberating statement—but of course one of those statements curled up in a doable negative. Is not Truth two-sided? Walking about the hillside in the shadow of the pines, listening to the gentle creaking of the wind and the pleasant susurrus of the cicadas, one has sudden moments of panic. Perhaps this is the moment—perhaps *today* the oracle is due to make its re-entry into the world. If it did, if from the heart of the rock we heard one of those terrific and yet ordinary judgements upon the world of affairs, would we be ready to receive it, act upon it? Delphi is a sort of mute challenge. All the other considerations seem vague, confused. Side by side with the confusion of periods and styles in the Museum one finds in the main street of the little town ample evidence that the Greeks, with their passion for novelty, are still busy accumulating influences. Among the many beautiful carpets hanging up for sale in the little shops along the main street my eye catches something; they hang like dead rabbits in a poulterer's shop. Closer examination reveals them to be the coon skin hats sacred to that great modern god Davy Crockett. His film must have passed this way! The small commerçants of Delphi are not slow to catch on to what the tourist public might need. Indeed the idea is a delicious one. That one should travel from New York to Delphi to buy a coon skin hat for oneself is typical of both modern and ancient Greece. After due reflection I bought one and had it despatched to Henry Miller. . . .

But the oracle, the Pytho? Once again the historians begin to stammer. Apollo killed the Dragon and left the corpse of this gigantic dead beast to rot. Out of this grew the oracular power of the Pytho. The word means 'to rot'. But what is one to make of this farrago of apparent rubbish? The modern Greek poet George Seferis ventures a thought. 'In such fertilizing compost the power of the god of harmony, light and prophecy took root and sprouted. Perhaps the myth means that the dark powers are the light's yeast; and that the stronger they are, the more intense the light when they are overcome.' One notices above all, the word 'perhaps'; for if anyone should know for certain it would be Seferis. But like the rest of us he is left guessing. This must excuse

my own small venture in interpretation. The word 'to rot' for me
is symbolical and suggests a spiritual truth into which the Delphic
visitor was initiated. One does not know out of what ancient rites
grew the notion of re-fertilizing ground with dead flesh. It is older
than Athens. But perhaps the 'ripeness' of Shakespeare's 'ripeness
is all' is not far from the Delphic notion of 'to rot'. The point at
which the body begins to rot is the fertilizing point of death; this
manner of trying to make death fertile may have had a symbolic
value. . . . From 'ripe' to 'rot' is a short distance in English, as
Shakespeare has told us in a famous passage. But there was something special about fruit that had dropped for the Greeks, in distinction to fruit that had been picked. Athenaeius, quoting from a
lost writer, says that the Athenians when they placed a ritual meal
for the Dioscuri (the twins) made sure that it consisted of cheese,
barley cake and *fallen* olives and pears, in remembrance of their
ancient mode of life. The gods preferred the perfect maturity of
the *fallen* fruit. Even today the oil of the *fallen* olive is reserved for
the use of the Church. And as for the twins . . . did they represent
perhaps (notice the perhaps) the dichotomy which resides at the
heart of man's psychology and which is reflected in his language?
The Truth-telling oracle of Delphi never lost sight of the double-
axe in man's mind, and the double nature of his consciousness,
the double sex of his psyche . . . Even today we have such an idea
in the American phrase 'double-take' and the English corruption
of French 'double-entendre'. Truth, like the sword, has a double
edge. . . . The oracle with all its theological sophistication knew
this only too well.

The fact that Apollo created the Delphi we know today does
nothing to qualify the confusion, for if you turn to read his biography in the *Dictionary of Classical Mythology* you come upon a God
who sprouts attributes as ivy sprouts leaves. . . . Most of them too

seem to be mutually contradictory. He is remarkably elusive, uses a number of different passports, while his personal behaviour on many occasions seems quite unsuitable for the god of harmony, light and prophecy. Once again it may be that our authorities are too late; they came here long after an age of darkness had settled over Greece. Now only these fragments remain to echo on in our troubled twentieth-century minds.

Nor will the long excursion to the Corycian cave do anything to clarify matters, though in itself it is worth making if only for the magnificent scenery of the Delphic hill complex, and the taste of the pure Greek air. It is so dry and clear, the atmosphere, that you can hear sounds a great way off—such as a distant shepherd's pipe in the valley and the tonk of sheep-bells; or sounds much smaller in the scale which startle one by their purity. I am thinking of the clicking of a tortoise walking over the burning rocks by the stadium, of the whiplash of a sudden gust of wind in the pines; of the steady susurrus of plain unstirred air among the dry grasses of the theatre. They utter a faint breath while remaining apparently quite still.

The cave of the oracle was blocked about a hundred years ago by a fall in the cliff, but the famous waters of inspiration still pour out into the glade and rush down the steep precipice to the bed of the Pleistos. Seferis records that the waters of the Castilian spring have a taste of thyme, but for me they have had always the faint flavour of mint. Cold and pure, they nourish the roots of the giant plane-tree which stands guard over this ancient precinct. Last year, peering up into the dense shadow of its leaves we saw a brown paper parcel hanging there, tied with string. A votive object? This was not as unlikely as it sounds for even today the folk-lore of Greece is full of the habit of leaving ex-voto's in sacred places. Alas! the truth was, though charming, more prosaic. The guide explained that the parcel contained his lunch; he kept it cool by hanging it in the shadow of the huge plane leaves. 'This tree is my ice-box,' he said, not without pride at his own perspicacity.

The traveller who stoops to take up some of the sacred water of inspiration should remember to drink to the poets of modern Greece who have now begun to take their rightful place in the European tradition to which they belong; it is a slender chain of gold links . . . Solomos, Palamas, Sekelianos, Cavafy, Seferis, Elytis. . . .

Perhaps one of them will recover for us the meaning of the oracle we so much need today?